Sampling Inner Experience in Disturbed Affect

EMOTIONS, PERSONALITY, AND PSYCHOTHERAPY

Series Editors:
Carroll E. Izard, *University of Delaware, Newark, Delaware*
and
Jerome L. Singer, *Yale University, New Haven, Connecticut*

Recent volumes in the series

THE COGNITIVE FOUNDATIONS OF PERSONALITY TRAITS
Shulamith Kreitler and Hans Kreitler

GUIDED AFFECTIVE IMAGERY WITH CHILDREN AND ADOLESCENTS
Hanscarl Leuner, Gunther Horn, and Edda Kleissmann

IMAGERY AND VISUAL EXPRESSION IN THERAPY
Vija Bergs Lusebrink

LANGUAGE IN PSYCHOTHERAPY: Strategies of Discovery
Edited by Robert L. Russell

THE PSYCHOBIOLOGY OF EMOTIONS
Jack George Thompson

THE PSYCHOLOGY OF EMOTIONS
Carroll E. Izard

QUANTIFYING CONSCIOUSNESS: An Empirical Approach
Ronald J. Pekala

SAMPLING INNER EXPERIENCE IN DISTURBED AFFECT
Russell T. Hurlburt

SAMPLING NORMAL AND SCHIZOPHRENIC INNER EXPERIENCE
Russell T. Hurlburt

THE TRANSFORMED SELF: The Psychology of Religious Conversion
Chana Ullman

A Continuation Plan is available for this series. A continuation order will bring delivery of each new volume immediately upon publication. Volumes are billed only upon actual shipment. For further information please contact the publisher.

Sampling Inner Experience in Disturbed Affect

Russell T. Hurlburt

University of Nevada, Las Vegas
Las Vegas, Nevada

Plenum Press • *New York and London*

Library of Congress Cataloging-in-Publication Data

Hurlburt, Russell T.
    Sampling inner experience in disturbed affect / Russell T.
Hurlburt.
        p.   cm. -- (Emotions, personality, and psychotherapy)
    Includes bibliographical references and index.
    ISBN 0-306-44377-5
    1. Depression, Mental--Psychological aspects--Case studies.
2. Borderline personality disorder--Psychological aspects--Case
studies.   3. Anxiety--Psychological aspects--Case studies.
4. Bulimia--Psychological aspects--Case studies.   5. Introspection-
-Case studies.   6. Content (Psychology)   I. Title.   II. Title:
Inner experience.   III. Series.
    RC454.4.H87   1993
    616.85'27--dc20   93-10777
                                                                        CIP

Cover art by James B. Krizman

ISBN 0-306-44377-5

© 1993 Plenum Press, New York
A Division of Plenum Publishing Corporation
233 Spring Street, New York, N.Y. 10013

To my wife

Preface

The descriptive experience sampling method described in the present book and its predecessor (Hurlburt, 1990) is a new method of examining inner experience that focuses attention on the details of people's everyday thoughts and feelings to an extent perhaps never before realized. The result of such a focus is the ability to draw some unanticipated (albeit tentative) general conclusions about people. The description of those particulars and their generalizations are the topics of this book.

It is perhaps not coincidental that researchers in other disciplines are also just now reexamining the role of everyday detail in understanding their own disciplines. I will cite here just one such instance.

The *Alltagsgeschichte* ("history of everyday life") movement within historical analysis originated in the late 1980s. *Alltagsgeschichte* analysis examines the everyday needs, wants, and desires of ordinary people, not simply large structures and long-term historical processes, and "has challenged the theoretical and methodological hegemony of *Strukturgeschichte* ["structural history"] within the German historical 'guild'. . . . [*Alltagsgeschichte*] has campaigned for the construction of a radically new paradigm of social historical research" (Crew, 1989, p. 395).

Just as our own method of studying the details of inner experience has led to new psychological perspectives, the *Alltagsgeschichte* examination of the everyday details of interpersonal activity has led to new historical perspectives. For example, structural (that is, conventional) historians generally present the influence of the Third Reich on the German people as being the result of Hitler's power/terror tactics. *Alltagsgeschichte* analysis of such nonofficial details as personal snapshots and letters of "ordinary" people, however, shows that Hitler's method of influence was much more ambiguous and contradictory. Rather than relying predominantly on power/terror tactics, the Nazis adopted a position that placed an extremely positive value on *Deutsches Qualitätsarbeit* ("German quality work"), thus engaging "the sympathies of a wide range of ordinary Germans, from factory engineer to skilled worker, regardless of their former political persuasions. . . . [They also] appealed to younger German workers' fascination with modern machinery" (Crew, 1989, p. 400). Thus, while it may be true that Hitler used power and terror tactics to some degree to control the working class, the finer-grained *Alltagsgeschichte* analysis shows that Hitler's everyday influence was built and maintained not only by power and terror but also by catering to the pride and interests of the workers.

It may be that one of the characteristics of the latter portion of the twentieth century is a growing appreciation by social scientists of the importance of viewing human personal or historical experience "from below" (Crew's term).

I wish to thank the subjects in this research, both those explicitly described here and others, who have generously shared the details of their experience. I also thank Jerome Singer for comments on an earlier draft of this manuscript and his consistent support of our attempts to describe inner experience, and Lisa Coffey for valuable editorial suggestions.

ACKNOWLEDGMENTS

This work was supported in part by a grant from the University Research Council, University of Nevada, Las Vegas.

Contents

1

Introduction and Method

What is it like to be depressed? Is the main characteristic of being depressed a sad mood, or does the thinking of depressed individuals have particular characteristics also? If depressed thinking has certain characteristics, are they characteristics of the content of thought or of its process—is it what we think *about* or *how* we think it? When depression lifts, is this just a change in mood or does thinking change also, and if so, does it change in content or in process? Do bulimics, who are often also depressed, simply use binge eating as a particular way of expressing depression, or is the inner process in bulimia decidedly different from that of depression? Do anxious individuals process thinking similarly to depressed people, so that the main difference between anxiety and depression is a mood difference? Do individuals diagnosed as borderline personality, who have rapidly changing episodes of severe depression as well as other mood fluctuations, share the same kind of cognitive processing as depressed individuals?

These seem like basic questions in the understanding of affective disorders, and one might think that the science of depression and anxiety would rest on a secure understanding of their answers. Surprisingly, this is not the case. There are a few theories which attempt to specify answers to some of these questions, but those theories are not based on solid data and are thus frequently contradictory. The fact is that we know very little about how depression, bulimia, anxiety, and borderline personality are experienced "from the inside."

It is beyond our scope to explain the historical reasons for this lack of data, although we do explore one aspect of this history in Chapter 2.

1

Rather, we wish to show that it is possible to answer the above questions, and we will provide some data which bear on all of those questions. We will show that careful reports of inner experience can provide fascinating and suggestive views into the phenomena of affective disorders.

This is the promised sequel to *Sampling Normal and Schizophrenic Inner Experience* (Hurlburt, 1990). In that book, we made the case that it was possible and profitable carefully to describe inner experience using the method we called descriptive experience sampling. That method will be described below, but for now, we may briefly note that the method involves using, for a number of days in the subject's own natural environment, a random beeper to signal a subject to take notice of her[1] inner experience that was occurring at the instant of the beeper's signal, and then describing the moments of experience thus obtained.

We showed in the first book that the method can be considered reliable and that it dramatically differentiated between schizophrenic and non-schizophrenic subjects. It was not our intent in that book to develop a complete picture of inner experience in either normals or schizophrenics, but we did provide some provocative observations of normalcy and schizophrenia which have generally been supported by our own continuing research project, and which should be validated by further research by others.

For example, our schizophrenic subjects (when not decompensated) had extremely clear emotional experiences, contrasting with the frequently-held opinion that schizophrenics have "blunted" affect. In fact, our subjects often had hyper-clear emotional experience which often included a clear awareness of precise bodily locations where emotion seemed to take place. As a second example, we found that images existed as concrete entities for our schizophrenic subjects. Whereas in our normal subjects inner visual experience is similar to external vision where the center of perception is most detailed and visual awareness tapers off gradually to indistinctness at the periphery, our schizophrenic subjects had images which included well-defined, clear, abrupt edges; the images of these subjects bent, twisted, and floated as if the images themselves were made out of some flexible material. Our schizophrenics often had images which were, as one subject termed it, "goofed-up": parts of the image were obliterated with black splotches, were the wrong color, or were tilted, etc. A third observation was that words appeared

---

[1]We will use feminine pronouns to refer to subjects because most of the subjects in the present book were female. There is nothing about the method which makes it more useful for females than for males; in fact, half the subjects in the previous books were male.

as visual/spatial presences for our schizophrenic subjects. Whole sentences were heard to "fly" past or through a subject's head; the words of a sentence were seen "piled up" in jumbled order, etc. None of our normal subjects have reported these kinds of experience. For more details, the interested reader is referred to our previous book (Hurlburt, 1990).

The previous book thus found major differences between the normal and the schizophrenic samples. But did those differences discriminate only normals from schizophrenics? Perhaps goofed-up images are characteristic of inner experience in *all* psychological disorders, not just in schizophrenia. Perhaps depressed or anxious individuals, as well as schizophrenics, hear whole sentences "flying by" them. Clearly, in order for us to consider the descriptive experience sampling method to be useful, it must be able to differentiate schizophrenics not only from normals but also from other diagnostic groups; and, furthermore, to distinguish the other diagnostic groups from normals and from each other. The primary goal of the present book is to demonstrate that that is indeed the case. I believe that you will find, for example, that the inner experiences of the depressed subjects in this book *are* similar to each other and dramatically different from those of the schizophrenics and normals of the previous book, as well as from the anxious, bulimic, and borderline individuals described here. Thus we believe that the primary goal of demonstrating that the descriptive experience sampling method is sensitive to different kinds of psychological disorders is successfully accomplished by the cases described here.

This book also has a secondary goal: sketching some of the salient characteristics of disordered affect. Just as we did with our schizophrenic subjects in the previous book, here we carefully observed the moment-by-moment inner experience of depressed, hypomanic, bulimic, and anxious individuals and those with borderline personality disorder, and carefully described what we found. Our second goal is thus to get a glimpse of depression and related states as they are experienced from the inside, and to begin to understand how the inner experience of depressed, bulimic, anxious, and borderline individuals are different from each other and from the normal and schizophrenic individuals we described in the previous book.

We should emphasize that we are not attempting to offer a complete description or theory of depression (or of bulimia, anxiety, or borderline personality), but are instead simply exploring the inner phenomena of those kinds of experience. Just as Lewis and Clark's task when exploring the American West was not to provide a complete catalog or explanation of the geographic phenomena of western America, but rather to report

accurately the major features of the landscape they happened to witness, so our own task is to describe the major landmarks that we found
when we explored the landscape of disordered affect.

We will present the results of those explorations in Chapters 3
through 14, and we shall see that many of the characteristics of the inner
experience of affect-disordered subjects are startlingly different from
what we might have expected. We will give here three examples, to
whet the appetite so to speak, but the reader will have to consult the
relevant chapters to fill in the details.

EXAMPLES OF OUR RESULTS

Example 1. Psychologists have accepted for at least a century that
human perception divides the world into regions called "figure" and
"ground," where the figure is the center of perception and is clearer and
more detailed, while the ground is less distinct and less differentiated as
it fades to the periphery of perception. We will see in Chapter 14 that the
perception of one subject did *not* have this figure/ground characteristic,
that the periphery of perception was just as clear as the center, and as a
result that many unrelated events could be simultaneously perceived.
We shall see in that chapter that such perceptions were distressing,
harrowing, constant events.

Example 2. We made the unsurprising observation in the previous
book that many individuals talk to themselves in their inner experience,
the phenomenon we called Inner Speech. For most of our subjects, this
Inner Speech has most of the same characteristics as external speech
except that no external sounds are produced: it proceeds at the same rate
of speed and pitch, has the same emotion and inflection, etc. as external
speech. Furthermore, Inner Speech is generally experienced as an active
creation: the speaker is aware of producing and directing the words
being spoken. This is by contrast to the phenomenon of hearing (including Inner Hearing), where the words are recognized as coming from an
external source, appearing by themselves, passively received by the
hearer. We shall see in Chapters 11, 12, and 13 that several of our anxious subjects had this active/passive distinction of speaking and hearing
reversed; that is, speech (both external and Inner) was apprehended by
the speaker as an automatic "rolling out" of the words, *not* under her
own perceived control or direction; hearing, by contrast, required directed effort, an active "going out to meet each word and bringing it
back." We will speculate that such reversal of the experience of the
production of meaning is a characteristic of at least some anxiety; further

research will be necessary to corroborate or refute that speculation. This study will thus sketch possible directions for future research which have previously not been imagined.

Example 3. We will see that the phenomenon we call Unsymbolized Thinking is a frequent characteristic of most of our affect-disordered subjects; Unsymbolized Thinking occurs occasionally but *not* frequently in our normal and schizophrenic subjects. One of our observations in Chapters 3–7 will be that Unsymbolized Thinking was strongly related to level of depression in our subjects: the inner experience of our most depressed individual was almost entirely Unsymbolized Thinking, while moderately depressed individuals experienced moderate amounts of Unsymbolized Thinking. Furthermore, we found that within single individuals, Unsymbolized Thinking occurs more frequently when subjects move into a depressive episode, and when the same subject becomes less depressed, Unsymbolized Thinking becomes less frequent.

UNSYMBOLIZED THINKING

Because Unsymbolized Thinking is such a frequent characteristic of almost all of the subjects in this book, we will describe this phenomenon here in some detail. Unsymbolized Thinking is the experience of an inner process which is clearly a thought and which has a clear meaning, but which seems to take place without symbols of any kind, that is, without words, images, bodily sensations, etc. For example, at one sample our depressed subject Diane (see Chapter 6) was grocery shopping, and was trying to decide whether to buy breakfast cereal. Diane clearly apprehended this attempting-to-decide as a thought process (*not* a feeling or bodily sensation, for example) which involved wondering whether she would eat the cereal or whether it would be wasted, a conscious recognizing that she didn't usually eat breakfast except that sometimes she had a glass of juice, and a conscious noting of how expensive the cereal was. However, there were no words (such as "cereal," "eat," "wasted," or "expensive," etc.), no images (of a box or bowl of cereal, for example), no bodily sensations (such as leaning toward or away from the cereal), etc. Diane "just knew" she was thinking about the possible waste and expense of breakfast cereal.

This breakfast-cereal thought was in many ways typical of the way most subjects experience Unsymbolized Thinking. First, subjects have no doubt about *what* they are thinking—the thought content is clearly and easily apprehendable. In our example, Diane knew clearly that she was considering the possible waste and expense of breakfast cereal and that she was clearly thinking that she didn't usually eat breakfast except for juice.

Second, the Unsymbolized Thinking can be complex and differentiated. In the cereal example, the Unsymbolized Thinking included separate components about wastefulness, cereal, juice, and expense.

Third, Unsymbolized Thinking can be quite specific. Here, for example, it provided a general description of breakfast habits (generally not eating breakfast) but included the particular exception of sometimes having juice.

Fourth, subjects generally have considerable difficulty describing *how* they experience an Unsymbolized Thought to take place. Many subjects apparently take it for granted that all thinking must be in words, and so initially report an Unsymbolized Thought as having taken place in inner words. When we inquire about the exact words said or heard, and the manner in which those words were apprehended, subjects typically initially become confused, uncomfortable, and seemingly dumbfounded, or their attempts at description become vague ("I sort of thought . . .") or take place in the subjunctive mood ("It was as if I were saying . . ."). When we assure subjects that we simply want to know how they themselves apprehend their inner experience, and that perhaps it is possible that there are no words apprehendable at the moment, many subjects become visibly relieved, as if they had doubted their own sanity when they had not been able find words or images in their thoughts. Some subjects refuse to believe at first that unworded thinking can take place, and only after they encounter repeated samples over several sampling days do they gradually convince themselves, much to their own disbelief, that Yes, I was thinking, and No, there were no words or symbols to support that thinking.

Fifth, when subjects have gained enough confidence to report such experiences, they report them with phrases such as "I don't know how I was thinking that, I just know it," or "I was *just thinking* (said with a resigned smile) . . .," or "It was just a thought." The notion that Unsymbolized Thinking is a strange or impossible phenomenon frequently never leaves a subject, even though they may have given 20 or more separate descriptions of Unsymbolized Thoughts over several days of sampling.

We should explicitly note that our task in these studies is simply to describe experience *as it is apprehended* by our subjects. We are *not* attempting to explain how thinking *really* takes place. For example, we are confident in our claim that subjects accurately apprehend thinking which takes place without words, images, or other symbols being immediately available to awareness. We are *not* claiming that there are *in fact* no words, images, or other symbols actually present somewhere in the thought process (perhaps "unconscious," "extremely dim," "systematically overlooked," or "destroyed by the beep itself"). Such words or images may or may not in fact exist. Our investigations do not answer such questions. What our results *do* show is that Unsymbolized Thinking is a very frequent phenomenon for some people and a very *infrequent* phenomenon for others, and that individuals who are depressed, anxious, or bulimic generally fall at the high end of the Unsymbolized Thinking frequency continuum.

THE POSSIBILITY OF "LEADING THE WITNESS"

We said above that many subjects do not recognize the possibility of Unsymbolized Thinking until we suggest that such a possibility exists. Might it be that we are suggesting the phenomenon to our subjects, who then simply echo it back to us? We cannot give a definitive answer to this question until other investigators attempt to replicate our work. There are, however, five preliminary comments we might offer.

First, some subjects describe the Unsymbolized Thinking phenomenon spontaneously, without any questioning from us. These subjects are not, apparently, bound by the preconception that thinking must take place in words, and they simply say, without apparent inner conflict, that they were "just thinking" and that no words or images or other symbols were present.

Second, we try to be extremely sensitive to the "leading the witness" issue. When we are engaged in the task of clarifying more precisely how a subject has described a particular sample, we typically give her two or three optional restatements of what she has said and allow her to accept or reject all or any of them. Our suggestions are always given tentatively, and we try to impress on our subject (and reaffirm for ourselves) that we are not "trying to put words into her mouth," that we want only to help the subject make her descriptions fit her own experiences as precisely as possible. It is, of course, the case that good intentions do not eliminate the possibility of bias creeping into an interview; nonetheless, it can be fairly said that the intention not to lead is constantly a priority.

Third, our subjects frequently contradict us when we give tentative clarifications of some aspect of inner experience, saying "that's not right," or "that's not what I meant." Clearly we were not leading the witness in those cases.

Fourth, we ourselves, at first, were greatly surprised by the existence of the Unsymbolized Thinking phenomenon. In the early phases of these investigations, when our subjects were confused about how to describe the manner in which a particular thinking (which later we came to call Unsymbolized) took place, we were equally as confused. And when early subjects said that thinking took place without words or images or other symbols, we ourselves (holding the same presuppositions as our subjects) were skeptical, and searched with our subjects diligently for the hidden words which "must" have been present. Only gradually did we let go of this presupposition and recognize that the Unsymbolized Thinking phenomenon was prevalent across subjects.

Fifth, even though the term Unsymbolized Thinking may be new to the modern reader, the phenomenon itself is not new, but was discovered in the early 1900s by the introspectionists, who called the phenomenon "imageless thought" (we return to the comparison between Unsymbolized and imageless thought in Chapter 2). The introspectionists did not claim that imageless thought was somehow related to affect disturbance, but they did describe the imageless thought phenomenon with almost exactly the same words that we use when we describe Unsymbolized Thinking. If we are leading the witness, then the introspectionists, even though their method was rather different from ours, must have been doing the same kind of leading.

SHOULD WE DISMISS THIS STUDY
BECAUSE IT IS "INTROSPECTIVE"?

The describing of inner experience is a venture that some would label "introspective" and dismiss because introspection has been discredited by a variety of studies. I tried to show in a preliminary comment to the first book that the criticisms most frequently leveled against introspection do *not* apply to the descriptive experience sampling method we are using, and in so doing urged readers to suspend their prejudices against introspective techniques while considering the evidence that we presented.

To admit, in 1993, that Unsymbolized Thinking is the same phenomenon as imageless thought is to walk directly into the lion's den of a modern psychology opposed to introspection, because the imageless thought controversy was the central point about which the modern criticism of introspection revolved. Students of the history of psychology have been taught that the introspectionists themselves couldn't agree as to whether imageless thought exists or not. Shouldn't we have learned our historical lesson to avoid anything that even remotely resembles imageless thought? Isn't it obvious by now that if our investigations find that something like imageless thought is one of the most important kinds of inner experience, then the present investigation technique must be doomed to failure just as was the introspectionist program of a century ago?

The answers to these questions are, we think, clearly, "no", however unpopular or improbable that might seem. In Chapter 2, we will attempt to point out that while the imageless thought controversy was a damning blow for introspection as it was practiced at the beginning of this century, it is *not* a problem for our own investigations. This is because of the little-recognized fact that *the introspectionists did agree on the existence of the phenomenon of imageless thought;* it was only when they tried to explain it that they disagreed. When the introspectionists simply described the phenomenon which was called imageless thought, they were in close accord with each other and with our own observations.

THE METHOD

We have given a complete description of the descriptive sampling method and its rationale previously (see Hurlburt, 1990). In brief, the method is as follows: Before sampling begins, we instruct subjects that they are free to participate or decline to participate at any time during the study, and we reiterate that instruction frequently throughout the sampling process. We tell subjects that we will be asking them to report their inner experience—thoughts, feelings, sensations, perceptions, awarenesses, etc.—at random moments. We inform them that they should feel free to tell us at any time if some aspect of their inner experience is none of our business; we all have thoughts or feelings which we might not want to share, so they have every right to decline. We would much rather they tell us up front that something is none of our business than simply evade it. If they evade, we generally feel as if a description is incomplete but we don't know why, and therefore continue to ask question after question trying to reach a sense of completion, so it is much better for both of us if they simply say, "I don't want to talk about that." [Such requests are very rare in our research.] We try to develop a co-researcher understanding with each subject: we are trying to find out something about which the subject is the only expert, namely her own inner experience. We will need to be guided as to what the characteristics of that experience are, and the subject is the only possible guide.

Subjects are equipped with a random interval generator (a "beeper") which emits a 400 hz tone over an earphone at random intervals. The interval lengths are randomly selected by the instrument itself, which is programmed to allow a maximum interval between beeps of one hour and a minimum interval of about one minute. The mean interval between beeps is 30 minutes. The volume of the beep itself is adjustable by the subject; the subject is instructed to adjust the volume so that the beep is sufficiently loud so as to be clearly and immediately recognized as the interval-generator beep, but not so loud as to startle the subject. The actual required volume depends on the ambient noise level in the particular situation the subject finds herself.

The subject is requested to use the apparatus in her own natural environments for a period of time sufficiently long to generate six to eight beeps—generally about three or four hours. [Early in this series of studies, we required subjects to wear the apparatus from morning to night, but we have subsequently found that the time of day is not particularly relevant in obtaining the results we find important.] We do request that subjects use the apparatus while engaging in different activities [primarily to avoid getting too many samples while subjects are watching television].

At each beep the subject's task is to "freeze" her ongoing experience and to write a description of it in a notebook which we supply. The notebook description does not have to be complete, or in complete sentences, but should contain enough of an outline of the experience so that the experience can be accurately reconstructed several hours later. We are interested, we tell the subject, in what her inner experience was like "one microsecond *before*" it was disturbed by the beep. We are *not* interested in what her *reaction* to the beep was, but instead, in what was happening *just prior* to that reaction.

It frequently takes several days of sampling for a subject to grasp exactly what we mean by freezing the ongoing experience. We have found the following analogies useful in conveying to subjects what we mean. "It is as if we were to take a flash picture of your inner experience. You know that when you have your picture taken, it always seems like you were blinking just when the flashbulb went off, but actually the picture catches you with your eyes open—the blink is *in response* to the flash. Our goal here is to catch, if we can, your experience just *before* the blink, so to speak, whatever the flash would catch before your body or thoughts have time to react to it." We also sketch the accompanying figure and give the following instruction: "Your experience changes, meanders around like a stream, which we can represent as this line [pointing to the curvy line in Figure 1.1]. Then the beep comes, and your experience is altered by it, as shown where the line representing your

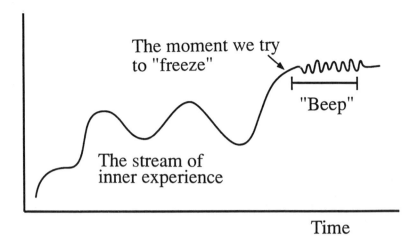

Figure 1.1 Sketch of the stream of inner experience indicating the moment we wish to sample. Note that the moment we wish to sample is just slightly before the onset of the beep.

experience becomes jagged. The moment we are interested in, the one we want you to "freeze," is the point *just prior* to that alteration.

We try to impress on our subjects that we are *not* particularly interested in explanations of *why* they are thinking or doing what they are doing, except to the extent that such explanations are required to understand the moment. (It is not, we say, that such explanations are uninteresting, as frequently they are genuinely fascinating, but that is not our focus.) Furthermore, we are not interested in whether a particular experience is frequent or typical or unusual, etc. We simply wish them to describe that single experience as it naturally occurred.

Subjects generally believe that what we mean by "moment" is much longer than do we ourselves, despite the fact that we emphasize the instantaneousness of the flashbulb, etc. In general, subjects initially report long durations—whole conversations, with questions and responses, for example—and only gradually learn to narrow their focus down to a single word, phrase or sentence.

After subjects have collected six or eight samples, they meet with us for an extended conversation about those samples. This conversation is almost without exception scheduled within 24 hours of the time of sampling—we need "fresh beeps," we say. This conversation is aimed at getting as exact a description of the sampled moment as possible. The subject refers back to her notes, and we question and requestion, attempting to iron out as many ambiguities of description as possible, until we think, and the subject agrees, that we have either obtained a complete description of the moment or that we have reached the limits of our abilities to describe that particular sampled experience.

It does frequently happen, especially early in the sampling process, that we "reach the limit of our abilities" to describe a sampled moment. We reassure the subject that complete, accurate descriptions of each beeped moment are not necessary; that it is preferable to leave a sample incompletely described than to make up details or pretend resolution; that if a difficult-to-describe phenomenon is important, it will happen again at a later sample, and by then we will have had more practice in describing; that we recognize that the subject has had no way of know-ing exactly what kinds of questions we would be asking, and so could not have known which details to pay attention to at the time of the first beep, but that subsequent beeps will probably be easier because of the practice that the present conversation is providing; that perhaps the phenomenon which was occurring at the moment of the beep is actually impossible to put into words, and so will never be able to be completely described; that we can ask questions which are impossible to answer or which do not make sense, and that the subject should tell us when we do that; etc.

After we have reached as complete a description as possible of the first sample, we move to the second sample of the day and repeat the process. It generally takes us between 10 and 20 minutes to discuss a single sample, and we have found that the interview process is tiring both for us and for the subject, so we limit the interview to about one hour, thus describing perhaps six samples. If the subject has collected more samples than time permits us to discuss, we discard the remaining samples.

This sample and discussion process is then repeated the next day (or the next convenient day), and is repeated again until we think we have obtained an adequate number of samples (or until some external factor forces the cessation of sampling). The criterion for "adequacy" of the number of samples is agreement between our subjects and ourselves that additional samples all seem similar to samples which we have al-ready discussed. This point is clearly arbitrary, but in my own practice, it is very clearly experientially defined: the sampling conversations are at first fascinating for me, a glimpse into a strange land with a unique viewpoint. After about 4 to 8 sampling days, that fascination dramat-ically lessens, and sampling becomes rather hard work that drains ener-gy rather than creates it. Subjects frequently have somewhat the same experience at approximately the same time, but that may be the result of my own decrease in excitement rather than the simultaneous recognition that "enough is enough."

It is our goal during the sampling period to write descriptions of at least some of the samples from each sampling day—that is, to have the writing of the sample descriptions keep up with the sampling itself. This is not always possible, but writing the descriptions soon after the discussions makes them more accurate for two reasons: the details are fresher in memory, and therefore easier to recall; and subsequent events (such as the discussion of later samples) cannot influence the description of the current sample.

At the conclusion of the sampling period, we identify the salient characteristics of the complete set of samples. Most frequently, these salient characteristics have emerged during the sampling itself, so that near the end of the sampling period, it is generally quite obvious what most of the salient characteristics will be. [This should not be surprising since we have spent 5 to 10 hours with this one subject and spent an additional number of hours writing single-sample descriptions.] We also go back through our notes for each beep in an attempt to identify any characteristics which emerge when all the beeps are considered at once. We then write descriptions of the salient characteristics, illustrating them with relevant samples which have already been described.

After the complete description of the salient characteristics of a subject's samples is finished and rewritten to our own satisfaction, we present it to our subject for her comments, encouraging her to be as critical as possible. We respond to any comments, questions, or suggestions the subject may have, integrating them into the final version. Very occasionally (twice, if memory serves, described in the chapters on Bob and Joe in Hurlburt, 1990), we cannot reconcile our own description with our subject's criticism. In those cases, we present both sides of the disagreement with interpretative comments. Our subjects' opinions of what took place during sampling are not infallible, nor are our own, and we attempt to provide as candid an accounting of any discrepancies in interpretation as possible.

The individual chapters which comprise the body of this book are the results of this procedure. Before we turn to those descriptions, we provide a reconstruction of the history of introspection, in our second attempt (the first was the "preliminary comments" chapter in the previous book) to show that introspective-type research can indeed be a source of reliable and valid scientific data.

A Comment to Suspend the Introspection Controversy

Introspecting Subjects Did Agree About "Imageless Thought"

Christy K. Monson and RTH

There is among psychologists a strong belief (some might say a prejudice) that holds that any method which might be labelled "introspectionistic" is unreliable and invalid. We wish to face that prejudice head on because we believe it is mistaken, and because sophisticated readers who hold it may reject our findings before they have considered them adequately. The risk of this prejudice to the present study becomes all the more acute because we will make the case that the phenomenon of Unsymbolized Thinking (which, as we have seen, is among the more important results of the present book) is the same phenomenon that the introspectionists called "imageless thought," and the concept of imageless thought was the battleground on which early introspection was soundly defeated.

This chapter will be structured as follows: first we will demonstrate that Unsymbolized Thinking and imageless thought are the same phenomena; then we will show how imageless thought has been seen historically as causing the demise of introspective methods "because introspectionists could not agree as to whether imageless thought exists"; next we will show that this historical position is mistaken: introspecting subjects did in fact agree about the phenomenon of imageless thought; and finally, we will conclude that the so-called imageless thought phenomenon actually supports our current observations, rather than serves as a cause to reject them.

UNSYMBOLIZED THINKING IS THE SAME PHENOMENON AS IMAGELESS THOUGHT

Let us consider two investigations typical of turn of the century introspection, one by Mayer and Orth (1901) and the other by Bühler (1907).

Mayer and Orth (1901) asked subjects (themselves included) to give free associations to an auditory stimulus word, and to note (and subsequently report) everything that went on in consciousness between the presentation of the stimulus and the response. Mayer and Orth found three kinds of contents of consciousness, the third of which is relevant here. They described the first two contents of consciousness (perceptions/images and acts of will) and continued:

> In addition to these two classes of conscious events we must set up also a third group of facts of consciousness, one that has not been sufficiently stressed in psychology up to the present day. In the course of our experiments we were, again and again, involuntarily brought up against the fact of the existence of this third group. The subjects frequently reported that they experienced certain events of consciousness which they could quite clearly designate neither as definite images nor yet as volitions. For example, the subject Mayer [also one of the paper's authors] made the observation that, in reference to the auditory stimulus-word "metre" a peculiar event of consciousness intervened which could not be characterized more exactly, and which was succeeded by the spoken response "trochee." In other cases, subjects could give a closer account of these psychic facts. For example, Orth [also one of the paper's authors] observed that the stimulus word "mustard" released such a peculiar event of consciousness, which he thought he could characterize as "memory of a common figure of speech." Thereafter the reaction "grain" followed. In all such cases, the subject could, nevertheless, not detect the slightest trace of the presence in consciousness of "presentations" by which they specified the psychic fact more closely in their reports. All of these events of consciousness, in spite of their obviously, often totally, different quality, we class together under the name *Bewusstseinslagen*—states of consciousness. The replies of the observers show that these states of consciousness are sometimes marked by feeling, but are, however, sometimes without any feeling tone. (Mayer & Orth, 1901, p. 6, cited by Humphrey, 1963, p. 33)

Mayer and Orth were the first to use the term *Bewusstseinslagen* to refer to those states of consciousness which did not have conscious image or volitional characteristics. Subsequent investigators also used the term, which gradually came to be one of the several kinds of experience known collectively as "imageless thought."

In Bühler's typical introspective study, seven subjects (including several of the most distinguished psychologists of the day) were given questions to which they were to respond "yes" or "no." The questions used generally required considerable thought, such as, "Was the theorem of Pythagoras known in the Middle Ages?" "Can you get to Berlin from here in seven hours?" and "The smaller the woman's foot, the larger the bill for the shoes?" The subject was to give his response, and then to describe in as much detail as possible his consciousness between the time of the question and the response.

The Yes/No answer itself was not the focus of the investigation; more important were the reports of the subject's consciousness between the question and the answer. Subjects gave frequent reports of words, sensory presentations (auditory, visual, kinesthetic, etc.), and feelings; but they also reported mental processes which were difficult to describe:

The most important bits of experience are something that, in all the categories through which these formations can be defined [sensations, images, feelings, etc.], are not touched at all. . . . Something which before all shows no sensory quality, no sensory intensity. Something of which we may rightly predicate degree of clearness, degree of certainty, a vividness by means of which it arouses our psychic interest; which, however, in its content is quite differently determined from everything that is ultimately reducible to sensations; something for which it would be nonsense to try to determine whether it possessed a greater or less intensity, or even into what sensory qualities it could be resolved. These entities are what the subjects, using Ach's term, have designated as awarenesses, or sometimes as knowing, or simply as 'the consciousness that', but most frequently and correctly as 'thoughts'. (Bühler, 1907, pp. 315–316, cited by Humphrey, 1963, p. 57)

Mayer and Orth's *Bewusstseinslagen* and Bühler's "thoughts" were quite clearly conscious awarenesses, knowings, or states of consciousness, which took place at a particular point in time (e.g., between the stimulus word and the response), were quite well defined, and had quite definite meaning, but with which no words, sensations, images, volitions, or other simpler conscious events could be identified.

That, however, is exactly the definition we provided in the previous chapter for the characteristics of inner experience we call Unsymbolized

Thinking: no words or images; the subjects "just know" what they were thinking about at the moment of the beep; the thoughts are quite specific and differentiated. Our own descriptions of Unsymbolized Thinking seem to us to be identical to the descriptions of imageless thought provided by Mayer and Orth, Bühler, and other introspectionists; our conclusion is that Unsymbolized Thinking is the same phenomenon the introspectionists called imageless thought.

IMAGELESS THOUGHT IS SEEN AS CAUSING
THE DEMISE OF INTROSPECTION

Although introspection held a central place in the early history of psychology, it has not received the historical attention it deserves (Danziger, 1980). Many, if not most, present-day psychologists either dismiss introspection entirely or are extremely critical of such methods, believing them to be inadequate and/or unreliable (Misiak & Sexton, 1972; Brennan, 1982). The term "introspection' does not even appear in the index of most modern introductory psychology textbooks; if it does appear, it is usually mentioned only in passing in connection with the historical significance of Wilhelm Wundt and the beginnings of modern experimental psychology.

Furthermore, most modern texts on psychological *method* do not mention introspection. Those that do are critical. For example, Wood (1981) concluded that "introspection has been used extensively by psychologists but, over the years, most psychologists have come to recognize the limitations of this approach. . . . If we rely on our . . . introspections we are likely to reach erroneous conclusions a good part of the time" (pp. 7–8).

The most frequent explanation of this omission or criticism of introspection is that many historians of psychology emphasize that the different introspective laboratories of the turn-of-the-century introspective era found different results, even under similar experimental conditions (Danziger, 1980). This introspectionists-can't-agree opinion was largely the result of the 1900–1925 controversy over whether imageless thought exists. The prevailing doctrine which served to explain the functioning of the mind was that of sensationalism, which held that every "experience has an elemental core and a meaning providing context. Perceptions have sensory cores and ideas have imaginal cores. The context can be sensory (as kinesthetic accentuation of rhythm) or imaginal (as in recalling the name of a familiar face). It is associated context that gives meaning to any experience." (Wertheimer, 1987, p. 111) For our purposes, the important part of the sensationalist position is the so-called "imaginal core" of an idea. According to the sensationalists, the essential feature—the very core—of every idea is an image. It was thus, according to the sensationalists, impossible to have an idea without having an image at its core; such images might be visual, kinesthetic, or auditory, etc., but the doctrine was clear: no image, no idea. This sensationalistic belief was the result of a long tradition extending back at least as far as Aristotle, and in the early 1900s was held by psychological investigators such as Titchener, Bagley, Okabe, Clarke, Book, Jacobson, Geissler, Fischer, Kakise, Tolman, Martin, and others.

As we have noted in our two examples, investigators applying introspective techniques observed that subjects sometimes reported that meaning, awareness, knowing, understanding, recognition, etc. occurred *without* images being present in consciousness. This kind of observation led some investigators to reject the "no image, no idea" position held by the sensationalists, and to propose, on the contrary, that some thinking can take place without imaginal cores; that is, they proposed that "imageless thought" exists. Among proponents of this imageless thought position were the Würzburg School investigators (Külpe, Mayer, Orth, Marbe, Ach, Watt, Messer, and Moore) as well as Binet, Woodworth, Betts, Aveling, and others. The battle lines were drawn between the sensationalists and the imageless thought proponents: did imageless thought exist or not?

For about twenty years, introspective studies were performed in both camps which attempted either to prove or to disprove the existence of imageless thought. After this time, neither the sensationalists nor the imageless thought proponents could claim to have convinced the opposition, and the resulting stalemate was taken as a sign of the impotence of introspection: if introspection could not resolve such a basic issue after so much investigation, then the introspective method itself must be inadequate and should therefore be abandoned.

The historical sketch we have just given is typical of most accounts of the demise of introspection. For example, Mook (1982) concluded, "Different investigators . . . have arrived at opposite conclusions . . . [to the question] Can you think without images? . . . There seemed to be no good way of finding out" (pp. 368–369); and Misiak and Sexton (1972) summarized, "The results based on introspection in various laboratories were conflicting, and at times the findings of one laboratory were exactly opposite to those of another, even when the conditions of experimentation were identical" (p. 47). Introspection was thus branded as being unreliable and therefore scientifically uninformative.[1]

The fact remains that many psychologists do still hold the summary idea that early introspectionists could not agree and therefore introspective methods are unreliable and should be avoided.

INTROSPECTING SUBJECTS DID IN FACT AGREE ABOUT IMAGELESS THOUGHT

The previous section presented a typical sketch of the history of the imageless thought controversy which holds that the introspecting sensationalists could not agree with the introspecting Würzburg School investigators over the existence of imageless thought. The present section shows that this introspectionists-can't-agree-generalization is a misleading characterization of the data reported by the introspectionists, a characterization which conceals the fact that, *for the most part, introspecting subjects did in fact agree with each other's reports of the phenomenon which was called imageless thought.* It seems to us, then, that subjects in both the sensationalistic and imageless-thought laboratories reported *similar observations.* It was only the *interpretation* of these observations, rather than the observations themselves, which differed from one laboratory to the next.

In both of the two examples above (Mayer & Orth, 1901; and Bühler, 1907), subjects in imageless-thought laboratories reported meanings, understandings, awarenesses, knowings, etc. which occurred with no conscious awareness of images. In fact, subjects in *all* the imageless thought studies reported such phenomena (that was, after all, the determining factor which led to their being imageless-thought proponents). It remains only to show that the subjects in the introspective experiments conducted by the *sensationalists* also reported that meanings, under-

---

[1]Danziger (1980) has shown that when modern historians attribute the demise of introspection to the disagreement among the introspectionists, they oversimplify the historical situation. In a more thorough consideration of the subject, he showed that the decline of introspection was due in large part to factors *other* than the different-laboratories/ different-results characterization. He concluded that such emerging interests as child and animal psychology, quantitative physiological observation, and the American interest in physical and mental performance ". . . redefine(d) the goals of psychological research and hence produce(d) a reselection of the methods needed to achieve these goals. Introspection was less a victim of its intrinsic problems than a casualty of historical forces far bigger than itself" (Danziger, 1980, p. 259).

standings, awarenesses, knowledge, recognition, etc. sometimes occurred without images being present in consciousness. Thus, we shall see that the introspecting subjects in experiments conducted both by the sensationalists and by the imageless-thought proponents *agreed about imageless phenomena* in the sense that they gave quite similar (no image present in awareness) reports about the contents of their inner experience. However, the sensationalists and the imageless thought proponents gave quite different *theoretical explanations* of these reports, and the sensationalists and the imageless-thought proponents never agreed about the theoretical explanation. We will conclude, therefore, that the unreliability attributed to introspection came not from the *subjects'* conflicting reports about consciousness, but rather from the *investigators'* attempts to fit these reports into a theoretical structure.

We are not the first investigators to note this similarity in data between the imageless thought and sensationalist subjects. For example, one of the imageless thought proponents of the Würzburg school (Moore, 1919) analyzed the results of the sensationalist Okabe (1910) and concluded that Okabe's subjects gave reports that the Würzburgers might call imageless. However, such observations of similarity have been, for the most part, lost from modern view.

We turn now to review a series of reports, all of which are from investigators who accepted the sensationalist position. We shall see that subjects in each of these studies reported phenomena during their introspections where some cognitive process (meaning, belief, etc.) was introspectively known to be ongoing, but which occurred without the simultaneous presence in consciousness of any image. In each case the sensationalist researchers accepted their subjects' reports of these experiences but did not assign to them the separate category "imageless thought."

Bagley (1900), the first of our sensationalist researchers, studied apperception of spoken language, and found that the subjects sometimes reported images "too faint to describe" (p. 117) and used verbal means to express the meaning that was present in their thinking. These subjects noted that the words used to express the meaning were not exactly the same as the meaning itself (implying that the meaning was known to the subject in some manner other than verbally), and that attempts to apprehend an image at such times failed. Thus, Bagley's subjects were reporting that meaning was sometimes clearly present with neither words nor images present in consciousness. However, rather than refer to such experiences as "imageless thoughts," Bagley called them "moods."

Clarke (1911) was a sensationalist who attempted to investigate directly the *Bewusstseinslagen* of Mayer and Orth. She presented to subjects words in Braille, because such words cannot be taken in "at a glance" in visual perception, and asked subjects to introspect during the period that the meaning of the Braille word was being grasped. Clark found that at times images were "inadequate, irrelevant, and contradictory" (p. 241) to the meaning that was known to be present in consciousness, which is to say that meaning was available to subjects but was not supported by consciously-apprehended images. Thus Clarke's subjects were reporting experiences of meaning without clearly apprehendable images; however, rather than call these meanings "imageless thoughts," she explained that thoughts which were accompanied by inadequate images were simply at the vague extreme of a graded continuum of increasingly vague images.

Okabe (1910) investigated belief by presenting written passages and requesting subjects to introspect while the process of belief or disbelief was forming. Okabe noted that his subjects sometimes had clearly image-based beliefs, such as when subject "V" reported at trial A102: "Verbal saying over to myself: Of course don't believe it," or at A88: "Clear verbal ideas: There's something wrong; it isn't a good comparison" (p. 569). At other times, however, the same subject experienced understandings which apparently preceded any image or sensation, as for example when she reported at A77: "Read and understood; did not believe it" (p. 569). However, Okabe did not identify this understanding or immediate disbelief as imageless phenomena, even though they were initially present without images available to consciousness.

Book (1910) studied the process of learning to use a typewriter. He noted that the thinking of neophyte typists is full of sensory images of the individual letters being typed, but as the typist becomes more skilled, the accompanying thought gradually loses its sensational qualities and eventually the meaning of the letters is apprehended directly without the aid of images. Rather than call this directly-apprehended meaning "imageless thought," he explained the meaning in terms of familiarity and recognition and suggested that sensational representations continued to exist at the less-clear end of an imaginal hierarchy.

Kakise (1911) investigated the problem of meaning and understanding through the presentation of words and phrases and found that subjects reported "a pure feeling of concept or meaning" (p. 52), where by "pure" he meant without the concomitant appearance of images in consciousness. However, instead of calling this feeling "imageless," he relegated it to a hierarchy of "concomitants of the process of understanding" (p. 42).

Jacobson (1911) asked subjects to introspect after having a printed word or phrase laid before them. He reported, for example, that when a subject was asked, "Did you see him kill the man?" (p. 570) there was "no meaning" for three seconds, at which time an image carrying the idea occurred. Clearly, the subject understood the meaning of this question throughout those three seconds, but rather than refer to this understanding as an "imageless" process, he concluded that there was no meaning present for the three seconds it took for an image to appear, since according to his theory, meaning must be carried by an image.

Langfeld (1910) and Geissler (1912) asked their subjects to suppress the real name of a familiar object and respond to a nonsense one. Their subjects reported that verbal ideas became unrecognizable, themselves even using the term "imageless" to describe this unrecognizability (Geissler, 1912, p. 194). However, Geissler termed this a "logical" process, rather than imageless thought, and assigned it a place outside the field of psychology.

Martin (1912, as cited by Woodworth, 1915; Spearman, 1923/1973) asked her subjects to recall a series of cards, first by using whatever mental method they believed to be most effective, and second by suppressing all images during the reproductive process. She found that the subjects "became skeptical as to the power of images to inform" (Martin, 1912, as cited by Spearman, 1923/1973, p. 191), but did not convert to an imageless-thought position.

Fischer (1916) presented her subjects with four groups of ten abstract drawings, the "Zalof," the "Deral," the "Tefoq," and the "Kareg" groups. She then asked subjects to introspect while attempting to arrive at the abstract generalizations which determined that one particular drawing was a "Deral" while another was a "Tefoq," etc. Her subjects reported "wondering" and "explicit awarenesses," (Fischer, 1916, p. 164) which she said were more or less fragmentary and which occurred without the immediate presence of images in consciousness, and which at times were noted as tension in the eyes. She also found that recall took place without waiting for imagery to appear in consciousness as the subject became familiar with the figures. Rather than refer to these "wonderings" and "explicit awarenesses" as "imageless thoughts," she noted that consciousness "was marked by the presence . . . (of) tensions, strains, organic contents, and the like" (p. 83).

We thus see that there are repeated instances where the introspecting subjects of these sensationalist investigators reported phenomena that the Würzburgers or others might call "imageless," but which the sensationalist investigators themselves interpreted otherwise (for example, as being at the vague end of an image continuum, or as being feelings). We are thus compelled to conclude that introspecting subjects

in both the sensationalist and the Würzburg laboratories were for the
most part in agreement about the existence of the *phenomena* of consciousness that some called "imageless" and some identified with other
labels. What the introspectionist investigators could not agree about was
the *interpretation* of those introspective observations: when, for example,
did consistent reports of meaning without conscious images necessitate
identifying a separate, "imageless," category of thinking?

Titchener himself, one of the leading sensationalists, accepted the
fact that introspecting subjects correctly reported "conscious attitudes,"
experiences that did not have clear images available to consciousness.
He wrote that one product

> of the attempt to analyze the processes of thought was the discovery
> of the conscious attitudes. What precisely these attitudes are, in
> their psychological status, is still a matter of dispute. They are re-
> ported as vague and elusive processes, which carry as if in a nutshell
> the entire meaning of a situation. . . . They are indicated, desig-
> nated by a single word such as 'hesitation,' 'vacillation,' 'incapacity,'
> or by a phrase, such as 'a realization that the division can be carried
> out without a remainder,' 'a remembrance that we talked it all over
> before and couldn't reach a conclusion.' (Titchener, 1910/1980,
> pp. 505–506)

Thus Titchener accepted the existence of such experiences as "vague
and elusive processes which carry as if in a nutshell the entire meaning,"
the experiences that others would call imageless. The question for
Titchener, however, was whether those experiences were analyzable
into sensory and imaginal elements:

> Some psychologists maintain, definitely, that there are awarenesses
> of meaning, and awarenesses of relation, which cannot be reduced
> to simpler terms, but must be accepted as nonsensory and imageless
> components of the higher mental processes. The author believes, on
> the contrary, that the attitudes, so far as they are conscious at all, are
> always analyzable. (Titchener, 1910/1980, p. 507)

Titchener's point was that introspecting subjects correctly observe the
phenomena of meaning or relation which occurs without the simultaneous perception of images. However, these observations should not
be assigned to a separate category of thinking called imageless thought,
since he held that if introspectionists were to go further in the correct
introspective analysis of those attitudes, they would find senso-
ry/imaginal cores for every idea.

We are led, then, to make extremely clear the distinction between
observing the events occurring in consciousness (where the subjects were

in substantial agreement) and *interpreting* those same events according to a theoretical perspective (where the investigators were in dogmatic disagreement). This distinction is not always made by modern historians of psychology.

THE IMAGELESS THOUGHT PHENOMENON
SUPPORTS OUR PRESENT WORK

We have seen that the sensationalists and the imageless thought proponents agreed about the phenomenon of imageless thought down to, but not including, its interpretation, and that our Unsymbolized Thinking is the same phenomenon as the introspectionists' imageless thought. Our conclusion is that the phenomenon of Unsymbolized Thinking is apparent to all investigators who attempt to analyze carefully the moments of inner experience. It has been our experience in describing the Unsymbolized Thinking phenomenon to colleagues that many do not believe that such a phenomenon is possible to recognize, much less to describe. The identity between Unsymbolized Thinking and imageless thought lends support to our observations; careful observers have been identifying this phenomenon for at least a century.

The history of the introspection of imageless thought provides two suggestions for any modern study which seeks to use reports about inner experience. First, we should recognize that it is probably impossible to use introspection to prove or disprove a theoretical position which is based on some a priori analysis of what thinking *must* be like; the descriptions of inner experience must come *before* the explanations.

Second, we should recognize that any categories we might advance to organize the phenomena of inner experience will not have clear, unambiguous borders; categories of inner experience do not end abruptly but fade into one another: for example, the introspectionists' referred to a "continuum of vagueness." There are frequent samples in our own present work which are "somewhere between" Unsymbolized Thinking and Inner Speech, or which seem in some respects to be both Unsymbolized Thinking and an Image. A science of inner experience must be content with the kind of concept which has imprecise boundaries. We should note that there is nothing inadequate or defective about such concepts; for example, the words "foothill" and "mountain" are extremely useful geographic terms even though there are many specific geographic formations which are "somewhere between" foothills and mountains.

We will see in the chapters which follow that it is possible to define middle-ground categories between, for example, Inner speech and Unsymbolized Thinking; and furthermore that it is sometimes difficult to determine whether a particular experience should be labeled Unsymbolized Thinking or Inner Speech or something in between. Even though these difficulties may present themselves at *individual samples,* it is usually not at all difficult to characterize a particular subject's *overall record* as reflecting *frequent* Unsymbolized Thinking or *frequent* Inner Speech. The judgments about individual samples may be unreliable, but the overall impressions seem quite reliable.

I

From Hypomania
to Depression

The four chapters that follow present sketches of the inner experience of four individuals whose everyday mood lies along the continuum from hypomania to depression, giving us a chance to see that as mood becomes more depressed, inner experience becomes more unsymbolized, and, conversely, as mood becomes more light-hearted and energetic, the perceptual aspects of inner experience become more distinct. Furthermore, mood fluctuated *within* three of the four subjects as we sampled their experiences, and, as we shall see, the same kind of relationship between mood and the clarity of symbolization of inner experience occurs *within* single subjects as well as between subjects.

A Slightly Hypomanic Student

John Michaels (not his real name) was a 27-year-old married male at the time of sampling. He volunteered for the project after hearing a brief description of it in a university abnormal psychology class, where I requested volunteers who felt that "emotions play what you take to be a larger-than-usual role in your life." John volunteered, explaining that what he meant by being emotional was that he had a very high energy level and was constantly engaged in one activity or another.

This high-energy state was evident to the external observer: John spoke somewhat more rapidly than the average person, was evidently extremely optimistic, was nearly always smiling, etc. He was a full-time premedical student, but also worked one full-time and one part-time job. The part-time job—as an assistant in the coroner's office—was taken not so much for financial reasons as because he was interested in the work. To maintain this schedule, he slept three to five hours per night, finding that such a regime was usually adequate: he would typically awaken refreshed and eager to proceed in whatever activity he had scheduled that day. His opinion was that every few weeks fatigue would catch up with him, and he would be tired for part of a day or so, but then the high energy level would return.

Thus it seems fair to say that John was slightly hypomanic, using that term in a nonpathological sense. His high energy level was quite adaptive for him: he was a good student and was evidently successful at both his jobs. The days of fatigue were an inconvenience, but he could usually predict them and had learned to adjust.

A graduate student who was becoming familiar with the experience-sampling method joined me in sampling with John for a period of 4 days, during which time he recorded 42 observations. Time in the hour-long daily conversations allowed the adequate exploration of 27 of these samples. On all four of these days he reported himself as being his "usual self," that is, "up" and energetic; we will describe those experiences in the next section, which we will call the "Slightly Hypomanic Period." At the end of those four days, we suspended sampling, asking him to resume sampling on a day during which he expected to be fatigued, which resulted in a fifth sampling day occurring two days later. This "Fatigue Period," as we will call it, provided 10 observations, all of which were adequately explored. The Fatigue Period will be described later in this chapter.

THE SLIGHTLY HYPOMANIC PERIOD

The Slightly Hypomanic Period was typical of John's usual mood and behavior: energetic, slightly euphoric, requiring little sleep, etc. Nearly all of the samples obtained during this four-day period involved Images; we will also describe Inner Speech and Feelings as they occurred in this period.

Images

Images were present as the focus of John's experience on 35 (95%) of the 37 samples in the Slightly Hypomanic Period. Our research has shown that this is an extremely high frequency of Images; most of our nonschizophrenic subjects report between 0 and 50% of samples which include visual phenomena. John's Images were generally clearly seen, in color and motion. They were frequently reseeings of scenes which John had actually seen in the near or distant past, in which case the scenes were accurately portrayed (as best John could remember). Other Images were visual creations of events which John was simultaneously reading about, in which cases they accurately portrayed John's sense of the passage being read, but also included details not explicitly described in the written passage but which were necessary to create a concrete visualization. The Images were usually experienced to be in front of John's head, at a place where they could be looked at directly, although sometimes they were located in the same physical space where an Imaged object was physically located. The experience of looking at an Image was generally identical to looking at physical reality, except that the Image was known to be imaginary and not real; that is, the focus and maximum clarity was in the center of the Image, with the periphery becoming increasingly indistinct.

Some Images were recreations of scenes which John had seen in reality earlier. For example, Sample #16 occurred while John was watching television with his wife. The television news had just shown a story about pit bull dogs being poisoned by neighbors, and John was about to tell his wife about a pigeon he had watched die earlier that day. He had left an optician's store, and while walking to his car had seen a pigeon in the bushes beside the sidewalk, unable to fly, acting as if it were sick or hurt. John had picked up the bird and smoothed its feathers, during which the bird did not protest or respond, so he carried it to his car and put it on the floor of his car to take it to a zoological park. En route to the park, the bird had begun to flap its wings vigorously and its eyes became beet red; then it had fallen over backwards, dead. Now, at the moment of the beep, John was seeing an Image of the dying bird flapping its wings, exactly as he had seen it earlier, viewed from the above left, that is, from the identical perspective as he had seen it in the original incident while driving with the bird on the passenger-side floor. The visual details were accurate, so far as John could remember, but there was no sound or other recalled sensations of reality. At the same time, he was feeling a little sad, a feeling which was centered around his chest area, but which could not be further described.

Another example of a recalled Image occurred at the next sample (#17). John was setting the dinner table and was teasing his wife about her wanting to be cremated, part of an ongoing conversation about that subject. At the moment of the beep, he was seeing an inner Image of ashes in the crematory oven at a mortuary he had visited about a year before. The Image was an accurate, colorful recreation, viewed from what was apparently the same perspective as he had actually had during that visit. The oven operator, a man named Bob, was standing slightly off to John's right, using a long pole extended into the oven to break up the bones remaining in the oven. Bob was seen rather indistinctly (as he would have been in reality, since he was in John's peripheral vision), but John could see that he was wearing his blue smock and blue pants and cowboy boots, just as he had a year earlier. The bones themselves were the center of John's attention, and were seen in accurate gray color, in motion as Bob's pole moved them. The only distinction between the present Image and the original seeing was that the bones being seen in the present Image were "known" to be those of his wife. This knowledge was not verbal, nor was it visual in the sense that there was some recognizable feature of the bones which identified them as being his wife's. He simply knew that they were his wife's bones. At the same time, John was smiling in a teasing way and feeling a fullness in his throat which he associated with a feeling of sadness, but he was not experiencing sadness at that moment.

Images were frequently recreations of scenes which John was reading about, in which case they were accurate constructions conforming to John's understanding of the text being read, although certain details had to be created to transform the written description into a visual Image. For example, at Sample #23, John was at work, reading the Bible during a break from activity. The passage he was reading was Judges 19:17, which is a description of a Levite traveling through a strange city and coming upon an old man. As he read the words of this passage, he said the words to himself in Inner Speech (see below), but his main focus was on an Image he was seeing of the old man with white hair, wearing a robe and sandals, sitting beside the door of an adobe-type house. The Levite was seen walking toward the old man, leading two donkeys, one of which carried the Levite's concubine, while the other was a pack animal. The characters in the Image moved as the story unfolded—the Levite and donkeys were now walking toward the old man, and the two men were looking at each other. This Image was full of rich visual detail: the men were seen in profile, as if from a distance of 10–15 meters, with the Levite on the right and the adobe house, connected to a row of other adobe houses, on the left. The old man was sitting at about a 45 degree angle outside the doorway. This Image accurately reflected the description in the Judges passage, but also contained details which went beyond the passage's explicit facts: for example, Judges does not say whether the old man is standing or sitting, nor does it say that he is near a doorway or that the house is adobe, etc. During this experience, John noted that he was interested and was anticipating what was about to happen, but these feelings were not the focus of his attention at the moment of the beep.

Another example of an Image created while reading occurred at Sample #24. John was studying physics as part of reviewing for the medical school entrance exam, which he was to take in a few months. He was listening to a physics review audiotape on his cassette player while looking at the associated page in the review workbook. The auditory and written descriptions were of the physics concept of "work," and the voice on the tape was saying, "Consider an object moving with constant velocity. . . ." John's focus was not on the words he was hearing and reading, but was instead on an Image of a flat black circle or disc, about 3 cm in diameter, which was moving across his visual field in a straight line from left to right. This disc seemed to be in the air between John and the page he was reading. After the onset of the beep, and in accord with the text and tape's description of work being done on the object, the disc took a sudden turn and moved downward across John's visual field. Here again, this Image was an accurate construction of what was being read and heard, but also went beyond the explicitly-described details. For example, the tape described an "object" which became the *disc* in John's Image, and the tape described this object as "moving," which became *moving left-to-right* in the Image. Also evident when responding to the beep was a feeling of pressed understanding, as if John were struggling to concentrate, which was experienced as a tenseness of his body particularly in the region of his solar plexus. This feeling of tenseness was not in his awareness at the moment of the beep, but instead was a state of John's body at the moment of the beep which came into awareness only when he focused on the experience triggered by the beep.

Images sometimes seem to be involved in problem solving. The "moving disc" Image just described (Sample #24) was one such example. Another came at Sample #45, where John was again reviewing physics, and was drawing on paper a coordinate system in response to the text assignment. His attention was focused not on the axes he was drawing, but instead on an Image of the axes he intended to draw. The Image was of a textbook-type coordinate system, with the axes being perfectly straight printed lines and a vector printed in bolder ink at a 40 degree angle. The Image was seen on the real paper that he was actually drawing on, and the lines he was drawing were in the same location as the Imaged lines, although he was seeing the Imaged lines more than the real ones. At the moment of the beep, he was physically drawing the coordinate axes, in the same place as the Imaged coordinate axes, but his attention was focused on the Imaged 40-degree vector which he was about to draw. It was not as if he would trace the Imaged vector onto the paper; instead, the Image represented an anticipation, a picture of what he was intending to draw, which was being formed slightly ahead of the actual drawing itself, more as a visual representation of his intention rather than as a pattern to be traced. John could also identify at the time of his response to the beep that he was a little tense, a feeling located in his solar plexus region. Here again, this tenseness existed as a bodily state but *not* as part of awareness at the moment of the beep.

Problem-solving Images were not limited merely to textbook physics problems, but extended into real life as well. For example, John was at work at his job as a medical technician, examining an employee who had just injured his ribs while lifting a heavy spool of cable (Sample #26). He had almost completed the examination and was giving instructions to the patient, telling him not to take aspirin for 48 hours because of the possibility of internal bleeding from torn muscle tissue. While explaining this to the patient, John was looking at the patient's rib cage, but instead of seeing the real ribs was seeing an Image of the rib muscle tissue, as if he were looking right into the man's chest. In the Image, he could see the ribs, the striations of the muscle, and the damaged muscle tissue which was bleeding. This was an accurate portrayal of the patient's ribs, so far as John could tell, with the exception that the Imaged muscle damage was a horizontal, straight-line cut a few centimeters long, which was the kind of damage one might find in a laceration, not in the strain that this man had actually suffered. There were in reality no outward signs (swelling, redness, etc.) of any muscle damage at all; John's no-aspirin advice was based on the possibility that there might be hidden damage. John could also report on feelings which were noted to be present upon responding to the beep: sympathy toward the man about his pain and frustration that John couldn't relieve it, both experienced as tenseness located in the region of his solar plexus. Once again, these feelings were states which did in fact exist bodily at the moment of the beep, but only came into awareness in the process of responding to the beep.

In Sample #45 above, John described an Image of a physics coordinate system which seemed to anticipate his drawing of the same coordinate system. Another example of this anticipation-Image phenomenon occurred at Sample #40, where John was again at work, typing out the occupational injury form for a patient he had just finished examining. John was a moderately efficient "hunt-and-peck" typist, and was, at the moment of the beep, typing the address of the patient. He was seeing the real form he was typing, but at the same time was visualizing, as if suspended in space just over the page, an Image of the particular letter he was about to type, printed as if typed by the typewriter. It was almost as if he would compare the actual character which he was about to cause to be printed on the page with the character which already existed in his imagination to check for accuracy of typing, but the process was quite automatic, not a back-and-forth sequence of comparisons. This Image was of the single letter about to be typed, and did not include the form itself or any of the previously-typed letters. At the same time, recognized only when he responded to the beep, John was feeling a little tense, apparently related to being about to return to studying for his upcoming medical school examination.

Atypical Image: The 'Bent' Perspective

The Images which we have described in the previous section, and nearly all of John's other Images, had in common the following characteristics: clarity, vivid color, richness of visual detail, movement in the Image, and clear focus in the center of the Image with a natural, gradual degradation of focus in the periphery. There were a few exceptions to this rule which bear enumeration. One of these atypical Images (Sample #19) occurred during this Slightly Hypomanic Period; the remaining ones occurred in the Fatigue Period and will be described there.

Sample #19 occurred just after John had had his hair washed at a barber shop. He was walking toward the barber chair, about to sit down, but his focus was on an Image of himself already sitting in the barber chair, wearing a barber's apron, viewed from the front, in motion as he put the beeper earphone back in his ear following the hair washing (he had been holding it near his ear as he walked to the chair). This Image had all the same characteristics as the previous Images which we have described. A split-second later, John experienced a second inner seeing, this time of the front portion of his ear with the earphone in place. It is this second Image which has the atypical characteristic we wish to describe. His ear was viewed from the front, but his experience was of looking straight ahead and having his visualizing 'bent' around and doubled back to look at his own ear. It was as if he were somehow looking down a tube which extended forward perhaps 15 cm, then turned to the right, and then pointed back at his ear.

We should note that this bent visualization was clearly different from merely viewing himself from an external perspective. For example, the first Image in this same sample involved looking at himself from the front as he sat in the barber's chair. This, of course, is an angle in which John could not possibly view himself. Yet in that Image, he did not experience his visualization as being bent; rather he simply experienced himself as looking straight ahead at an Image which was itself a view from an external perspective. Several other of John's Images were of himself viewed from external, impossible perspectives. The bent visualization occurred only on this one occasion.

Inner Speech

We have seen that all but two of John's samples included some focus on an inner Image. The remaining two samples occurred while he was speaking in an inner voice, one an Inner Speaking of an exclamation and

the other an Inner Speaking of the words that he was simultaneously reading. Five more samples occurred while he was reading the Bible
or his physics review text, and during those samples he was also
speaking the words in Inner Speech as he read them, simultaneous
with the creation of and focus on a visual Image. Thus, out of the 27
Slightly Hypomanic Period samples, there were 7 (26%) total examples of Inner speech: 1 "pure" Inner Speech, 1 Inner Speech while
reading, and 5 Inner Speech while reading but with the focus on an
Image.

The one pure example of Inner Speech occurred at Sample #13,
where John was watching a television movie which was set in the 1920s.
The scene at the moment of the beep showed a young black couple and
their white friend in a soda shop, and the owner was telling them he
would serve the friend but the black couple must sit outside. John was
speaking to himself the words, "What a jerk!" directed to the soda shop
owner. This was experienced to be in his own voice, under his own
control, at John's normal rate of speaking, and with an angry inflection,
exactly as if he had said the words aloud. Noticeable at the time that
John responded to the beep was a mixture of empathy and embarrassment for the couple and anger at the shop owner. These feelings were
clearly differentiable, but he could not describe how they presented
themselves to him.

The six remaining examples of Inner Speech all occurred while reading. In all but one of these cases, the Inner Speech was not the main
focus of attention, but was observed to be taking place in the background while an Image occupied the center of attention. In all cases, the
Speech was experienced to be in his own voice, under his own control,
at his normal rate and with natural inflection.

Emotional Processes Outside of Awareness

John reported emotional processes ongoing at every beep (100%),
including tenseness, expectation, anger, empathy, embarrassment, etc.
There are two generalizations we can make about these emotional experiences. First, these emotions were never a focus or even a part of John's
attention at the moment of the beep, but they were instead apparently
ongoing bodily processes which were occurring outside of his awareness. When John responded to the beep, he would notice that these
processes were ongoing; that is, he would bring them into awareness at
that time. However, his sense was that had the beep not interrupted
him, the emotional processes would have continued in John's body but

outside of his awareness, perhaps running their bodily courses without his ever becoming aware of them. We have reserved the term "Feelings" with a capital F for emotional experiences which are part of awareness at the moment of the beep, so John's emotional processes do *not* fit our definition. (This distinction between ongoing bodily emotions which are easily discernible when looked for an instant after the beep, and Feelings which are emotional aspects of awareness immediately present at the moment of the beep, is a subject which needs further study. Most subjects initially make no distinction between the two kinds of phenomena, but once they understand the difference, most subjects confidently discriminate between them.)

Second, while the significance of this emotional experience was clearly differentiated (that is, he could easily differentiate embarrassment from anger, etc.), how each of these emotions presented itself to him could not be differentiated. He just knew that one emotion was embarrassment and another was anger, etc. Most of the experiences seemed to reside in his chest in the general region of the solar plexus, and were described only in general terms such as "an emptiness" or "a tenseness." An exception to this seemed to be embarrassment, which was experienced along with a hot feeling in his face.

THE FATIGUE PERIOD

The first four sampling days had occurred on occasions when John reported he was feeling "up" and energetic (his most frequent state), and produced the series of experiences which we have just described. As we have seen, these experiences were quite uniform: nearly all involved Images which were clear, colorful, and in motion, etc. John had said originally that he occasionally had days or portions of days where he was fatigued, and that these "fatigue days" were predictable on the basis of how many activities he was engaged in and how much sleep he would get. We asked him to predict when the next fatigued state would likely take place, and he said that would be two days later. We therefore requested that he suspend sampling until that day, to be resumed during that predicted fatigue day; he readily agreed to this plan. The Fatigue Period sample thus occurred on one day and produced 10 samples, all (except possibly one) of which involved the inner visualization of Images. Of those 10 Images, 5 had characteristics which were in some way atypical of the Images which he had reported in the Slightly Hypomanic Period.

Abrupt Edges of Fatigue Period Images

Sample #46 occurred at work while John was talking to a patient about steroids and the fact that they deplete vitamins in the body. At the moment of the beep, he was describing how the vitamins in beef have been reduced by the administration of steroids to cattle in the effort to fatten them, and he was seeing an Image of a cow being given a shot of steroids. He did not in fact know whether steroids were administered by injection or orally, but the Image was of an injection. He was seeing an image of an approximately circular portion (30–40 cm in diameter) of the hindquarter of a brown cow, in clear detail and in color; he could see, for example, the short hair of the cow, uneven as if someone had brushed part of the hair against the grain. The cow was being given an injection of steroids, and John could see the 20-cm-long syringe which was being held motionless like a dagger, with the needle in the cow's hide. Thus far, the description is similar to the typical Images described above. However, this Image was different from the others in that it did not have the increasingly-indistinct periphery that all the Hypomanic Images had had; instead, the Image abruptly ended at the border of the 30–40 cm circle. The remainder of the cow was not seen, either clearly or indistinctly in peripheral vision. Furthermore, the hand which held the syringe could be seen only up to the beginning of the wrist, and the forearm, like the remainder of the cow, was not seen either distinctly or indistinctly. By contrast, the Images which had occurred in the Slightly Hypomanic Period had had a focus in the center of the Image and then a gradually increasing indistinctness in the periphery. Also, at the time of responding to the beep there was a feeling of disgust about the steroid-administration practice, which was detected as an emptiness in John's chest.

Lack of Motion in Fatigue Period Images

One of the characteristics of the steroid-injection sample (#46) described above was that the hand holding the needle was seen without motion, while almost all of the Slightly Hypomanic Period Images had included accurate motion of the objects and people in the images. At least 5 of the 10 fatigue-day images had this lack-of-motion characteristic. The most striking of these was Sample #49. John was talking on the telephone to a friend who was describing an incident where a disgruntled glazier union worker threw a rock through a large plate-glass mirror as it was being transported on a truck. As the friend described the scene, John was creating an accurate, colored Image of the event (it was common for John to see an Image of what was being described to him in conversation). However, this Image was clearly a picture, frozen in time, of a fist-sized white rock hitting the mirror and the cracks in the mirror radiating away from the point of impact. These cracks were not moving or extending; that is to say, the glass was not seen to be in the process of shattering. Furthermore, the rock was not falling to the ground after striking the mirror or passing through the mirror. It was simply there, at the point of contact with the mirror, suspended as if stuck to the surface of the mirror itself. A moment before, John had had an Image of the white truck with blue "Olson Glass" printed on the side; then, with no transition, appeared the Image of the rock hitting the glass, like two snapshots viewed back to back. On any of the Slightly Hypomanic Period sampling days, it seems likely that this would have been viewed as one continuous moving scene from the initial viewing of the truck to the final shattering of the glass and its falling in smithereens to the ground.

Indeterminacy of Visual Detail in Fatigue Period Images

At Sample #48, John was beeped while still writing down the experience of the previous beep. At the moment of the present beep, he was focused on an Image of the present writer's office where our daily sampling conversations took place, viewing the three of us (John, the graduate student, and me) engaged in a conversation. The scene in the Image was accurately constructed, with John sitting in the center, holding his sampling notebook, and gesturing with both hands slightly outstretched as if to emphasize a point. Here again, the motion was frozen as it was in the previous sample: his hands were not moving, for example. But moreover, the visual details were relatively indeterminate. For example, he could not say whether he held the notebook at its bottom or top; he could "see" that the graduate student was wearing a dress, but could not describe its color or anything else about it; he could "see" the shirts that he and I were wearing, but could not describe the color of either shirt; he could not see any of our faces, and yet our heads seemed to be present in the image; etc. He said that perhaps the Image was blurred or fuzzy, but was not confident of that. All of these characteristics were strikingly different from those in the Slightly Hypomanic Period, where details were abundant and John was confident of them. It seemed that he had to some degree temporarily lost the ability to see clearly in inner experience. At the time of responding to the beep, he was feeling some tenseness, located in the region of his solar plexus, but was feeling in a generally good mood.

Perhaps No Symbolized Inner Experience in a Fatigue Period Sample

One sample (#50) occurred while John was eating dinner. He was thinking about asking a friend to play golf with him the next Sunday, but the experience at the moment of the beep was difficult to describe accurately. A moment *after* the beep began, an Image appeared of John and his friend standing near the first tee of a local golf course. At the instant of the beep's onset, however, it seemed that perhaps this Image was in the process of being formed but was not yet visible. However, John was not confident that he was actually aware of the Image forming; perhaps the Image was instead triggered by the beep itself. At the actual moment of the beep, John was "thinking about" asking his friend to play golf, but he could not be sure about how that thinking was experienced. This kind of phenomenon occurred only once, so we did not have a chance to explore it further. Perhaps the beep occurred at the beginning of the formation of an Image, or perhaps this thinking was an example of what we are calling Unsymbolized Thinking. John's indecisiveness in describing his experience is quite typical of subjects' first encounter with Unsymbolized Thinking: many subjects who subsequently become confident that their thinking proceeds without words or images in awareness at first do not believe their own observations, since they contradict their notions about how thinking can possibly take place. With John, we must leave the question as to whether this was Unsymbolized Thinking or the relatively slow formation of an Image undecided. Either way, this sample is in contrast to the quick, clear Images of the Slightly Hypomanic Period.

Lack of Awareness of the Atypicalness of These Experiences

The reason we had elected to conduct the Fatigue Period sampling was because John had initially told us that his experience was different on those days in which he was fatigued. We have just seen that he was right: the Fatigue Period samples included Images which were fixed instead of in motion (as they were in the Slightly Hypomanic Period); which had abrupt edges instead of fading gradually into indistinctness; which were generally less detailed, less distinct, or fuzzy; and which included the possibility of Unsymbolized Thinking rather than clear Images.

However, we note here that John himself, at the beginning of the conversation which explored the Fatigue Period samples, said that, to his surprise, there were *no* differences between the fatigue day's samples and those of other days. Even well into the course of that fatigue-day conversation, after he had described Images which were, to us, strikingly different from any previous samples, he still did not detect any differences between his current Images and those he had described in the Slightly Hypomanic Period. Once differences were pointed out to him, he could recognize them, but even then these differences seemed slightly elusive to him. Thus we observe that in periods of low energy, John lost not only his ability to form bright, complicated, detailed Images, but also apparently lost his ability to notice the absence of those characteristics. This is, indeed, an observation we can frequently make in our other subjects as well: major changes in inner experience can occur without the subjects themselves noticing them.

It is possible that John's lack of awareness of the difference between the fatigue-day Images and other Images might be that the characteristics we are describing here as "changed" were in fact also characteristic of his usual (Slightly Hypomanic) Image experiences, but that he had simply not been beeped during samples with such characteristics. This explanation is plausible, and cannot be refuted given our data, but it seems rather unlikely, given that half of the Fatigue Period samples had these atypical characteristics, while only 1 (the bent visualization Sample #19) of the remaining 27 non-fatigue-day samples was atypical.

DISCUSSION

Of all the subjects we have described in this or the previous book, John is the most euphoric and energetic. His inner experience is also the clearest of all of our subjects. He almost constantly saw Images in his inner experience, and these Images were bright, detailed, gripping, moving, colorful, complicated visual presentations. It is rare for our nonschizophrenic subjects to report as many as 50% images—much more frequent are subjects whose samples include between 0 and 20% visual phenomena.

We will see in subsequent chapters that our subjects at the depressed end of the continuum from hypomania to depression report few or no images, which will lead us to speculate that clarity of symbolization in inner experience is inversely related to depression. John's sample provides one data point: the least depressed subject has the clearest, most symbolized inner experience.

John's sample provides more than merely a single data point, however, since his own Fatigue Period sample can be contrasted with his own Slightly Hypomanic sample. During the Fatigue Period, his euphoria and energy lessened significantly, and at the same time the clarity, brightness, and complexity in his Images also lessened. Images became fixed rather than in motion, fuzzy or indeterminate rather than clearly detailed, and narrowed down to the center rather than extending throughout his visual field. Furthermore, there was one Fatigue Period sample which may have included no symbols at all—that is, it may have been an Unsymbolized Thought.

Thus we may observe that John's sample provides both a data point between subjects (least depressed subject = most symbolized inner experience) and a trend or direction within subjects (more depression brings less symbolization). We shall see that these same generalizations apply to the other subjects in this section.

Normal Affect

We are exploring here the continuum from hypomania to depression, and the next logical step in this progression would be a subject with normal (nonmanic, nondepressed) affect. We provided six such examples in the previous book (Hurlburt, 1990), and because they are rather typical of dozens of others in our own research, it seems redundant to present another normal subject here. We can present some general characteristics of those normal subjects, although the reader should be aware that we have not amassed sufficient numbers of subjects, nor chosen them with sufficient regard for how they represent the population at large, to give confident statistics about the frequencies of characteristics of inner experience in the general population.

With that caveat, as perusal of the previous book will show, we can tentatively sketch the following characteristics of normal inner experience: It is frequently verbal, with Inner Speech comprising from 20% to 90% of subjects' samples; Images occur with frequency from 0 to about 50%; and Unsymbolized Experience occurs occasionally, with frequencies ranging from 0 to somewhat over 50%, with the higher frequencies occurring in individuals who could be judged to be most "emotional."

We turn now to a subject who may be said to be slightly depressed.

4

A Medical Student With a Period of Dysphoria[1]

Michelle Winter (not her own name) was a 22-year-old Dutch medical student at the time of sampling. She had volunteered for the sampling project, having heard about it in her role as student assistant in the department where the author was a visiting professor. Michelle's native tongue was Dutch, but the sampling discussions were carried out almost entirely in English, in which she was also fluent. During some of the sampling discussions, a fluent Dutch translator was also present and discussions of nuances in the English conversation were carried out in Dutch. We sampled with Michelle during two periods separated by about a month. The first sampling period lasted about three weeks, with a few days off for illness and vacation, and resulted in the collection and discussion of 48 samples. The second sampling period began about a month later, lasted three days, and resulted in the discussion of 23 samples.

Michelle's affect was distinctly different during the two sampling periods. The initial sampling period occurred during a time when Michelle was experiencing what she called "low self-esteem," at which time she continued to be engaged in her academic activities (including volunteering for this project), but her mood was quite depressed and she had little true interest in any of her activities. By contrast, this dysphoric

[1]This work was supported by the Vakgroep Sociale Psychologie, Rijksuniversiteit Limburg, Maastricht, The Netherlands, where the author was visiting professor.

mood had lifted by the time of the second sampling period, and there was more confidence and "sparkle" in her life, as seen by both herself and others (including me). We will describe the two sampling periods separately below, referring to them as the Dysphoric Period and the Normal Affect Period, respectively. It turned out that Michelle's inner experience was considerably clearer during the Normal Affect Period than during the Dysphoric Period, and so for ease of exposition it will be convenient to describe the characteristics of the Normal Affect Period first, even though it was chronologically the second sampling period.

THE NORMAL AFFECT PERIOD

There were three sampling days during the Normal Affect Period, which resulted in 23 samples being taken and discussed. These samples had four rather clear salient characteristics: Inner Speech, where Michelle experienced herself as talking within her inner experience without making any external speech-related movements or sounds, an experience she called "subvocal speech"; Feelings, which were rather clearly defined specific emotional experiences; Just Listening, where Michelle was paying attention to an ongoing conversation and was absorbed in it; and Just Doing, where Michelle's attention was engaged in the task she was performing.

Inner Speech

Of the 23 samples in the Normal Affect Period, 14 (61%) involved the sort of self-talk that we call Inner Speech; Michelle herself referred to it as "subvocal speech." In these samples, Michelle experienced herself as talking to herself without making any external speech-related movements or sounds. She experienced speaking in her own voice, and of creating the words being experienced; this was more an experience of speaking than of hearing. In some cases (e.g., Sample #59), the words were actually spoken aloud after they had first been thought in Inner Speech. In Sample #59, she was talking to a friend, and was aware, through a Feeling of tension and hesitation in her upper torso, that she found the public place where they were standing uncomfortable for the private nature of their conversation. The words, "No, I don't want to talk in this room[2]," were first said to herself in Inner Speech, and then

[2]These words, as well as all others in Michelle's sample, were in her native Dutch language; we provide here her own translation into English.

were repeated aloud. The characteristics of both the Inner and the outer Speech were the same: same rate of speaking, same inflection, etc.

Inner speech accompanied reading and writing, sometimes synchronized with the words she was reading or writing, and sometimes just prior to a word which she was about to write. For example (Sample #48), Michelle was reading a medical textbook, and the words "1. Heparin" occurred, being said in Inner Speech. These words were the first line of a list she would write as she took notes about the things which could be done in the treatment of the disease she was reading about. The words were experienced just as if they were being said aloud, said in her own voice with all its normal inflections and at her normal rate of speaking. In another example (Sample #67), she was underlining a phrase in a medical text, and as she read and underlined she spoke the phrase in Inner Speech, ". . . not in patients with cirrhosis . . ." As she "subvocally" spoke the words, she emphasized the word "not," as if to stress the exception which caused her to underline that particular phrase. In another sample, she was writing down a list of signs of a patient with blood loss. She had written the name of the disease already ("anemia"), and was currently writing the first of its symptoms, "fatigue." At the same time, she was saying, in Inner Speech, the word "palpitations," which was to be the next symptom that she would add to the symptom list. Again, the characteristics of the Inner Speech were just as if the words were being said aloud.

These examples of Inner Speech are very similar to examples which are given in other chapters of this book and elsewhere (see Hurlburt, 1990). With Michelle, as with most of our subjects, it is as if there is a "speaking consciousness" which works rather autonomously, and which sometimes produces Inner Speech and sometimes vocal speech, both with the same characteristics. Furthermore, the speaking consciousness functions as if it were an unchanging gestalt, capable of producing a wide range of words and sentences, but itself staying unmodified throughout. However, Michelle (to some degree in this Normal Affect Period and even more so, as we shall see, in the Dysphoric Period), unlike our non-depressed subjects, seemed to have many different speaking consciousnesses which seemed to be related to what was being said. For example, in Sample #58, she was at school, deciding whether to leave her pencil case on the copy machine, a decision which depended on whether the magnetic copy machine card (the only thing of value) was in the pencil case. At the moment of the beep, she was experiencing two quick verbal thoughts, both of which were in Inner Speech: "I will leave this [the pencil case] here," and, "Is the copy card here [in the pencil case] or in my pants pocket?" What differentiated these Inner Speakings from the others previously described is that they "involved energy," that is, they were very active, energetic thinkings. Michelle's inner experience itself, which included this word-producing process, was active and energetic. The words themselves were spoken slightly faster than they would have been spoken aloud, but the point we are trying to highlight here is that it was not only the characteristics of the words which were active and energetic, but more fundamentally, the mental state which produced the words was experienced to be active and energetic.

This is a fine distinction which bears repeating. Other subjects frequently report differing levels of energy in their Inner Speech. For example, Sue Melancon's level of energy (described in Hurlburt, 1990, Chapter 8) could be quite low in matter-of-fact inner experience, but also could be quite high, as for example once when she said, in Inner Speech, "This is going to be totally fuckin' great!" In Melancon's example, as with most of our other subjects, the experience of producing the words was the same in the matter-of-fact and in the animated examples; the phrases themselves and the contemporaneous affect, however, were quite different, one flat and the other excited. For Michelle, by contrast, high energy thinking seemed to be a qualitatively different kind of thinking from her normal energy thinking. That is, the energy level was not merely one attribute of a process whose other attributes remained the same, but was instead a feature which distinguished two experientially different processes from each other.

We have seen examples where Michelle experienced a mental state which produced calm words, and by contrast, experienced what was apprehended as a different, active and energetic, mental state which produced active and energetic words. An example which illustrates the experience of yet a different mental state which produces words was Sample #49, where Michelle was having an inner conversation with herself about her relationship with her boyfriend, saying at the moment of the beep in Inner Speech, "It's not pleasant like this." At the same time Michelle felt a clear but complex emotional experience: Feelings of sadness, anger, and uncertainty, which were represented in her body as a wringing feeling in her stomach, and this emotional involvement seemed to produce the words. The words themselves seemed about the same as in other Inner Speech samples, for example, they seemed similar to the words "1. Heparin" in Sample #48, but the production of the words was experienced much differently. In the present sample, she was much more emotionally involved, and the "It's not pleasant like this" thinking seemed to be a very primary, central experience. By contrast, in Sample #48 the words "1. Heparin" seemed just a reaction to what she was doing at the time. Here again, we are emphasizing that it seemed to be the thinking process itself that was primary and central, not merely that Michelle's attention was more centrally focused on this thinking.

Yet another example of differing manners of Inner Speech came at Sample #55, which took place while Michelle was walking out of the bathroom. She said to herself in Inner Speech, "I have to do a bit with my hair," reflecting the fact that she glanced in the mirror and noticed that her hair needed rearranging. These words also had the same speaking-to-self characteristics as the "1. Heparin" example, but here the experience that included the words was just calm—not particularly active or energetic, not central to her experience, not just a reaction—but instead was experienced to be part of a process of setting a task for herself. This task-setting process could not be further described, but Michelle was emphatic that it was a decidedly different kind of thinking process from those which produced other Inner Speech examples.

A final example of the Inner Speech phenomenon occurred at Sample #60. Michelle was idly walking out of the cafeteria, waiting for a friend to catch up to her, and watching a young man walking out ahead of her who was wearing very bright green and orange pants. She said to herself in Inner Speech, "The pants he is wearing look like a climbing suit," and this sentence was repeated three times, the beep occurring on the second repetition. The first time this sentence had been said, it was said as a straightforward declarative sentence, but the two repetitions were said in a sing-song, amused manner. Here again, our point is not merely that the vocal characteristics of the words were different from other samples, but rather that Michelle's experience of creating those words, her apprehension of the process which produced the words, was different from other samples. Here, the intention was to idly kill time while noticing the rather outrageous colors of the pants. Michelle also reported an emotional experience of relaxation associated with this experience, experienced as not-clear Images of people wearing climbing suits. The Images and the people in them were not clear, but the colors and their recollection were clear: neon green with neon orange, black with gold, yellow with pink and green, etc., all on shiny material.

We will recapitulate this last set of observations because the point we are trying to make is rather speculative, and we should get it as clear as possible here before we later consider the Dysphoric Period. There can be little doubt that Michelle experienced different characteristics in those experiences which involved her mentally saying words to herself: calmness, activity, centrality, reaction, task-setting, and amusement. Most of our other subjects also experienced such a range of characteristics of experience. The difference between Michelle's descriptions and those of our other subjects is that the other subjects understood this variety in terms of rather differing displays being created by a rather unchanging thinking process, while Michelle understood her thinking process itself to change from one sample to the next. That is, Michelle reported that she herself changed in the apprehension of the different experiences, rather than being a constant self simply experiencing different moods, energy-levels, etc. We will return to a discussion of this point in the section on the Dysphoric Period.

Feelings

In the Normal Affect Period, 10 of the 23 samples involved relatively clear emotional experience at the moment of the beep. These experiences ranged from a simple feeling of calm to a relatively complex recollected emotion of past events. We will present some examples of this type of experience in order from the more simple to the more complex.

In a simple example (Sample #56), Michelle was combing her hair. She was busy with the combing, Just Doing it, engaged in the activity without premeditation, so to speak, simply combing her hair to get it the way she wanted it. At the same time, she was experiencing a Feeling of being peaceful and quiet, which could be identified with a relaxed sensation in her body and mind. This mental calmness was an inner quiet; thoughts were not "flying around" as she sometimes experienced them. Another simple example occurred at Sample #59 (described above in the Inner Speech section), where Michelle was thinking and later saying aloud, "No, I don't want to talk in this room." The Feeling of discomfort and hesitation was easily localized in the region of her upper torso— from her stomach to her neck, and the meaning of these feelings was also clear and simple—she did not want to talk there.

The simple Feelings could be positive as well as neutral or negative. We have already described one example of a simple positive emotion, the amused Feeling accompanying "He is wearing a climbing suit" in Sample #60. That amused Feeling could be said to exist both in her body and in the sing-song nature of her inner voice at the time.

A somewhat more complex example took place at Sample #69. Michelle was reading a medical text, and had just read the phrase "noncirrhotic fibrosis of the liver" which was part of the text on the right-hand page of the book. She glanced at the chapter title, which appeared on the left-hand page, and then sighed. The beep occurred during this sigh. The sigh had several different but related significances for Michelle: that there was much that Michelle didn't know, that there was much that she needed to do, that she didn't know where to start, and that she felt a bit desperate about the whole process. These Feelings had a precise bodily representation, occurring in a very specific region of the upper part of her chest, on the inner surface of her chest cavity. The sigh was like an effort to get the Feeling out; in fact, following the sigh, the Feeling lessened somewhat (but did not go away completely).

At the more complex end of this spectrum, Michelle was in an exercise room fastening her feet into a rowing machine (Sample #65). She was actively engaged in this task, not thinking about it or anything else, but at the same time aware of a complex Feeling which could be said to be in her body but could not be further elaborated. It had happened that two young men and a young woman, all about her age, were involved in using the rowing machine, and the two fellows had just proposed a race, boys against the girls, using the meter readings on the machine. The proposal had been made in a friendly, flirting, teasing way which Michelle found pleasant. She had declined, saying that racing in the rowing machine destroys her rowing form. However, the fellows had persisted and the race was about to take place. At the moment of the beep, the following Feelings could all be said to be present at the same time: of being flattered at being asked and enjoying the attention, of wanting to participate in the social situation of the race, of wanting to win, of not wanting to destroy her rowing form, of enjoying being talked into participating, and of enjoying knowing that she really wanted to be talked into it all along. These Feelings were all present at the moment of the beep, even though they could not be differentiated into distinct bodily referents or other explanations.

Another example of complex emotional experience was Sample #63. Michelle had been watching a video recording on which a doctor communicated with a patient about depression, and had said to herself in Inner Speech just before the beep occurred, "my mother would also go to the priest with this problem if she would trust him." At the moment of the beep, Michelle said in Inner Speech, "Yes," and simultaneously remembered a whole situation which was the cause of her mother's lack of trust in the priest. This recall experience was difficult for her to describe: it did not involve words or images, and yet it could be said that the whole situation, not just details from it, was recalled. The recollection was of the feelings associated with the experience—her own at knowing about it and her mother's while undergoing the situation. These feelings were not reexperienced, that is, there was no bodily feeling at the moment of the beep; instead, the feelings were remembered, in a way that was impossible for her to explain further: she knew which feelings she was remembering, and knew what those feelings were, but could not explain how she knew.

The deepest of Michelle's experiences seemed to be primarily emotional. At Sample #62, she was working at her job as a research assistant, and her task was to score the videotaped interview which she was then watching according to the presence or absence of particular behavioral characteristics. The portion of the videotape she was then watching was irrelevant to the scoring task, and she had drifted off into a dreamlike state during which she was not hearing what was being said in the videotaped conversation. The beep occurred as she was leaving this dreamlike state, although Michelle acknowledged that it might have been that the beep itself had interrupted her reverie and caused her return to awareness. She could describe in general terms the content and quality of the dreamlike state, but it was not possible to give details. The state consisted of Feelings, words, and Images of moments of situations, with the predominant characteristic being emotional. The general content of this experience concerned a love affair which had just ended unhappily for her, her Feeling of love for the man, and her recognition that he did not love her anymore. But exactly how those feelings were represented, or which words or images were used, she could not state.

Just Doing

Four of Michelle's samples involved merely paying attention to what she was doing, without any particular cognitive process taking place in awareness. For example, in Sample #61 Michelle was walking into the library, passing through the door at the moment of the beep. At that moment, there was no cognition nor emotion present to her awareness; she was simply walking into the library. The walking was purposeful, in the sense that she was entering the library to complete a certain task, and that she knew what that task was. However, at the moment of the beep, that knowledge, or any other for that matter, was not present in awareness. Some of these Just Doing experiences had an emotional component also, for example, the hair-combing sample (#56, described above in the section on Feelings) where she was also Feeling relaxed.

Just Listening

Two of Michelle's samples involved paying attention to conversations in which she was engaged. In these samples, Michelle was paying attention to what the speaker was saying, more or less involved in listening, with no other thoughts or emotions present at the moment.

THE DYSPHORIC PERIOD

We turn our attention now to the characteristics of the first sampling period, which we are calling the Dysphoric Period. We sampled for approximately three weeks, four to five days per week, with a few days off for competing time commitments. This resulted in the collection of about 75 samples, of which we had time in our daily interviews to discuss 48; our description is based on those 48. We will structure our discussion parallel to the discussion of the Normal Affect Period; that is, we will first consider the characteristics of Inner Speech, then of Feelings, then Just Listening, and then Just Doing.

The discussion of 48 samples over 13 sampling days during Michelle's Dysphoric Period is more discussion than we usually find necessary to clarify salient characteristics of inner experience, and this reflects the fact that Michelle's reports were confusing, both to her and to us. There could be no doubt that she was trying to report honestly about the details of her experience and that I was trying to listen carefully, but we found the going difficult. It should be said that subjects who experience frequent Unsymbolized Thinking frequently take longer than other subjects to become confident about their ability to report accurately. As we shall see, Michelle had frequent samples which may or may not have been Unsymbolized, and our attempts to clarify the nature of this phenomenon were quite intense and time-consuming.

Inner Verbal (?) Experience

Nearly two-thirds of Michelle's samples (31 [65%] of 48 samples) in the Dysphoric Period could be described as being to some extent verbal. However, neither Michelle nor I was able to become confident of the nature of the verbalness of many of these experiences. We have seen in the previous section that during the Normal Affect Period, Michelle frequently (in 61% of the Normal Affect samples) gave straightforward, clear descriptions of verbal characteristics in her inner experience: she experienced herself as saying such and such in Inner Speech, and could easily report the exact words she was saying, along with their inflection, rate of speed, etc. However, Michelle's Dysphoric Period experience of inner words never seemed to become clear, and thus neither did our conversations. During those conversations, when we asked questions such as, "Was that particular word present in your experience, or would some other synonym suffice as well?" Michelle frequently responded with a sentence such as, "I don't know exactly what you mean by words being present in my experience." By contrast, this kind of question was answered with a straightforward Yes or No in the Normal Affect Period (remember that the Dysphoric Period *preceded* the Normal Affect Period).

There were two phases during Michelle's Dysphoric Period, differentiated by the characteristics of her inner verbalizations. The first phase occurred in the first week of sampling, during which Michelle described her inner verbal experiences as taking place "inside the balloon"; during the second phase, the in-the-balloon aspects had disappeared from our sampling conversations. We will describe both of these phases in separate sections below.

First, however, we ask what a subject might mean when she describes a portion of inner experience as being "in a balloon." We might expect that such a statement could have either one of two distinct meanings, which we will refer to as the "perceptual" meaning and the "metaphorical" meaning. If Michelle were using such a phrase in a perceptual sense, she would mean that at the moment of the beep she saw, or felt, or had some other (inner) sensory apprehension of a sphere-like balloon and of something which appeared to be inside that balloon. If that were the case, then the sampling conversations would seek to differentiate those perceptions and make them descriptively vivid. If, on the other hand, Michelle were using the reference to the balloon in a metaphorical sense, then she would mean that at the moment of the beep she was *not* seeing or otherwise perceiving something that resembled a balloon, but instead was using the linguistic reference to a balloon to call attention to some characteristic of her inner experience which could be elucidated by referring to a balloon. For example, if certain aspects of her experience seemed cut off from other aspects, or were bunched together, etc., it might be an apt metaphor to say that it was "as if they were in a balloon."

As part of our general procedure, when we seek to understand a subject's description of experience, we always attempt to ascertain whether the language used is perceptual or metaphorical,[3] and Mi-

---

[3]This is not always easy, since many people switch quite cavalierly from perception to metaphor without having any awareness of doing so. One of the major tasks involved in the training of subjects in the present study is to encourage perceptual and discourage metaphorical statements. The reader may recall that in Chapter 12 of the previous book (Hurlburt, 1990), we discussed a decompensating schizophrenic's inability to distinguish between perception and conception. The perception/conception confusion may well be in

chelle's case was no exception. With most of our subjects, it is rather easy to feel confident in making the distinction. However, with Michelle, we could never confidently conclude whether the balloon was a perception or a metaphor. The reader should be assured that both Michelle and I worked assiduously at attempting to distinguish between the metaphorical or perceptual nature of these descriptions, but we simply could not differentiate adequately.

Why might we have had difficulty making this distinction? One possibility is that Michelle did not have the intellectual capacity to make such a distinction, but we can reject that possibility: Michelle was a bright student, quite capable of recognizing a metaphor when, for example, she read one in a novel; she simply could not differentiate perception from metaphor as applied to her *own* inner experience during the Dysphoric Period. Another possibility is that Michelle's experience during this period was *neither* perceptual *nor* metaphorical. That, we believe, is the explanation here, and we shall attempt to show why we arrived at that conclusion in the following section.

Words in the Balloon

We shall describe a few experiences which Michelle understood to take place "in the balloon" and then return to the question of whether the balloon was perception, metaphor, or some other kind of phenomenon. The first experience was Sample #5, where Michelle was pouring lemon juice over apples in preparation for cooking. The words, "one half will be enough" were somehow present to her awareness. These words were not experienced as heard, or said, or seen, and yet Michelle was aware of them. These words seemed to be in her head, although her head, or more precisely the space inside her head, felt bigger than it actually was. The words were experienced as being in the space inside her head, or rather in a small part of that space. The words appeared to move through that subspace smoothly, from right to left, faster than the words could be said aloud, even though there was no feeling that the words were speeded up. The experience of the passing of these words was not visual or auditory, but rather was felt. Furthermore, there was no experience of the creation or production of those words, that is, she didn't feel herself to be actively speaking them, even though the words were experienced as being her own. During her description of this par-

some way related to the perception/metaphor confusion we are describing here. Further research is needed to clarify this issue.

ticular experience, which was one of the early samples, she never used the word "balloon," but later she came to divide the space inside her head into subspaces, one of which she called the balloon.

The next sample (#6) was a rather complex visual and verbal experience which further clarified Michelle's understanding of the spaces inside her head. She was thinking about a walk she might take with friends the next morning, and there were three rather distinct aspects of this experience, the quasi-verbal, the visual, and the emotional, and we will describe each in turn. The quasi-verbal portion of the experience consisted of many thoughts which moved up and down and back and forth through the same subspace as described in the previous sample. These various thoughts moved simultaneously through this inner space, rapidly but without any frantic sense of speed and "without colliding with each other." The thoughts, if they were put into words, might be, "I could take coffee," or, "Maybe we can also take some sherry," but the words themselves did not seem to be present to her awareness. It was more as if the meanings themselves, in some ways similar to sentences but without the structure or words of sentences, traveled by within this inner space, as if they were flying through air. The space itself was described to be like a balloon, although Michelle didn't see the surfaces even though she was aware that definite surfaces existed.

The visual aspect of this experience was described to be like a "movie," an excerpt from a motion picture which started black, then faded into a scene and then faded to black again. The scene was of Michelle and three friends walking in the heather. It was in color, and the four people were visually present, but the details were not clarified. Michelle knew who the people were, but that knowledge was not carried by the perceptual details of the scene; she simply knew who they were. The movie was perceived to be on a screen which was on the right side of her head, and was viewed from the left side, although the point of view was not clearly specified. The screen was clearly outside the "balloon" but inside the space of her head.

There was also an emotional aspect of this experience, which could be described as relaxed, calm, feeling free of obligations and connected to nature. The emotion was felt to exist in her body lower than her head, in the region of her heart, and its meaning was felt to be definitely attached to the film, not to the thoughts in the balloon. The emotion seemed to "know" the emotional content of the film, and was representing that emotional content to Michelle. It was *not*, however, that Michelle was actually experiencing the emotion at the moment of the beep; rather, the emotional awareness merely knew that the emotion was present.

The next sample (#7) occurred when Michelle was opening a box of photographic slides to look at them. At the moment of the beep there were again the three aspects of experience described previously: the verbal, the visual and the emotional. The verbal aspect involved the sentence, "If I remember correctly, that picture of the dogs is on the side." This sentence was experienced to be a rather clear sequence of words, not telegraphically compressed or implied, which moved through the balloon in a straight line from the lower right to the upper left extent of the balloon. This path or trajectory was experienced to be the same as that of the lemon juice path above (Sample #5), but the balloon itself was "not so light" as it was in the lemon juice experience. This time the balloon was heavier, as if the air inside it were thicker, and it seemed to take a bit more energy to move the thought through the balloon. The heaviness of the balloon was seen to be a characteristic of thoughts which occurred when Michelle was tired, as was the case here.

At the same time this thought moved through the balloon, there was an Image of the slide in question. It was viewed as if illuminated from the back and was thus bright and clear. Also visible in the Image, though not so distinctly (as if unfocused-upon) was the grey paper border of the slide. The Image seemed to be in the general area of the actual box of slides, as if Michelle were holding the slide next to the box and looking at it there, although the Image did not include her fingers or hand. The slide itself was seen to be accurately perceived; the colors were veridical, and the Image included a slight bend or crease in the slide which was an actual characteristic of the real slide.

Also present in this experience was an emotional recollection of the dogs which were the subject of the slide. Here again, the emotion was not so much reexperienced as it was merely recalled.

The next sample (#8) occurred a few minutes later while Michelle was still working with the slides. She was in the process of cutting the film and putting the slides into the plastic windows, and at the moment of the beep had another experience which had the same three aspects we have been describing. The verbal aspect included two sentences which were perceived to move one after the other through the balloon, like cars in a train. The sentences were, "I'm going to have just enough windows [slide frames]," and, "Oh, no, one Belgium slide cannot be windowed." The trajectory which these thoughts appeared to take through the balloon was the same as in the lemon juice thought and the slide of dogs thought described previously: from lower right to upper left in a straight line. The two thoughts of the present sample were experienced as separate but connected, as two parts of a train of thought. They moved through the balloon faster than in the lemon juice thought, and the impression was of more activity, more spirit. It was felt to be moving smoothly, but with greater energy.

At the same time, there was an Image of the Belgian slide for which there might not be enough windows. It was seen the same way as the slide of the two dogs (Sample #7, described above), at arms-length as if held in her hand, and the Image also included the rather indistinct unfocused-upon window, even though in reality this slide had not yet been put into a window. The slide itself was also illuminated from the back, but the slide's details were not as clear as those of the slide of the dogs (which Michelle attributed to the fact that she had not yet seen the slide projected and so only knew in general that it included a white house, etc., but knew no other details).

There was also a Feeling aspect of this experience—this time a reexperiencing (not just a recollection or expecting) of the emotion which had taken place the day she had taken the photograph. This emotion was complex: idly jolly, relaxed, and relieved.

The next sample (#9) also involved a thought which took place in the balloon. Michelle was walking into her kitchen to put on water for tea, and was irritated to find dirty dishwater left by one of her roommates, who had washed the dishes the night before. The thought, "I must throw it away but . . ." was mostly in words, but the conclusion of this sentence, that first she would put on the tea water, occurred without words, even though the meaning was clear to Michelle (thus the end of this thought was clearly an example of Unsymbolized Thinking). The verbal part of the thought moved through the balloon at the same steepness of trajectory as the lemon juice thought and the thought about the dogs, but was in the other direction—from upper left to lower right. This time, however, the words did not seem to arrive at the end of the balloon and disappear as had the earlier thoughts, but instead, they seemed to get blurry or foggy at the lower right, as if they had gone out of focus. Michelle felt the subspace inside her head to be bigger than her head actually is, perhaps twice as big (about 40 cm in diameter). Despite this, the experience was that this space was inside her head, and that the balloon was only a part of that total inner space. The fogginess at the lower right of the balloon seemed to accompany the occurrence of the conclusion of the sentence in actions, rather than words.

The next sample (#10) also contained a thought taking place in the balloon. Michelle was sitting at her desk looking for an exercise book. At the moment of the beep, the sentence, "Where is that purple exercise book?" emerged in the balloon. This time, however, the thought did not pass through the balloon in a straight trajectory, but instead came forward from the back of the balloon, as if a card on which the words were written were picked up and brought into view from the rear. The words of the sentence all appeared at the same time, rather than sequentially as in the previous samples, and seemed to be on two lines, as follows:

> where is that
> purple exercise book?

At the same time, there seemed to be an oscillation or flashing of the word "purple," which carried the meaning that the term "purple" was not the correct word for the approximately burgundy color of the book. However, this experience was not the clear seeing of an Image of these words, one of which was flashing. Rather, the words were thought, not seen, despite the fact that they seemed to have a particular visual orientation.

To sum up, Michelle described these experiences as if they had really taken place in a balloon. The balloon was described as a region within the space of her head, although this space was bigger, perhaps twice as big, as her head in fact was. Thoughts seemed to move through this space on fixed trajectories, sometimes the same trajectory repeatedly, and sometimes on separate, seemingly random trajectories. The speed with which a thought moved through the balloon could vary from thought to thought, as could the amount of energy that was associated with the thought. Sometimes the thoughts seemed to move through the balloon by themselves, and sometimes it seemed as if Michelle had to move them through the balloon herself. The air within the balloon sometimes seemed to be light and fresh, and sometimes seemed to be heavy and thick. The inner space inside her head seemed to be divided into three regions, the balloon, the screens, and the remembering part. (We have not described the remembering part because a beep never occurred while it was in use, but during the course of the conversations, Michelle described it as a space near the back of her head which was not full of air as was the balloon, but instead was closely packed. In the remembering part, thoughts had their own place, a fixed position within that area, and did not move around on trajectories or at random as they did in the balloon. A thought which started out in the balloon might move through the balloon more or less quickly and then travel into the remembering part where it stopped and became fixed.)

We have seen that Michelle described the balloon experiences using the language of perceptions. We now return to our question of whether this phenomenon is perceptual, metaphorical, or of some other nature. First, we ask whether the balloon was *perceptual*, that is, was it seen, felt, heard, etc.? Our descriptions of all of these experiences taking place in the balloon have doubtless given the impression that the way Michelle apprehended these words was quite visual. That is, when we have used descriptive terms such as "appeared to move from right to left," or "a flashing of the word 'purple'," it seems that Michelle must be *seeing* these words as they passed through the particular trajectories in her visually perceived balloon. That is a misleading impression, however.

From the very beginning of her Dysphoric Period descriptions, Michelle had difficulty with my questions about how she apprehended the particular words of her experiences. For example, she told me confidently that the sentence, "Where is that purple exercise book?" was present in her awareness. But when I asked her how that sentence appeared, how she knew that sentence was there, she was hard-pressed to give an answer which satisfied either of us. I would ask whether the words were more seen or more heard, or more heard or said, and it seemed that my questions were not meaningful to her; they were more confusing than helpful. "The words were thought," she said. I inquired how she knew that they were thought, and she replied that she just knew. If they were just thought, I asked, how did she experience them as moving from right to left? She wasn't sure, but said that it "felt" like they were moving in that manner. I asked how she experienced that feeling. Her response was that when she tried to convey the feeling, it came out in visual terms. There was no doubt that Michelle was trying to answer my questions as honestly and candidly as she could. My conclusion was that she was unable to differentiate clearly between inner seeing, inner speaking, inner unworded knowing (Unsymbolized Thinking), or inner feeling during this period.

A second oversimplification present in our descriptions may leave the impression that the words themselves were easily and directly apprehended by Michelle. This was not actually the case. For example, when I would ask whether one of her thoughts had been in the exact words she had reported, or would other words—perhaps synonyms for the words she had used—have been just as adequate, she would respond that when she used the particular words, those were the right ones, and that synonyms in general would not do. How did she know that it must be those words and not others? She couldn't be sure, but she did know that other words weren't right. It seemed that she was answering these questions *not* by referring back to a recollection of the words in the experience in question (as most of our subjects seem to do in response to such questions), but rather by considering alternative wordings and discovering that these alternatives just did not seem to "fit" the experience she was describing. This sense of fitting was more a current feeling than it was a recollection of the words that had been experienced at the moment of the beep. Thus we came to an uneasy understanding that words themselves were usually *not* clearly perceived in her inner experience, but instead seemed to be just beneath the surface of awareness, as it were. The experiences could be described in only one set of words, but those words themselves were not present at the moment of the beep. These just-below-the-surface thoughts were reported as verbal because the particular moving or flashing words she used seemed to "fit" the felt/known characteristics of the experience better than any other words or any other type of description.

During the second week of sampling, Michelle stopped describing her thoughts as taking place inside the balloon. The beginning of this change seemed to take place when we were following up a seemingly minor detail in what turned out to be one of the last experiences which took place in the balloon. The detail was that in the course of our conversations about a particular sample, Michelle reported that the thought moved from upper right to lower left in her experience. Then, later in the discussion of the same thought, she reported that it moved from upper left to lower right. As a general rule in the sampling process, I tend to be alert to details with such discrepancies because they provide an opportunity to check on the consistency with which subjects report their experience. So when presented with such a conflicting report, I routinely try, without leading the witness, so to speak, to ascertain the source of the disparity. For example, I might ask, "So as this thought moves from upper left to lower right, does it travel in a straight line?" giving the subject the opportunity to say something like, "Oh! No, I didn't mean upper left to lower right, I meant upper right to lower left!" resolving the discrepancy as a slip of the tongue, which I would find very convincing. With Michelle, however, the attempt to resolve this left/right discrepancy did not result in an immediately clear outcome: instead, she became confused over whether she really meant left-to-right or right-to-left. I provisionally interpreted (to myself) such confusion as evidence consonant with the interpretation that Michelle's descriptions were metaphorical rather than perceptual.

Later evidence caused me to question that interpretation, however. For whatever reason, the balloon descriptions stopped during the second week of sampling. I occasionally asked, where appropriate in subsequent discussions, how a particular thought was similar to or different from a thought that had taken place in the balloon, and our understanding of the balloon phenomenon deepened somewhat. The reason that Michelle occasionally confused the side-to-side directions in her descriptions was that she "viewed" her experiences from two different perspectives: from the inside looking forward, as they would naturally be perceived by herself, and from the outside looking backward, as they might be seen by me; of course, these two perspectives had contradictory right-left orientations. Our best reconstruction of Michelle's general sampling procedure is as follows. The beep occurred, and Michelle's attempt to "freeze" the experience so that she ·could report it to me resulted in her immediately creating a "view" of her experience as seen from my perspective, that is, from the outside. This view had two characteristics of particular interest: first, it was a primarily visual apprehension or her inner experience as occurring inside a balloon; and second, it was characterized by the near (but not entirely complete) certainty that the visualization was an accurate embodiment of what occurred at the moment of the beep. We must emphasize that it took many hours of attempts at clarification before Michelle arrived at this understanding, and in the meantime she was not aware (much less surprised) that she frequently took two different, inside-out perspectives on the same event without noticing it. Our conclusion is, then, that Michelle did not have a stable point of view on her own inner experience during the Dysphoric Period. Her point of view was sufficiently diffuse to allow two opposing, contradictory perspectives to occur without her noticing the discrepancy despite constant, detailed questioning. We further concluded that Michelle's balloon experiences were *not* seeings or other inner perceptual experiences, since she could never give consistent perceptual details of those experiences. Thus, we concluded that the balloon was not the result of inner perception.

If the balloon was not perceptual, was it, then, metaphorical? In general, we use the term 'metaphor' to refer to two phrases which are connected by the (expressed or implied) words "as . . . as," the first phrase, called by linguists the tenor, is the thing being described, and the second phrase, called the vehicle, is the unrelated thing to which we compare the tenor from the point of view of characteristic aspects of the vehicle. For example, when we say, "This cake is as heavy as lead," we are using the characteristics of the vehicle, the weight of lead, to call attention to characteristics of the tenor, the cake, namely that it is heavy, not light and fluffy as cake should be. The point is that the metaphor is a linguistic device which refers directly to one thing when it intends to highlight another. Michelle's balloon experiences were similar to these linguistic metaphors in that they seemed to refer to one thing (balloons) to highlight another (that there seemed to be certain groupings, orders, and subspaces in her inner experience).

However, metaphors are intentional. For example, the person who says "the cake is as heavy as lead" knows full well that the cake is not actually lead; the speaker is quite aware of the metaphorical nature of the communication. An important characteristic of Michelle's balloon experiences was that she had no awareness of the metaphorical nature of her description, and in fact consistently denied its metaphorical nature. We therefore concluded that the balloon reports were *not* metaphorical.

Thus, we came to conclude that her reports of the balloon were neither perceptual nor metaphorical, but instead reflected an unstable and/or diffuse basis which allowed neither alternative. At the time this sampling took place, I was under the (mistaken, as I now believe) impression that communication must be either perceptual or metaphorical. When I pressed her to clarify the perceptual/metaphorical distinction, she became confused (legitimately, I came to believe) because neither option was correct. Both perception and metaphor require a stable point of view and a clear, secure organization of experience; she apparently had lost that necessary stability or clarity during her Dysphoric Period. She was trying her best to describe what she understood as a perceptual reality, but she was honest enough to recognize that her descriptions of this perceptual reality were "not quite right." Only later did it become clearer to us that her inner experiencing was itself insufficiently clear or stable to allow discrimination between perception and metaphor. By the time she could clarify the distinction, her inner experience had clarified, and the balloon descriptions were no longer needed.

Words After the Balloon had Disappeared

After the first week of sampling, the descriptions Michelle gave that included words (18 remaining samples in the Dysphoric Period) no longer included words in the balloon. However, they were still not the clear perceptual realities that they became in the Normal Affect Period. In the Normal Affect Period, as we saw, Michelle could say with confidence that particular words were present in her inner experience, and describe how she perceived them: spoken in Inner Speech, as though in her own voice, with natural inflection, but without external movement or sound. However, during the Dysphoric Period, even after the balloon period had ended, Michelle had great difficulty, just as she had in the balloon examples, in describing exactly how words occurred to her.

For example, in Sample #15, Michelle was getting ready to go to work when the sentences, "Oh, yeah, I remember. It is in the kitchen," occurred in her mind. These sentences were clearly in words, Michelle said. But when I inquired how she knew the words were there, she replied that they must have been there, because they were implied by the actions which she subsequently performed—she did in fact go to the kitchen. This was an "active consciousness," she said, an intention to act, and the word production was a portion of that action. When I asked whether those particular words were the correct ones, or whether others could have sufficed, she paused and replied, "I couldn't think of any other words that could be said; I could have spoken those words aloud." However, she went on to add that it was more as if she were speaking the words, and described the rate of speaking as being faster than could be spoken aloud, but not uncontrollably fast. The self-contradictory aspects of her own description discomfited her. The characteristic we are emphasizing here is Michelle's inability during this phase of the sampling to describe confidently the inner-perceptual basis which made the words evident to her. When, for example, I asked whether the words she used in her descriptions were the exact words present at the moment of the beep, instead of recalling the perception which had occurred at the beep, again it seemed she now tried new, substitute words and rejected them on the basis that the present feeling accompanying the trial words was not quite right; after exhausting the possible alternative wordings, she concluded that only the specific words initially reported could suffice. We conclude that Michelle did not have clear access to the original words; instead, the thoughts were apparently present to her either as Partially Wordless Speech, where verbal characteristics such as rhythm and inflection are present but words themselves are not, or as Unsymbolized Thinking, or some phenomenon between the two.

Such distinctions are sometimes easy, but at other times (as here) difficult to make. Michelle's lack of confidence about the perceptual details of her experience, as we described it in the previous paragraph, is quite similar to the "it's-in-words-no-it's-not" difficulty many subjects have when they grapple with reporting Unsymbolized Thinking for the first time. Most of those subjects eventually become confident that the correct description is "not-in-words." We then report that the subject was engaged in Unsymbolized Thinking and infer that the earlier samples were also Unsymbolized Thinking. Michelle, however, never reached this closure. On the other hand, when we described Partially Wordless Speech in the previous book, we said that subjects could confidently report that they had a clear sense of inner speech even though no words were present. Because Michelle could not be confident about any such sensations, we could not definitely conclude that these experiences were Partially Wordless.

You may recall that in Chapter 1 we discussed the fact that the categories of inner experience which we would be describing do not necessarily have clearly demarcated boundaries. Occasionally we find that we must remain undecided as to the category in which a particular sample belongs, or whether a new category deserves to be created. This is one such instance. We should, however, emphasize the narrow range of our indecision: while we cannot decide confidently between Partially Unworded Speech, Unsymbolized Thinking, or some as-yet-to-be-defined category, we can say with confidence that Michelle's inner experience at these moments was much less distinctly verbal than her Inner Speech samples of the Normal Affect Period.

Sample #23 was another such instance, when Michelle was walking down the stairs in a university building, and she could see the door of the classroom where she was going to meet a fellow student. A moment before the beep, she had wondered whether the student's group meeting would be finished when she got there, and at the moment of the beep, the words, "Most groups are ready early in the first meeting of the new block. So it is possible," were present in her inner experience. Again, Michelle had a difficult time answering the questions about exactly how the words presented themselves. It was as if she were saying the words, but no voice or sounds were present; it was more like a movement. The words were there, and yet they were not there in words. She felt and knew that somehow those exact words were there; it was not just the meaning of the words that was present, but those particular words themselves. Yet she did not experience the words directly. The rate that these words appeared was, again, slightly faster than in worded speech. Furthermore, this was an effortless consciousness, in that the production of these words required no effort—they just occurred, and we conclude again that what occurred at this beep was either Partially Worded Speech, Unsymbolized Thinking, or something in between.

We will consider one more example, Sample #41. Michelle was in class, and was following along while a fellow student wrote the words "physiological discharge" on the blackboard. She was following his writing, and this was experienced as a kind of speaking of the words again as he was writing the letters, but the speaking was being done more with her eyes than with her mouth. Michelle had just spoken the words aloud, and the sound of them was still "in her head," as if they were being spoken there again. But her impression was that she was not speaking the words as they resounded. Here again, we notice the relative lack of perceptual clarity in her descriptions of the words: hearing was not clearly separated from the sense of speaking, and the eyes were not clearly separated from the ears or the voice apparatus.

Our conclusion is that, during this after-the-balloon phase of her sampling, much of Michelle's thinking was in the general arena of Unsymbolized Thinking or Partially Worded Speech. Again, we do not now see it as essential to resolve the issue of choosing between the two categories. It is clear that whether we call this phenomenon Partially Worded or Unsymbolized, words were much less clearly present, much more Unsymbolized, during the Dysphoric Period than they were in the Normal Affect Period.

Feelings

Of the 48 samples in the Dysphoric Period, 10 involved some Feeling or emotional experience. This emotion occurred along a continuum of clarity, from extremely clear emotional experience including the ability to say exactly where in the body the emotion was experienced, to emotion which was experienced vividly but without such bodily clarity, to emotion which was remembered and not directly experienced at the moment of the beep. Of these 10 Feeling samples, 4 also included some kind of inner visual experience. All the samples which included inner visual experience were accompanied by a relatively clear emotional experience.

An example of a clear, bodily Feeling occurred at Sample #12, where Michelle was in the medical school anatomy room preparing to dissect a cadaver with two fellow female students. She was angry at one of the women, who had borrowed her dissection instruction book but had not returned it, leaving Michelle unprepared for the day's class. This anger was a clearly experienced bodily Feeling, located in the region of Michelle's heart. The words, "It would have been nice if she would have put the book in the mailbox so I could have prepared," were experienced in the balloon, moving from right to left. Even though this was a long sentence, it still was understood to "fit on one line" in the balloon (rather than on two lines as in the "purple" sample described earlier (Sample #10), but Michelle felt that something "had to happen" inside the balloon, to allow the sentence to fit because it was so long. Here again, as with other examples in the balloon, this experience was not clearly visual, but more felt. The primary part of this experience was felt to be the anger, and the anger was understood to evoke the words. The anger came first and then the words, in rapid succession.

In Sample #25, the Feeling was not so clearly experienced in her body. Michelle was looking at her calendar making an appointment. One of her friends had asked another friend whether she was going to a fitness class on Friday night, and the second friend had replied, "Yes, I am." At the same time, which was the moment of the beep, Michelle was nodding in agreement and saying aloud, "Yes," meaning that she, too, was going. The prominent Feeling was a reaction to these events, a Feeling of wanting to go on Friday night. This Feeling was not felt in the body, but nevertheless was a Feeling that, Yes, she wanted to go, although she couldn't be sure that wanting to go was actually a feeling—perhaps it was just a knowing that she wanted to go.

An example where the emotion was more recalled than experienced was Sample #33A, where Michelle was on the telephone with her sister, talking about the wedding of a daughter of one of their parents' friends. The daughter had been the flower girl at Michelle's parents' wedding years ago. Michelle was saying aloud, at the moment of the beep, ". . . actually, it's quite nice to see that," which were words which meant and paralleled the Feeling that it was nice for her sister to see her mother's bridesmaid marrying. The Feeling was described to be very faint, and included a faint recollection of seeing the daughter's wedding, but the Feelings had no particular bodily referent.

Images and Indeterminate Inner Visual Experience

Four (five, if we include the faint recollection of the wedding in the previously described sample) of Michelle's Dysphoric Period emotional experiences included some kind of inner visual experience. In all these cases where an Image was present, an emotional experience was also quite clearly present. The clarity of these inner visual experiences varied greatly. The Image of the photographic slide of the two dogs (Sample #7, described above in the section on Words in the Balloon) was seen clearly, including the photographic film itself illuminated from the back, which showed the slight crease which was an actual characteristic of that film. The second Image of a photograph slide of Belgium (Sample #8, also described above in the section on Words in the Balloon) was not as clear: she could see the "window" (the frame of the slide) rather dimly and out of focus, and she could tell that there was a white house in the slide, but she could make out no additional details.

The third of these inner visual experiences, where four people were walking in the heather (Sample #6, also described above in the section on Words in the Balloon), was even more perceptually indeterminate. Michelle was confident that this experience was visual, and she knew that there were four people somehow being seen, but no other visual details were available to her inner experience. The experience seemed to be a seeing, but the sensations of seeing were not clear or defined; it seemed to be the visualization in inner experience of four people, but the four people (or other details) were not clear or defined. The experience was somehow visual; exactly how was difficult or impossible to report. We thus call this kind of experience Indeterminate Inner Visual Experience.

The remaining example (Sample #18) was even more visually indistinct. It occurred while Michelle was in conversation with two other women, one of whom was talking about driving long distances and the difficulties when there was no one to share the driving at night. Just before the beep, Michelle had said, "Yes, that's true," and as the beep was occurring, Michelle still was very engrossed in the conversation and experiencing a "sort of very, very vague image" of a car with two persons in the front seat, at night, viewed from the back seat. This inner visual experience was a recreation of scenes from Michelle's childhood when she had travelled long distances with her family. The two people were seen in silhouette, but the entire scene was not clear, and we therefore would call this another example of Indeterminate Inner Visual Experience. There was also an emotional aspect to this experience, which was itself very clear: the Feeling of being alert to make sure the driver doesn't fall asleep. However, the emotion was not reexperienced, but instead was remembered.

Thus we see that Michelle reported a few visual experiences during her Dysphoric Period. Only one of these Images was reported to be perceptually clear, and the others ranged along a continuum from clear Images to what we call Indeterminate Inner Visual Experience, where inner experiences are understood to be visual but the exact visual nature of these experiences cannot be adequately described.

DISCUSSION

The case of Michelle is the third (counting the normal subjects) data point on our continuum between hypomania and depression, and our general between-subjects observation still obtains: the more depressed our subjects are, the less distinct and more unsymbolized is their inner experience. Furthermore, Michelle also corroborates our within-subjects observation: in that period where Michelle herself was more depressed, her *own* inner experience was more unsymbolized. We might review the several aspects of Michelle's inner experiences which seemed to be different during her two sampling periods. For example, during the Normal Affect Period, in contrast with the Dysphoric Period, her descriptions of her inner experience were clearer and easier to understand; she was more confidently able to identify features of her inner perceptions, and had more clear-cut examples of what we have called Inner Speech. Furthermore, her experience in the Normal Affect Period had less of the "unconstancy of the perceiver" phenomenon which we will review in the next paragraphs. Thus, we are led to speculate that Michelle's dysphoria was associated with relative unclarity of inner experience, with failure to maintain a constant point of view on one's own inner experience, or with failure to maintain awareness of inner perceptual reality, or with all three.

There is one additional aspect of Michelle's case which bears discussion, the phenomenon we call the "unconstancy of the perceiver." All the descriptions which we have given of Michelle's experiences, more so in the Dysphoric Period but also to some extent in the Normal Affect Period, share this so-far undescribed characteristic. We have become accustomed, with our nonschizophrenic subjects both in the present and the previous book, to find variations in the inner experiences of words, Feelings, Images, etc. For example, a subject might describe a range of Images: sometimes brightly colored and sometimes black and white, sometimes recollected scenes and sometimes creations of imagination, etc. The different characteristics of these experiences of inner seeing would typically be described as different kinds of Images, while the inner seer itself stayed constant. Or, again, a subject might experience a range of inner verbal experiences: sometimes spoken and sometimes heard, for example; here again, the differences were experienced as fluctuations in the words being perceived, while the experiencer remained constant. With Michelle, however, it seemed that the perceiver changed with each new experience. That is, for our typical subjects, the variations in inner experiences occurred "before the footlights of consciousness," so to speak, while the "footlights" themselves stayed constant. For Michelle, however, the footlights themselves seemed to differ with each new experience.

Let us examine some concrete examples. As we saw above, Michelle described in her balloon examples that sometimes thoughts moved freely through the balloon, and sometimes they required energy. The point we are making is that this difference was not experienced as a characteristic of the thoughts themselves, but was rather a characteristic of the *thinking process* of that thought. Sometimes the thinking process was experienced as requiring energy; when on another occasion less energy was involved, it seemed to Michelle that a *different* thinking process, one which had less energy as a constituting feature, was involved. The distinction we are trying to make here is subtle but important enough to bear repeating: Michelle's descriptions were qualitatively different from those of other subjects; while other subjects might have reported different energy levels associated with different experiences, those energy levels were understood to be merely aspects of the experience being described. That is, the energy level was part of the experience, not part of the experienc*ing process*. Michelle, on the other hand, described the experiencing process as being more or less energetic at different times.

We pursued this distinction to the limits of our abilities, and concluded (rightly or wrongly) that the differences in description were not merely different ways of describing similar phenomena, but did in fact reflect distinctly different phenomena.

As another example from the Inner speech sections above, we saw that sometimes words were experienced as part of an "active thought process," and sometimes they were part of what was experienced as a "calmness." Here again, the distinction is not that the words being thought had different characteristics, but instead, the "active thought process" and the "calm thought process" were experienced as two different ways of thinking.

A third verbal example is the inner verbalization that Michelle must fix her hair (Sample #55). We have described this sample as an example of Inner Speech, but from Michelle's perspective, this was not an example of the set of Inner Speech thoughts, but rather a unique occurrence of a particular kind of thinking that Michelle called "setting a task for herself." The phrase "setting a task for herself" was meant to describe the experience of thinking itself, and was not meant merely to describe its outcome. That is, the words, "I must fix my hair a bit" were experienced to be created by a setting-a-task-for-myself consciousness, and this consciousness was experienced to be different from the active-thinking consciousness, the calm consciousness, or the involving-energy consciousness.

Thus, part of Michelle's descriptions were focused on the differing aspects of the experience of consciousness itself, and not just on the differing characteristics of the objects of that consciousness. None of our other subjects found it necessary to make that distinction, being content to describe only the differing aspects of the objects of consciousness themselves.

We might note in passing one last difference between Michelle's sampling and those of our other subjects: often, our sampling conversations with Michelle about each of the beeped experiences seemed rather incomplete when compared to the subjective feeling of completeness with other subjects. In both the Dysphoric and the Normal Affect Period, it seemed that there were details of Michelle's experience which were not being completely described. These details were frequently small, and perhaps unimportant, but nonetheless seemed to occur more often with Michelle than with other subjects. Each of the examples, taken by itself, is assuredly innocuous. But taken together, I was left with the impression that I was not getting as complete a picture of Michelle's experiences as I was accustomed to getting. For example, in describing a conversation, Michelle said, "Someone said, 'I've already got a group,' " and I sensed the very slight, unspoken message that the "someone" was being kept a bit private. A different subject might have said, by contrast, "A girl named Pam said . . .," or "One of the students I don't know very well said . . .," or some such similar expression. I could, and much of the time did, ask for the details, but that is a delicate issue in this kind of research, because the descriptions which we ask for are very private by their nature, and this privacy is an issue at every step of the procedure. Our conversations are always conditioned by (usually unspoken) considerations such as, "Do I need to understand that possibly private detail in order to grasp the nature of the experience at the moment of the beep?" or, "What is my motivation for wanting to understand that possibly private detail?" or, "Would delving into that possibly private detail distract us from the more important tasks at hand?" For whatever reason, it seemed that there were more such possibly private details not discussed with Michelle than with other subjects. There are at least two possible explanations: first, for some reason which is a characteristic more of me than of Michelle, I may have interpreted some rather indeterminate characteristic of Michelle's presentation as being avoidance, and reacted to it with undue circumspection; and second, Michelle herself may have been in fact somewhat more reticent with details than the other subjects with whom I have worked. There is at present no way to disentangle these possibilities, so our interpretation must be left unresolved. We should, however, at least note the possibility that the episodic low self-esteem or dysphoria is associated with relatively incomplete sampling descriptions.

We will now turn to an individual who was somewhat more depressed than Michelle.

A Graduate Student with Periods of Depression

Susan Taylor (not her own name) was a 42-year-old married mother of five children at the time of sampling. She was a graduate student, and was recruited to participate in the study because she had a history of depressive episodes. While she did not have a clear recollection of the onset of depression, she could recall a depression-spawned suicidal gesture as early as age 14. Episodes of depression had occurred periodically thereafter, gradually becoming severe enough by age 37 to render her incapable of performing routine household chores for a period of three months, and she was subsequently suicidal. At the beginning of that period she had sought professional help, began taking the antidepressant medication Elavil (later Desyrel), and began seeing a psychotherapist regularly about a year later. Serious depressive episodes still occasionally occurred, with the most recent serious episode, an agitated depression with suicidal ideation, taking place about 18 months before the present study began and one month after she had discontinued medication. Since that time, Susan had experienced considerably less depression, except for occasional depressive periods. She had continued occasional binge eating, which had been an ongoing problem throughout these periods. She had discontinued taking antidepressant medication 19 months before sampling and had not resumed.

We sampled with Susan during three different periods of time, separated by several weeks. At the time of the initial sampling, she was not particularly depressed but was somewhat upset due to the fact that she was currently trying to decide whether to transfer from her present university to one in another state, a decision which would have major consequences for her husband and children. During this period she had two general reservations regarding her participation in the sampling project: she was upset because of her life situation and so was afraid she would become emotional during the sampling interviews, causing her embarrassment and me discomfort; and the sampling procedure might force her to look at personal issues which she was not yet ready to deal with. (I reassured her that participation was voluntary on a day-to-day basis, and that either of us could suspend sampling at any time if the procedure became difficult. With those reassurances, we began sampling. Both fears were for the most part unrealized during the subsequent sampling sessions, although there were occasional tears which seemed more related to her life situation than to the sampling per se.) We will refer to this initial sampling period as the "Mildly Depressed/Upset Period."

Following the six days of sampling in the Mildly Depressed/Upset Period, we discontinued the sampling procedure for eight days while I prepared several drafts of the first portion of the present report. Each draft was reviewed with Susan and corrected until we both agreed that the descriptions of salient characteristics accurately reflected her inner experience during the initial sampling period. We then began a three-day follow-up sample designed to provide a new set of samples on which to check the validity of the initial salient-characteristic descriptions. As part of the validity-checking procedure (see Hurlburt, 1990), each of the 37 samples in this follow-up period was examined in light of the descriptions of the salient characteristics which we had prepared following the initial sampling period. We found that all those characteristics were satisfactorily described; in no case did we have to alter a description to reflect the follow-up data. During this follow-up sampling period, Susan's affect was somewhat brighter than it had been during the Mildly Depressed/Upset Period: she smiled more frequently, there were no tears, she reported herself to be feeling better, etc. We will therefore refer to this second, follow-up sampling as the "Brighter Affect Period."

At the conclusion of the Brighter Affect Period, I left the beeper with Susan and asked her to sample again if any significant alteration in her mood or experience might occur. Approximately five weeks later, she hurt her lower back and experienced muscle spasms which made relaxation impossible for her. During the period of prescribed rest, while several medications were tried to facilitate relaxation, Susan experienced a depression deeper than had occurred for several years. For four days, she cried almost constantly and had frequent suicidal ideation. The depression lessened somewhat after these four days, and on the fifth day of this depressive episode she resolved to sample again as I had requested (the depression had been too severe to contemplate sampling until that day). She sampled for three days, responding to 26 beeps. During these three sampling days, Susan could be characterized as being quite depressed (although not as debilitatingly depressed as had been the case on the previous days). This third sampling will be referred to below as the "More Depressed Period." We will describe each period in turn.

THE MILDLY DEPRESSED/UPSET PERIOD

Susan sampled initially for a period of six days, collecting 76 samples, of which 57 were fully discussed in the sampling interviews (the remainder were omitted for lack of time). The first day and a half of sampling was marked by Susan's uncertainty about whether the apparatus was functioning properly, because occasional intervals were longer than the programmed one-hour maximum, but beeps which did occur seemed adequately responded to. We substituted a different random interval generator and the problem stopped.

During this period, Susan was not nearly as depressed as she had been some months or years earlier (or would be again later), but neither could she be described as being free of depression. She was frequently on the verge of tears, and she cried occasionally during the sampling conversations. This weeping seemed to occur spontaneously, but not because the topic being discussed was particularly sad or upsetting. She was considering changing universities, which would result in an uprooting or separation from her family, and she said that prospect weighed heavily on her (although it did not appear as a major characteristic of her samples during this period).

Unsymbolized Thinking

By far the most salient characteristic of Susan's inner experience during this period was the predominance of Unsymbolized Thinking, occurring in 24 (42%) of the 57 Mildly Depressed/Upset Period samples. (By comparison, Unsymbolized Thinking occurred in 41% of the Brighter Affect Period samples and in 72% of the More Depressed Period samples.) The reader should be advised that Susan herself did not use the term "Unsymbolized Thinking," using instead a variety of words which we understood to refer to the same or similar phenomenon: "thinking," "wondering," "questioning," "general thought," "puzzling," and "feeling-thought" gives some idea of the range of labels she used. All these labels described experiences where Susan was quite unequivocally "mentally" involved with some particular, quite differentiated idea or problem, and she was "thinking" about it or "wondering" about it, etc. There were no words, images, or any other clearly definable perceptual characteristics of this thinking. Occasionally it seemed to Susan that words might somehow be dimly present in this kind of thinking, but she never became able to determine how (or even whether) this presence of words was experienced. If words were present, they certainly were much different and far less easily apprehendable than were the words in the Inner Speech experiences described below.

For example, at Sample #13A, she had just walked by the bulletin board where several days earlier she had posted the grades for a course in which she was the teaching assistant. At the moment of the beep, she was "thinking about" a mistake she had made on one of the grades and "wondering" if she had made other mistakes. Even though this was a highly differentiated experience, involving inner apprehension both of one particular event and the possibility of other occurrences, there were no words or images or any other describable characteristics of experience which could be said to carry this complex meaning. Nonetheless, Susan was quite confident that she was "thinking" and "wondering" about those particular topics; thus, this is an example of Unsymbolized Thinking.

In another sample (#38), Susan was sitting in the front row of a church-related lecture, and the speaker was addressing the class from a position behind her, standing between the first and second rows. At the moment of the beep, she was Unsymbolized Thinking (she called it "feeling-thinking") that he was rude to be standing behind her. Here again, this meaning was not verbal, nor was there any ongoing imagery, but nonetheless Susan "knew" that she was "feeling-thinking" that he was rude.

In a third example (Sample #41), she was reading, and saying in Inner Speech (described below) the words "to bring forth grass" as she was reading them. At the same time, she was Unsymbolized Thinking (she called it "puzzling") about the concept which was being described and trying to understand it. She could not say precisely how she knew she was puzzling except that it seemed as if she were approaching the concept first from one direction and then from another. This approaching/reapproaching was not verbal, imaginal, or bodily; it seemed to be mental or cognitive, but could not be described more adequately. Nonetheless, it was understood to be taking place.

The following features are characteristic of these examples and all of Susan's 21 other episodes of Unsymbolized Thinking. Susan had a clear awareness that some type of mental activity was taking place; she knew the specific nature of the ongoing process (that is, she could distinguish between "wondering," "puzzling," and "thinking-about," etc.); she could easily identify the content or target of this mental process (that is, she knew exactly what she was thinking about); and no words or images or specific bodily sensations could be confidently identified as being part of the process. As a rule, it was mildly frustrating for Susan to try to describe these experiences because she could provide so little detail about what was taking place. She occasionally said that it seemed that words might be present "beneath the surface" or "at another level," but careful questioning failed to establish whether such dimly perceived words were actually part of her experience.

Feelings

Emotions were identified as being present at the moment of the beep on 14 of the 57 Mildly Depressed/Upset Period samples. Of these 14 samples, 9 (16% of the total Mildly Depressed/Upset Period samples) included Feelings directly experienced in awareness at the moment of the beep. (By comparison, Feelings occurred in 8% of the Brighter Affect Period samples and in 28% of the More Depressed Period samples.) In addition to the experience of Feelings (but including 3 samples where Feelings also occurred simultaneously), 8 samples (14% of the 57 Mildly Depressed/Upset Period samples) included emotional experiences where emotional processes were noted to be ongoing in her body but were present to awareness only when brought into focus by responding to the beep (that is, they were not present in awareness at the immediate moment of the beep itself). Susan occasionally (in 4 samples) had difficulty making this distinction between Feelings which are present to awareness at the moment of the beep and emotional processes not present in immediate awareness but present in the body.

An example of experienced Feelings took place at Sample #53. Susan was walking back to her car which was parked near a construction site on the university campus because by mistake she had left her sampling notebook in the car. While walking back, she was about to pass the worker who was directing traffic around the construction site, and with whom she had exchanged pleasantries a few moments before while walking in the other direction. The beep occurred after the conclusion of a sentence which she had spoken to herself in Inner Speech (see below): "I forgot my notebook." At the moment of the beep, she was Feeling somewhat foolish, hurried, and silly, knowing that she was about to pass the same worker twice more while retrieving the notebook. Susan could not specify exactly how the foolish, hurried, silly Feeling presented itself to her; that is, she could not be sure whether it was a bodily or mental feeling, or, if it was bodily, exactly where and how in the body it was manifested. Nonetheless, the Feeling was somewhat clearly "there" at the moment of the beep.

Another example (Sample #8A) occurred late in the evening when Susan's son was making what she considered an unreasonable request to avoid going to bed. The beep occurred at the immediate conclusion of her saying aloud to her son, "Too late!", and she was Feeling impatient and tired of the hassle with him. Here again, she was not sure how this impatience presented itself, whether it was bodily or not, but she knew it was clearly present, experienced at the moment of the beep.

Emotional Processes Outside of Awareness

In the previous two examples, Susan apprehended her Feelings as being part of her awareness at the moment of the beep. On 8 (14%) of the samples in the Mildly Depressed/Upset Period, however, there were, at the moment of the beep, emotional processes which seemed to be outside of her momentary awareness, but were nonetheless ongoing in her body, behind the scenes, so to speak, experienced only when Susan examined her experience in responding to the beep. For example, at Sample #21, Susan was wondering whether the sampling device worked or not by trying to figure out what time she had turned it on, since the beeps should never be more than an hour apart. (This wondering was in Unsymbolized Thinking.) At the same time, she was vaguely apprehensive or anxious, which seemed to be a bodily sensation extending from her throat downward through her chest. This experience could be differentiated from the previous two Feeling examples in that the emotional process did not seem to be part of the ongoing awareness at the time of the beep, but was recognized as being present only when "going back" to examine what she was experiencing. That is, the apprehensive or anxious bodily process was present at the moment of the beep, but was an unfocused-upon ongoing aspect of her experience, rather than being a part of awareness at that moment.

Since our task as we have defined it is to describe awarenesses as they occur at the moments of the beeps, we exclude such bodily processes from our count of Feelings. However, the existence of such bodily processes which are clearly occurring but which are outside of awareness seem quite possibly to be important phenomena, so we include discussion of them.

Another example of an emotional process which was present upon examination but which did not seem to be an immediate aspect of awareness occurred at Sample #26. Susan had heard mentioned in passing the previous day that the present writer's son had to be taken to the doctor. At the moment of the beep, she was saying in Inner Speech (see below) "your son," which was part of a sentence directed in imagination to me. At the same time, she was wondering (an example of Unsymbolized Thinking) what was wrong with my son. In responding to the beep, seconds after it occurred, Susan asked herself whether emotion was present, and discovered that, yes, a feeling of stress could be located in her body, particularly across her chest. This emotional process did not seem to be part of her awareness at the moment of the beep, but was nonetheless present bodily at that moment.

Sometimes, several kinds of emotional processes existed at the same time. For example, at Sample #24, Susan was lecturing her son about his not doing his reading homework. The beep occurred just after she had said aloud, "I expect you to do it!" Present at the moment of the beep, but available to awareness only in retrospect, were the emotions of annoyance, skepticism, and perhaps anger directed at her son. But also present was a general feeling of anxiety. This anxiety was not particularly related to the homework incident, but instead had been more or less present for some hours and seemed more related to Susan's own life decisions. In fact, it seemed that this anxiety was the same anxiety that Susan had reported three hours earlier at Sample #21 (see above).

The next beep (#25) occurred about 45 minutes later, and Susan reported that similar emotions were still present, but now more interwoven than they had been earlier. She was involved in another disciplinary action, this time with another son, who had not done what Susan and her husband had told him to do. Now, Susan was beeped while saying to him, "Go to the bathroom, brush your teeth and go to bed!" She was again angry and frustrated, and also feeling some of the same "uptightness" that she had been experiencing for several hours that evening. Furthermore, she felt like she didn't know what to do about her son's behavior, a feeling described as "being at a loss." Thus, Susan reported having three different emotional processes occurring at the same time. The three emotions (anger/frustration, "uptightness," and "being at a loss") were not experienced as being quite as separated as were the emotions in the previous sample; at the present beep, the three emotions were distinct and yet blended together. These emotions, again, were not in immediate awareness, but were observed to be present only when she retrospected.

In summary, it seems that Susan's emotional experiences existed for her on a continuum of presence to awareness, sometimes being clearly available Feelings but often being quite differentiated, ongoing emotional processes which were not focused upon but which nonetheless existed at some deeper level. Susan's emotional processes and Feelings could be differentiated, allowing for multiple emotions to exist at the same time, either separately or blended together but without losing the distinct nature of the individual emotions. Occasionally, it was possible for Susan to identify the bodily region where a particular emotion was experienced, but for the most part, emotions were resistant to further reduction. Susan knew what her emotions were and what they referred to, but she could not say how she knew.

Inner Speech

Susan experienced herself as speaking in an inner voice in 7 (12%) of her 57 Mildly Depressed/Upset Period samples. (By comparison, Inner Speech occurred in 41% of the Brighter Affect Period samples and in 33% of the More Depressed Period samples [0% if Inner Speech while reading is excluded; see below].) In all of these experiences, the Inner Speech was perceived to have the same characteristics as her own voice would have when speaking aloud: the words seemed to be created by herself, under her own control; the speech was in complete sentences; the sentences were perceived to be punctuated and inflected just as her speech would have been had she said that sentence aloud; and the words were uttered at the same rate of speed and seemingly at the same pitch as her external speech, etc.

Three of these samples have been described in previous sections of this chapter: Sample #53, where Susan was Feeling somewhat foolish while saying in Inner Speech, "I forgot my notebook," was described in the Feelings section. Sample #26, where the words "your son" were part of an inner sentence inquiring about why the present writer's son must visit the doctor, was described in the section on emotional processes outside of awareness. Sample #41, where Susan was reading the words "to bring forth grass" and saying them in Inner Speech as she read, was described in the section on Unsymbolized Thinking. In Sample #26, the inner words were directed to a particular external person, namely me. In Sample #53, the words were directed to Susan herself, while in Sample #41 the words were a mere accompaniment of reading, apparently directed to no one in particular. All of these examples had the same characteristics as exterior speech, and could be distinguished from exterior speech only because Susan "knew" they were inner and that there were no audible sounds being made.

Inner Speech, when it was present, was the most clearly apprehendable portion of Susan's awareness. For example, at Sample #35, Susan was beeped while she was sitting in a university laboratory room. At the moment of the beep, she was Inner Speaking the sentence, "Should I say anything to Joe (the janitor) or not?" The question referred to a professor's request that that room be left unlocked. This sentence was, again, perceived as actively spoken, in Susan's own (inner) voice, accurately inflected and mirroring how an external utterance would have sounded. Again in this case, the question was directed to Susan herself. At the same time, Susan had the impression that there was "a lot going on underneath" this awareness, and that she might have apprehended it had she "gone back" during the moment just following the beep and examined this carefully (as we have described above in the section on Feelings). She did not, however, do this.

In summary, Susan's Inner Speech had the following characteristics: when present, it was the clearest part of her inner experience; it was apprehended as having the same phenomenal characteristics as external speaking except with no sound or movement; and the speaking was at the same rate, pitch, and inflection as external speech would have been.

Indeterminate Inner Visual Experience

Of the 57 samples in Susan's Mildly Depressed/Upset Period, 3 (5%) involved what seemed to Susan to be inner visualizations, but she was extremely uncertain about any of the visual details of those experiences. This uncertainty about perceptual characteristics leads us to refer to them as Indeterminate Inner Visual Experiences. (By comparison, Indeterminate Inner Visual Experience occurred in 0% of the Brighter Affect Period samples and in 5% of the More Depressed Period samples.) We will begin by describing the sample which involved the visual experience which was the *most* clear.

The clearest (least Indeterminate) example of Visual Experience (Sample #22) occurred while Susan was driving her car, focused on the traffic pattern. She had seen some bicyclists at the upcoming intersection, and now it seemed that she had turned her attention back to the traffic, but an image of these bicyclists seemed to "stay with her." It "almost seemed like I was both watching the real traffic and seeing an image of the bicyclists superimposed on it. But I'm not sure. It did seem like there was a mental image." The "image" was of two bicyclists, mother and child, coming around the corner. What makes this experience to some degree indeterminate is that Susan was indefinite in describing the image, using phrases such as "it almost seemed . . ." etc.

On the other hand, Susan *was* able to provide some perceptual details (such as the approximate ages of the bicyclists and in which direction they were moving), which may have implied that there was in fact an image being seen. However, Susan had external perceptual knowledge of that information, and she could not be certain that any of that kind of perceptual detail was actually being seen in the imaginal experience. (At the same time as Susan was watching the traffic and indeterminately seeing the image, she was also listening to a tender song, "Sara", playing on the car tape player. This song was about a girl's experience with incest and the boy that fell in love with her, and Susan was Feeling, in her heart, an emotion which matched that being conveyed by the song.)

The next-clearest example of Indeterminate Inner Visual Experience occurred at Sample #30, where Susan was thinking about a sample (#23, see below in the section Sensory Awareness) which had taken place the previous day, and which would be one of the topics in our upcoming sampling meeting. She was now trying to decide how to describe to me the Sample #23 experience: whether it was in words, etc. (this portion of Sample #23 was an example of Unsymbolized Thinking, a phenomenon which subjects frequently have difficulty describing). While this conversation was not tape recorded and so cannot be transcribed verbatim, the following reconstruction from my notes may adequately characterize her description of the present sample: "It was like seeing myself saying something, seeing my face. Like almost having an image, almost picturing myself. Like I was rehearsing it in my mind— almost like a mini-videotape, but not quite like I was looking at it. I must have sensed seeing it because I noted my facial expression. But maybe there was no real visual experience, although it seemed I saw my expression." Here again, we have a visual experience of questionable determinacy as evidenced by phrases such as "almost like . . .," "I must have sensed . . .," "maybe . . .," etc. There is something about the experience which seems visual, but it is difficult or impossible to pin it down.

The last (and most indeterminate) example of Indeterminate Inner Visual Experience was Sample #54, where Susan was walking into a shopping mall to do some window shopping, and thinking about a conversation she had had earlier with her therapist. Susan was about to transfer to another university, and she and the therapist had talked in a light-hearted manner about Susan's taking a picture of him with her and hanging it in the new university. Just before the beep, Susan had said to herself in Inner Speech, "I could put it up on my wall." Susan wrote in her sampling notebook that at the moment of the beep, she was "picturing" this picture hanging on the wall at the university in the city where she was going. At the same time, she was "mentally chuckling," remembering the conversation "but also trying to picture it." During the sampling conversation, which took place the following morning, I asked Susan for the details of what she had seen. Was it in color? Viewed from what perspective? Profile or full face, etc.? Here again, we have no exact transcript, but an adequate reconstruction of her response is: "I don't know . . . I didn't see his face specifically. What I saw was a picture up on the wall. (Exactly what did you see?) I'm not sure I saw a vivid picture. It was like a flash of a picture on a wall. I was trying to imagine that. The image is not the key thing there. The key thing is probably the imagining . . . the trying to imagine a picture of him. (But what did you *see*?) An institution-type wall, yellowish, with a picture on it. The face was not clear, but that wasn't important because I knew what it was. (Exactly what did his face look like?) I knew it was a picture of him, but I didn't necessarily see the details. I almost think I saw the (picture) frame more clearly than the face. It's almost like I was imagining myself seeing the picture, rather than actually at that moment seeing the picture, except that it seems that I almost actually saw the wall. It was yellowish." As Susan struggles to describe accurately her inner experience in this passage, we see that she is unable to provide straightforward descriptions of the perceptual details of her experience, using phrases such as "I'm not sure I saw . . .," " I was trying to see . . .," "I didn't necessarily see . . .," or "it seems that I almost actually saw. . .". These phrases do not indicate careless description, but instead reflect a careful attempt to describe a difficult-to-describe phenomenon. What makes this experience difficult to describe seems to be that the seeing itself is not clearly apprehendable. It is not "not seeing," but it is also not clearly "seeing."

In my view, the lack of confidence in providing detail is not in itself sufficient reason to conclude that an experience was not visual. On the other hand, the simple assertion that an experience *was* visual is not sufficient reason to accept that it was. What is required, in Susan's case and for all our other subjects as well, is to attempt to understand what the subject means by her descriptions. In this sample, we concluded that Susan's experience was less visual than simply seeing in the external world or seeing an image, but was somehow more visual than the wondering or thinking that we described in the Unsymbolized Thinking section. It seemed that she was "sort-of" seeing, and we have come to call this phenomenon "Indeterminate Inner Visual Experience."

There is one further aspect of Susan's description of this sample that bears discussion, and that is her statement, "It's almost like I was imagining myself seeing the picture, rather than actually at that moment seeing the picture." When Susan used the term "imagining" here, she was not referring to seeing an image but rather to conceiving what such visualizing would be like. Thus Susan is saying that it's almost as if she were having a *conceptual* experience (conceiving herself seeing) rather than a *perceptual* experience (perceiving a visual image of the picture). We make this distinction to demonstrate that Susan was not sure whether her experience was conceptual or perceptual, and this lack of certainty may be the core of the indeterminacy in her visual experience. We have noted in our description of Michelle (Chapter 4) that during her Dysphoric sampling period in particular, she also had difficulty distinguishing between conceptual (metaphorical) and perceptual experiences.

In summary, Susan's visual experiences seemed to exist along a range of clarity of the visualness of the experience. She had *no* samples which were undeniably clearly visual; that is, she did not report seeing images in which visual perceptual details were the center of attention and could be confidently described. She did, however, have experiences which seemed more visual than other samples. We called these samples Indeterminate Inner visual Experiences to connote the indefinite visualness of the experiences. We should be careful to note that Susan was *not* describing experiences which were clear visualizations of images seen to be "out of focus," "cloudy," or "misty." Instead, Susan was describing experiences where the sense of seeing was itself equivocal. She could not be absolutely confident in determining whether she was "seeing" or not. Thus, Susan's indeterminacy was a characteristic of the visualizing, not of the image being seen.

Sensory Awareness

Susan was particularly aware of some aspect of her external sensory environment in 3 (5%) of the 57 Mildly Depressed/Upset Period samples. (By comparison, Sensory Awareness occurred in 19% of the Brighter Affect Period samples and in 44% of the More Depressed Period samples.) For example, at Sample #14, she was pressing a yellow stick-on note onto a book. At the moment of the beep, she was particularly aware of the yellowness of the paper, as if the yellow note paper had become enlarged in her awareness. This enlarging did not seem to be an intensification of the yellow color, nor was there any particular emotional reaction to the color. She was merely focused on the yellowness, and the note seemed somehow magnified in her experience.

In another example (Sample #23), she was reading her Church News about periodic extra instruction for Sunday School teachers and wondering (in Unsymbolized Thinking) if she would have to attend since she taught a short-term Sunday School class. At the same time, she was also enjoying a piece of bacon, being particularly aware of the taste of it. This awareness of the taste was not evaluative, although she knew she liked the bacon; and was clearly nonverbal. Instead, it was merely an attentiveness to the taste of the bacon. This paying attention was only the secondary focus of that particular experience, the first being the wondering about the Sunday School training.

THE BRIGHTER AFFECT PERIOD

Eight days after the conclusion of the Mildly Depressed/Upset Period, we resumed sampling as part of our procedure to check the validity of the descriptions we had written of the initial period's samples. By the time of this second sampling, Susan's affect had brightened somewhat. She was no longer continuously on the verge of tears, she smiled frequently, she had a more easily available sense of humor, etc. From Susan's perspective, she was experiencing considerably less anxiety and upset now than she had during the initial sampling period, and for these reasons we refer to this second sampling as the Brighter Affect Period.

We found that the salient characteristics of samples taken during this second period were quite similar to those seen in the first sampling; for example, our description of Susan's Unsymbolized Thinking, generated during the first sampling period, quite accurately reflected those moments of the second period where Susan was engaged in Unsymbolized Thinking. There were, however, three aspects of the Brighter Affect Period samples which bear discussion: an increase in frequency of Inner speech, the emergence of a new (to Susan) salient characteristic which we call Words Present, and an increase in relative complexity of experiences during the Brighter Affect Period.

Inner speech

During the Brighter Affect Period, 15 (41%) of the 37 samples included Inner Speech; by contrast, during the Mildly Depressed/Upset Period, Inner Speech had occurred only 12% of the time; the difference between these two percentages is significant ($z = 3.16$, $p < .01$). Furthermore, we shall see that there were *no* freely-produced (excluding Inner Speech as an accompaniment of reading to self) Inner Speech samples during the More Depressed Period. The relative frequencies of the other characteristics of inner experience were also somewhat different between periods, but this was by far the most dramatic change. The degree to which words were present in Susan's inner experience decreased systematically as Susan became more depressed. This is especially evident if we count the Words Present experiences (described below) as verbal experiences; then we see that there were 57% verbal experiences in the Brighter Affect Period compared with only 12% in the Mildly Depressed/Upset Period and 0% in the More Depressed Period (if we exclude the examples of Inner Speech which simply accompanied reading to herself).

Words Present

There was one salient characteristic which emerged during Susan's Brighter Affect Period which had not appeared during the Mildly Depressed/Upset Period—the characteristic we call Words Present. This aspect occurred in 6 (16%) of Susan's 37 Brighter Affect Period samples (but not at all in either of the more depressed periods), and involved the recognition that words were somehow distinctly present in inner experience without, however, being "spoken" in Inner Speech. In five of these samples, a complete sentence was apprehended as existing as a unit, with the words of the sentence present all at once. That is, the words did not follow one another in a temporal sequence as they did in Inner Speech, but were instead all present simultaneously. Susan could not positively describe how these words occurred to her, but was confident that they were not heard, spoken, or seen; she somehow just knew that those exact words were present.

For example, at Sample #F12 Susan was engaged in her work as a teaching assistant, stamping the university name on a series of Rorschach Ink Blot plates. At the moment of the beep, she was looking at the plates and the words "Yes they've been stamped" existed as "mental words." Susan was confident that the words were there, almost like they were a "thought, or an idea that embodies those particular words." She didn't "actually directly experience those words, but those exact words were meant, or were there below the surface." These words had no temporal, punctuational, or inflective characteristics as did the Inner Speech samples we have described above. Rather, they all seemed to be equally present simultaneously.

This Words Present characteristic could be present at the same time as an ongoing Unsymbolized Thinking. For example, at Sample #F25, Susan was making photocopies, trying to fit a large page into the copy machine window. While she was adjusting the position of the page, the words "I wonder how to fit it in" were available as Words Present to her awareness. These exact words were somehow simply there in awareness, not spoken, heard or seen, and present as a unit rather than sequentially. At the same time, Susan was wondering, in Unsymbolized Thinking, which part of the page was the most important. Furthermore, Susan had a direct visual Sensory Awareness of the page, looking at it as she held it on the copy machine window.

As we said above, five of the six Words Present experiences involved complete sentences present to her awareness as a block or unit. In the remaining experience (Sample #F27), just a few words were present from an idea whose totality seemed to exist as Unsymbolized Thinking. Susan was eating a chocolate bar, aware of the sweet chocolate taste (an example of Sensory Awareness described above). At the same time, she was engaged in Unsymbolized Thinking about yogurt, that she would like to have some but she didn't care for the strawberry. For the most part, as in the other Unsymbolized Thinkings, this idea was nonverbal, but somehow "strawberry" and "yogurt" were rather distinctly individually present to awareness. These "words" were not spoken, heard or seen, but instead seemed to be "more highlighted out of the whole glob" of the Unsymbolized Thinking. Susan could not give perceptual details of how this highlighting took place, relying instead on metaphorical descriptions: "it was as if those particular words were printed in bold face type"; "it seemed that those words were emphasized"; and "It's like when popcorn pops—some of the kernels pop higher than the others"; but none of those descriptions of the words referred to details which Susan could see or hear. This example does lead to the speculation that Susan's Unsymbolized Thinking may in fact be in some way verbal or preverbal. We recall from the initial descriptions that "it seemed to Susan that words might somehow be dimly present" in Unsymbolized Thinking, even though she could not specify in what way this dim presence occurred.

The strawberry yogurt sample thus seems to be a case where Unsymbolized Thinking takes place "nearer the surface of verbal awareness," so to speak, so that a few words make themselves directly available to awareness. If we follow that speculation further, it may then be the case that Susan experiences a continuum of clarity of verbal experience, ranging in order of increasing clarity: Unsymbolized Thinking, Unsymbolized Thinking with a few Words Present, Words Present, and Inner Speech.

Complexity of Inner Experience

The third difference between the Brighter Affect and the Mildly Depressed/Upset Periods was that Susan's reports of her inner experiences were much more complex during the Brighter Affect sample than they were in the initial sample. As we saw in the previous section, Susan confidently described two experiences which involved Words Present, Unsymbolized Thinking, and Sensory Awareness all occurring simultaneously (the copying Sample #F25 and the strawberry yogurt Sample #F27). Many other samples had two clearly distinguishable aspects. In general, Susan's descriptions were more varied and complex during the Brighter Affect Period than during the Mildly Depressed/Upset Period.

Taken together, these observations lead to the conclusion that Susan's inner experience was more focused, coherent, and differentiated during the Brighter Affect Period than during the initial period. We will see that the opposite was true in the More Depressed Period.

THE MORE DEPRESSED PERIOD

Five weeks after the Brighter Affect Period, Susan experienced a relatively severe depressive episode which involved four days of almost constant crying and frequent suicidal ideation. During the initial sampling periods, I had requested that Susan contact me if and when depression became more severe so that we could sample during those times. During these four days, the depression was too severe for such a request to be contemplated, but on the fifth day of that depressive episode, the depression had lessened somewhat, and although she remained depressed, Susan resumed sampling for a period of 3 days, collecting 18 samples that we fully discussed. These samples afford a glimpse into Susan's inner experience while depressed.

In our discussion of the Brighter Affect Period, we noted that an adequate characterization of Susan's inner experience during that period called for the identification of a new salient characteristic of inner experience (Words Present). The More Depressed sample did not necessitate the construction of any new characteristics, but some of the characteristics we have already identified appeared with very different frequencies.

Unsymbolized Thinking

Unsymbolized Thinking was present at 13 of the 18 (72%) More Depressed samples, a percentage which is significantly larger ($z = 2.40$, $p < .05$) than the 42% of the other two sampling periods). Furthermore, 5 additional samples did not include any symbolization (two Sensory Awarenesses, two Feelings, and one Indeterminate Inner Visual Experience at the most indeterminate end of the continuum we have described). In fact, the *only* clear symbolization which occurred in Susan's

More Depressed samples was Inner Speech which directly accompanied reading, words which she was more or less forcing herself to read, and even then this Inner Speech was a process secondary to an unrelated Unsymbolized Thinking (see below). Thus, *all* of Susan's 18 More Depressed samples involved Unsymbolized Thinking as a major aspect, or involved no symbolization at all. Thus our first observation is that Susan's inner experience was much less symbolized when depressed.

Inner Speech

Inner Speech could be said to be present at 6 of the 18 More Depressed samples. However, all 6 of those cases involved Inner Speech while reading as she tried to catch up on homework. Furthermore, in all these cases, Susan was not really focused on what she was reading, but was simply going through the motions, with her main focus being engaged in Unsymbolized Thinking about some related or different topic. Thus, it may be fairly said that Susan had *no* freely-produced Inner Speech samples during the More Depressed period.

Feelings

Feelings were a focus of attention during 5 (28%) of the 18 More Depressed samples, about the same percentage as the combination of Feelings and emotional processes which had occurred in the Mildly Depressed/Upset Period. However, the emotions during the More Depressed Period seemed stronger and more prominent—more directly experienced—and thus all qualified for our definition as Feelings. Moreover, the experienced Feelings were *all* negative during the More Depressed period, being namely "frustrated," "frustrated and annoyed," "perplexed—wondering what is wrong," and "annoyance, anger and disgust." Thus, our third general observation is that Susan experienced considerably more strong frustration and anger during her More Depressed sample. Susan continued to have difficulty describing the perceptual details of her Feelings, just as she had had in the previous sampling periods.

Sensory Awareness

Susan was focused on some sensory aspect of her environment in 8 (44%) of the 18 More Depressed samples. Thus, Sensory Awareness was significantly ($z = 3.53$, $p < .01$) more frequent here than in the two previous sampling periods, where its frequency averaged 11%. In all these examples, she was just taking in a characteristic of the environment, without processing it or commenting on it or integrating it into her experience. She was merely noticing the characteristic. Thus, our fourth conclusion is that is that Susan had more "raw" experiences, awarenesses which were relatively passive and unprocessed, during her More Depressed sample than at other times.

Samples during Suicidal Ideation

The following two samples took place 12 minutes apart, during the More Depressed Period on a Monday evening at 6:05 and 6:17, and I am recounting them here for two reasons. First, they are rather typical of Susan's samples during the More Depressed Period. Second, they flanked a moment of strong despair which culminated, at about 6:15, in serious contemplation of suicide. Sample #D6 occurred at 6:05 while Susan was reading a draft of the sampling account by Susan Melancon (Chapter 9 of Hurlburt, 1990). The topic of the paragraph she was reading was "glossolalia" (Speaking in tongues). She was reading the words "speech accompanied by unrelated thought," and was speaking the words to herself, an example of Inner Speech while reading. At the same time, and more centrally in her experience, she was wondering specifically what an example of glossolalia would be. This wondering was an example of Unsymbolized Thinking. At the same time, Susan was aware of, but was not thinking about, tears which were rolling down her face, an example of Sensory Awareness.

Ten minutes later came the suicidal ideation (during which the random beeper did not happen to signal); two minutes after that came Sample #D7. She was thinking about what to wear to her next psychotherapy appointment: should she wear dressy or casual flats—since she could not wear high heels—and also what color should she wear given the possibility of a bladder accident. This consideration was nonverbal, an example of Unsymbolized Thinking. However, there was also present simultaneously an Indeterminate Inner Visual Experience of the blue and white stripes of a particular top which Susan was considering wearing. This visual experience was just of stripes of color, perhaps a white stripe bordered on each side by blue, and did not include visual details of the top itself. Susan was confident that this experience did in fact include an inner seeing of color, but was not able to give confident descriptions of the visual characteristics (that is, she could not confidently answer such questions as, "Were there in fact only three stripes?" etc.). Thus, this aspect of her experience seemed to be an example of

Indeterminate Inner Visual Experience, somewhere in the middle of her range-of-clarity continuum.

Perhaps surprisingly, despite their close temporal proximity to a time of despair and suicidal ideation, these samples do not evidence any stronger characteristics of depression than the other samples during this period.

In general, we can characterize Susan's inner experience during the More Depressed period as including more Unsymbolized Thinking, more passive awareness of "raw" sensory data with no symbolization, and more Feelings of anger and frustration.

DISCUSSION

The case of Susan is the fourth (counting the normal subjects) data point on our continuum between hypomania and depression, and our general between-subjects observation still obtains: the more depressed our subjects are, the more unsymbolized is their inner experience. Furthermore, Susan also corroborates our within-subjects observation: the more depressed Susan became, the more Unsymbolized became her inner experience.

In fact, when Susan became very depressed, symbolization disappeared almost entirely from her awareness. The only examples of clear symbolization in Susan's More Depressed Period are those Inner Speech examples of words being read. However, in those examples, Susan was not focused on the reading; it was a rather automatic activity while her attention was actually on an Unsymbolized Thought about a distinctly different topic.

Conversely, when Susan's affect was at its brightest (in the Brighter Affect Period), symbols, in the form of words, became much more frequent. When we combine Inner Speech with Words Present, we find that 57% of Susan's Brighter Affect samples included words, compared with 12% in the Mildly Depressed/Upset Period and 0% (if we exclude the background Inner Speech while reading) in the More Depressed Period.

6

A Depressed Resident of a Halfway House

Diane King (not her own name) was a 31-year-old female resident of a psychiatric halfway house at the time of sampling. She had been a patient in the state mental health system for about five years, and for some years before that had been in and out of private psychiatric hospitals. There had been a number of widely varying diagnostic impressions over the course of her treatment, including schizophrenia, schizophreniform disorder, and borderline personality, but the most frequent, and also the most current, diagnosis was depression. Her history was marked: by frequent suicidal gestures involving medication overdose and threatening to jump from the top of buildings; by rather petty involvements with the law such as shoplifting, frequent enough to result in spending nine months in jail; by presenting herself at the county jail and refusing to leave, resulting in her being charged with trespassing and jailed; by accusing others, including mental health workers, of raping her, sufficiently frequently so that the police became reluctant to take subsequent reports; by other contacts with public agencies such as police, fire department, ambulance services, etc., as a result of frequent calls for help, suicidal and otherwise; and by problematic personal relationships. Over the years, Diane generally ascribed these incidents to being the result of desperation following some kind of pressure situation. Following the diagnosis of depression a year and a half earlier, she had been taking Lithium (400 mg bid) regularly, and she was confident that the Lithium calmed her down. She had in fact recently been progressing well through the progressively-less-restrictive transitional housing system. At the time of sampling, she was taking the Lithium and also the antidepressant medication Desyrel (100 mg at bedtime).

She volunteered to participate in the sampling study after hearing me describe it in a brief presentation to the halfway house residents. Diane sampled for seven days over a three-week period, the sampling days being interrupted by holidays, illness, and Diane's move from the halfway house to a supervised apartment setting. The procedure produced 42 samples, about 6 samples each sampling day.

UNSYMBOLIZED THINKING

In 20 (48%) of the 42 samples, Diane was focused on a particular idea or event, and was thinking or wondering about it without any words or images or any other clearly definable characteristics, the type of experience we call Unsymbolized Thinking. For example, at Sample #9, Diane was resting quietly in bed, and was "a little bit debating" whether to go to a seminar on medications that evening, and hoping the seminar would be interesting. She had no doubt that she was engaged in this debating- and hoping-type of cognitive activity, and knew quite specifically that it referred to the medication seminar, but she could not provide any more detail about how this debating or hoping took place except to rule out the possibility that words, images, or any other recognizable symbols were involved.

Another example (Sample #40) illustrates that two different Unsymbolized Thoughts occasionally occurred simultaneously. Diane was in a grocery store buying groceries for the first time since she had moved from the halfway house to her independent apartment. She was standing in front of the shelves of breakfast cereal wondering if she should buy a box. This wondering involved a recognition that she didn't usually eat breakfast (or had only a glass of juice), a consideration of whether she would in fact eat the cereal or whether it would be wasted, and a consideration of the expense involved. All these aspects were part of one mental process which occurred without words or feelings or images; she "just knew" that she was thinking about exactly those aspects of eating breakfast. At the same time, she was Unsymbolized Thinking that she didn't like buying her own groceries because it was too hard to make decisions. She herself called this Unsymbolized Thought a "feeling," although it was not a bodily feeling nor an emotion. It was "almost as if" the words "I don't like buying my own groceries" were present in a faded, general way, but the words themselves were not actually present. The meaning of the thought was simply there.

Diane's Unsymbolized Thinking was thus quite typical of the Unsymbolized Thinking phenomenon we described earlier: she knew the specific nature of the ongoing process (that is, she could distinguish between "debating" and "hoping," etc.); she could easily identify the content or target of this mental process (that is, she knew exactly what she was thinking about); and no words or images or specific bodily sensations could be confidently identified as being part of the process. We observe that this kind of process was quite common for Diane, being present in about half of her samples.

INNER SPEECH

During 17 (40%) of her 42 samples, Diane experienced herself as speaking in an inner voice, which was perceived to have the same characteristics that her own voice has when speaking aloud: the words seemed to be created by herself, under her own control; the Inner Speakings were in complete sentences; the sentences were perceived to be punctuated and inflected just as they would have been had she said the sentences aloud; the words were uttered at the same rate of speed and seemingly at the same pitch as her external speech; etc.

For example, at Sample #31 Diane was eating raisins while watching TV, and at the moment of the beep was saying to herself in Inner Speech, "I'm going to fix lunch so I won't forget to do it tomorrow." These words were said in her own voice under her own control, and seemed to be located somewhere inside her head. The sentence was inflected as a simple statement of fact, just as it would have been had she made the statement aloud.

IMAGES

Diane was experiencing some kind of inner visual experience in 4 (10%) or her 42 samples. These visual experiences existed along a continuum of clarity, including 2 experiences which were of perfectly clear and visually detailed Images and 2 experiences which seemed to be seeings but in which no visual details could be confidently said to be seen, phenomena we are calling Indeterminate Visual Experience. We will present the two Images and then the two Indeterminate Visual Experiences, which happen to coincide with the order in which the samples occurred.

At Sample #8, Diane was eating an ice cream cone just outside a shoe store where she had just been shopping with her sister and her sister's children, and was remembering the shopping visit. This took the form of an inner reexperiencing of the shoe store: the whole store was seen accurately, in motion and color, with the visual details clearly present. She saw her sister's children and some other children in the store, the shoe displays, shoes lying on the floor including particular shoes that Diane had liked, etc. This reexperiencing seemed to last for a long time, perhaps a minute or two, while Diane "looked around the store," focusing first on one aspect and then another in her inner experience. Furthermore, the experience was more than merely seeing an Image, but was instead just like being in the store (although Diane was clearly aware that this was just a recollection). For example, one of the children (not her sister's) was crying, and his cries were clearly heard in inner experience, apparently just as they had originally occurred. At the same time as this reexperiencing was taking place, an Unsymbolized Thought was ongoing. This thought was not verbal, but if it were to be put into words, it could be expressed by 'I found a swimsuit! It's not expensive, it's pretty and fits fine!' There was also a Feeling present in this sample, as if a big load had been lifted off her shoulders—she was happy and relieved. This Feeling was generally experienced in her body, particularly in her shoulders, but it was not possible to describe it physically in more detail.

The other Image occurred at Sample #20. Diane was with her boyfriend watching an old John Wayne movie on television. At the moment of the beep, she was recalling the dinner they had had earlier that evening and was saying in Inner Speech the words, "Nice dinner and good conversation," inflected as a simple statement of fact. At the same time, she was seeing an Image of the restaurant where they had eaten, in color, viewed from a perspective of being suspended above the restaurant looking down on the dining room and the parking lot, as if the roof had been removed from the restaurant. This Image seemed to have been constantly present in Diane's awareness for 15 minutes or so, and while the whole panoramic view of the restaurant and parking lot remained present, she shifted the focus of her attention from one aspect to another. She was quite sure that the whole panoramic Image had remained unchanged for the past 15 minutes, and that it was just her focus of attention which moved from one point of the Image to another.

INDETERMINATE INNER VISUAL EXPERIENCE

Diane's inner experience in 2 (5%) of the 42 samples included some kind of visual aspect which seemed to be more "knowings about" visual scenes rather than actual inner seeings, the phenomenon we call Indeterminate Inner Visual Experience. For example, at Sample #27, she was watching TV but not really paying attention to it. Instead, she was thinking about talking with her doctor the next day about her medication, hoping he would change or reduce one of her prescriptions. This "thinking about" and "hoping" were examples of Unsymbolized Thinking, in that Diane was aware of what she wanted to tell the doctor and of what she wanted him to say, but the actual words were not present in her awareness. She could be quite specific about what the particular words would be, but it was as if they were implied in her experience rather than actually being present. At the same time, she was "sort of picturing" herself in the doctor's office, but this did not involve actually seeing an image—it was perhaps more that she was imagining herself in the office, or projecting herself into the imagined office even though it was not actually seen in her imagination.

The second example of Indeterminate Inner Visual Experience came at Sample #35. Diane was with a group which was visiting a courtroom, and had spent the last half hour watching the courtroom procedures and personnel. At the moment of the beep, she was remembering what she had gone through when she had been to court a few years before, and was feeling nervous about that experience. She described this recollection as seeing an image of the courtroom, and the description, as reconstructed from my notes, continued as follows:

R.T.H.: Please describe the details of this image.
DIANE: I can remember what the judge looked like, and there were a few people in the courtroom. I was standing next to the public defender and I was nervous. (Note that rather than providing visual perceptual details such as colors, positions, details seen, etc., Diane responded with a *con*ceptual rather than *per*ceptual description: "I remember" rather than "I see.")
R.T.H.: At the moment of the beep, did you see a particular picture?
DIANE: Pretty much. I can remember what the people looked like.
R.T.H.: There is an important distinction between seeing an image and being able to remember visual details. At the moment of the beep, did you see an image or were you remembering what the scene looked like?

DIANE: It's sort of faded—it's like it's partially visual. My lawyer and the judge, I can remember them, where they were standing.

R.T.H.: Were the lawyer and the judge in the image?

DIANE: I remember being very nervous, wondering what was going to happen. (Throughout this excerpt, Diane gave conceptual responses ["I remember . . ."] to questions about inner perception. She did not give inner perceptual details; for example, she did *not* say, "I see the judge *on the right* and the lawyer *on the left; the lawyer is wearing a blue suit*." These are the kinds of details given by our subjects who see clear Images.)

This reconstructed excerpt gives the flavor, I believe, of the indeterminate or at least difficult-to-determine characteristics of this inner experience. This sample lies somewhere between a visual (perceptual) experience and a non-visual (conceptual) recollection of fact, perhaps best understood to be like remembering a seeing than an actual seeing per se. At the same time as this 'seeing' was taking place, Diane was wondering (an example of Unsymbolized Thinking) if anyone else who went to court felt as nervous as she did.

These Indeterminate Inner Visual Experiences are quite similar to those described in Susan's Indeterminate Inner Visual Experience (see Chapter 5). It should be noted that Susan's sample did not, however, include any clearly-perceived Images, contrasting with the fact that Diane's first two Images were apparently seen clearly. We don't know whether Susan would also have seen clear images had she sampled further.

FEELINGS

In 16 (38%) of Diane's 42 samples, Feelings were ongoing characteristics of her experience at the moment of the beep. Feelings could be a relatively minor aspect of Diane's experience. For example, at Sample #7, Diane was with her sister shopping for a swimsuit. She had seen some suits she liked, but they were too expensive, and at the moment of the beep she was wishing (in Unsymbolized Thinking) she had more money and that she did not have to watch what she spent. Also part of Diane's awareness was a slight Feeling of jealousy of her sister, who was financially better off than Diane. The Feeling was clearly jealousy, but Diane could not describe how that Feeling presented itself to her.

Feelings could also be a major focus of Diane's inner experience. For example, Sample #25 occurred a few hours after she had broken up with her boyfriend. She was hurt, frustrated, and angry, experiencing very strong Feelings which seemed to occupy her entire body from her head to her toes. There was no particular thought ongoing at that moment— just an awareness of the pain and her attempt to deal with it. Although Diane could confidently describe the Feelings as being a combination of hurt, frustration, and anger, she could not describe how frustration, for example, was experienced, or how it was different from anger, even though those two Feelings were clearly differentiated for her.

COMPLEXITY OF INNER EXPERIENCE

Almost all of Diane's experiences were complex in the sense that two or more aspects of an experience were present simultaneously. For example, a particular thought might be expressed as both an Image and an Unsymbolized Thought, or two separate thoughts might be ongoing simultaneously. We have seen examples of this multiple-aspect complexity, such as the swimsuit sample (#7) described in the section on Feelings. An example of two different thoughts occurring at one time was Sample #29, in which Diane was reading the "Garfield" comic strip in the Sunday newspaper. She was reading the comic strip's words and simultaneously saying them in Inner Speech. At the same time, she was saying to herself, "I'm going for a short walk later," also an example of Inner Speech. The two sets of words were experienced as being spoken simultaneously, both in her own voice, inside her head, and with her own natural inflection.

ALTERNATING THOUGHTS

Frequently when two or more thoughts were present simultaneously, her focus on the thoughts seemed to alternate in her awareness in a manner that Diane called "tick-tock." For example, Sample #13 occurred when Diane was struggling to cope with breaking up with her boyfriend. She was in her room crying, and had two simultaneous Unsymbolized Thoughts, which, while nonverbal, could be expressed by the words, 'I'm crying because Calvin disappointed me,' and 'I just want to cry and be left alone for awhile.' These thoughts were clearly apprehended to be separate from each other, and seemed to exist side by side in her chest. She would focus first on one of the thoughts, at which time the other would remain present to awareness but recede into the background, and then later she would switch her focus to the other thought, at which time the first would remain in awareness but recede to the background. This alternation of focus seemed to be like the tick-tock of a pendulum, a regular, clock-like oscillation, with the period of time spent with each focus seeming to be about five minutes.

THE LONG DURATION OF INDIVIDUAL EXPERIENCE

Many of Diane's thoughts and feelings were experienced to last for long periods of time. For example, the shoe store Image (Sample #8, described in the Images section) had been present to experience for "a minute or two" at the time of the beep, the Image of the restaurant (Sample #20, described in the Images section) was present for 15 minutes or so, and the tick-tock crying thoughts (Sample #13, described in the Alternating thoughts section) were present for a long series of 5-minute oscillations. Thus not only Images but also Unsymbolized Thoughts and Feelings were experienced as having durations of many minutes or perhaps even hours. During some of these long-duration experiences, for example the restaurant Image (Sample #20), and also the "tick-tock" thoughts (Sample #13), Diane experienced herself as focusing on first one and then another aspect of the thought, so that her attention could be said to have shifted during the time span that the particular thought existed. However, she was quite confident that this shifting of attention was *not* a change in the thought itself; the thought stayed constant and present to awareness as her attention shifted. This shifting attention was experienced to be an attentiveness to some aspect of the thought while other aspects remained in awareness but receded to the relative background. When, however, these background aspects were subsequently focused upon, they would have identical characteristics as when that aspect had been focused upon previously.

THOUGHTS LOCALIZED IN THE BODY

Diane experienced most of her cognitive experiences (Inner Speech, Unsymbolized Thinking, and Images) as taking place inside her head, while Feeling experiences were generally understood to take place in her body. On Diane's third sampling day, however, her *cognitive* experiences were understood to exist in particular parts of her body. We have already encountered one such sample (#13, in the Alternating Thoughts section) where the two tick-tock Unsymbolized Thinkings were felt to exist side by side in Diane's chest.

Sample #14 took place while she was lying in bed resting. Two thoughts were occurring simultaneously in Inner Speech. The first, "I ate too much dinner," was perceived to be in her own voice, under her own control, and was normally inflected, just as other Inner Speech experiences had been. However, this thought did not take place inside her head, but instead the words were clearly experienced as being said in Diane's stomach. The second thought, "I need to talk to Linda," was also a typical Inner Speech experience, and was occurring simultaneously. This thought was perceived to be inside Diane's head, as was more usual for Diane's Inner Speech.

Sample #15 was a straightforward Inner Speech thought, "Linda helped me calm down and she understood my problem/frustration/disappointment," except that these words were understood to be being said throughout her entire body.

Sample #16 involved two thoughts. The first was an example of Unsymbolized Thinking that, while nonverbal, could have been expressed by the words, "I'm still disappointed, but able to cope better." This thought was experienced as taking place in Diane's heart, rather than in her head as had most other Unsymbolized Thoughts. At the same time the words "I'm going outside for awhile and sit and think about my problem," were being said in Inner Speech in her head.

Thus we see that both Inner Speech and Unsymbolized Thinking could be experienced as taking place outside Diane's head. We should note that these experiences occurred on only one sampling day. On subsequent days, I inquired as to the location of her thoughts (as indeed I had done on the first two days), and Diane consistently identified them as being in her head. She recalled that the third day's thoughts were located outside her head, and found it slightly strange that such experiences occurred on one day but not others. Nonetheless she was confident that all the descriptions were accurate.

We should also note that by the third day Diane had become rather skillful at identifying her inner experiences, so there is no reason to suspect that her descriptions were merely the result of lack of practice in the method.

DISCUSSION

Diane is the fifth (counting the normal subjects) and last data point on our continuum from hypomania to depression, and this case to some extent corroborates our general between-subjects observation: the more depressed our subjects are, the more unsymbolized their inner experience. We did not sample in periods of varying depression with Diane, so we cannot comment on the within subject variation.

Diane's inner experience, while involving largely (48%) Unsymbolized Thinking, also included a larger percentage of Inner Speech (40%) than we might have predicted from observing the trends in our previous subjects. Clearly we need to sample with many more individuals to be confident of any explanation of this phenomenon—perhaps a low percentage of Inner Speech is not actually a characteristic of depression. However, we may also speculate that Diane's high frequency of Inner Speech was the result of the fact that Diane was not a typical depressed individual. Her diagnoses had ranged over the years from depression to borderline personality to schizophrenia, and her actions had caused skirmishes with the law and with authority which are not at all characteristic of pure depression. Some of the characteristics of her inner experience (e.g., her long durations of experience and the complexity of her inner experience) seem more similar to the borderline personality individual described in Chapter 14 than to other depressed individuals.

Inner Experience from Hypomania to Depression

We have seen that there are some striking similarities among the cases of John, Michelle, Susan, and Diane with respect to the relationship between depression and inner experience, and we will elaborate on those similarities here. The four cases are instructive because they represent points spaced widely along the range of affect: slightly manic (John in his Slightly Hypomanic Period); normal affect (Michelle during her Normal Affect Period, as well as the first six subjects in the previous book [Hurlburt, 1990]); dysphoric mood (Michelle in her Dysphoric Period, John when "fatigued," and Susan during her Brighter Affect Period); mild depression (Susan during her Mildly Depressed/Upset Period); and deep depression of clinical significance (Susan in her More Depressed Period and Diane).

Furthermore, we had the opportunity to observe how inner experience was related to mood *within individuals* by sampling each of these subjects except Diane during two or more periods when their moods were rather different. Thus, our data for the mood-related characteristics of inner experience come from both inter-subject comparisons (contrasting Susan's depression with John's slight hypomania, for example) and intra-subject comparisons (contrasting Susan's deeper depression with her own more usual dysphoric affect state, for example).

We must recognize that these generalizations are based on only four cases. Because generalizations from small numbers of cases have attendant risks, we must underscore the tentativeness of these speculations. However, the four subjects provided eight sampling periods (three for Susan, two each for Michelle and John, and one for Diane), and the most important of the generalizations was true for *all* eight periods, so we feel justified in presenting the observations. Furthermore, I have, with less completeness, sampled with perhaps a half dozen other depressed individuals in a clinical setting, and the general observations hold true for them also.

We will comment on five characteristics of our affective samples which we found striking, namely (a) the relation between Unsymbolized Thinking and Affect; (b) the relation of inner perceptual clarity and affect; (c) the inability of depressed individuals to distinguish perceptual from conceptual descriptions of inner experience; (d) the unconstancy of the perceiver in depression; and (e) the prevalence of emotional processes outside of awareness in these subjects. These characteristics may all be overlapping aspects of a single inner process or may in fact be separate entities; further research is required here. We will describe them as if they were separate.

UNSYMBOLIZED THINKING

Our first observation is that the *frequency of inner symbolization decreases as depression increases.* This observation can be stated in two ways which are opposite sides of the same coin: that the frequency of words and images decreases as depression increases, and that the frequency of Unsymbolized Thinking increases as depression increases. Let us consider our examples starting with the slightly manic and progressing towards the quite depressed. In our slightly manic example (John during his Slightly Manic Period), symbols were present in inner experience at *all* beeps, usually in the form of images. In our normal examples (subjects of the previous book and Michelle's Normal Period), symbols were present in inner experience *most* of the time, usually in the form of Inner Speech or Images. In our dysphoric samples (Michelle's Dysphoric Period), thinking occurred in some *indeterminate* manner between Partially Unworded Experience and Unsymbolized Thinking. In our moderately depressed samples (Diane and Susan during her Mildly Depressed/Upset Period), Unsymbolized Thinking was present about *half* the time. In our most depressed instance (Susan's Depressed period), there were *never* any samples which were not in some important way unsymbolized. This is a dramatic effect, ranging as it does in regular sequence from *always* in slight mania to *never* in depression. In our subjects, depression is strongly related to the lack of symbolization (and to the presence of Unsymbolized Thinking) in inner experience.

INNER PERCEPTUAL CLARITY AND AFFECT

Our second observation is that *inner perceptual clarity decreases as depression increases.* John, in his Slightly Manic Period, almost always saw Images which were perceptually crystal clear. His Images in this period were always visually complex, with one or more central figures moving against a differentiated background. It was easy for him to report exactly what he saw: colors, details, and movement were all unambiguously seen. In John's two samples in his Slightly Hypomanic Period when Images were not present, Inner Speech was observed, and had the same extremely-clear perceptual characteristics. All of our depressed individuals, however, at least sometime, did not have this clarity of experience. In Michelle's, Susan's and Diane's chapters, we described visual experiences which took place without clarity, calling them "Indeterminate Inner Visual Experience," experiences which seemed to be in some way visual, and where the subjects knew the content of their experiences, but in which there was no clear or definite detail available for either the thing seen or the act of seeing. Furthermore, our depressed individuals reported that their visual experiences were sometimes more and sometimes less indeterminate; thus indeterminacy was not an all-or-none phenomenon but instead existed in gradations, with some visualizations clearer that others.

Now, an unclear inner perception can be understood in at least two different ways: it may be that the image itself is unclear, but the seeing of that (unclear) image is itself precise; or, on the other hand, it may be that the seeing process itself is "cloudy" or unclear. Our impression is that in depression, the latter explanation (or possibly both) is the more correct interpretation: the inner perception process itself becomes unclear.

This lack of clarity of inner perception applies to the perception of words as well as visual phenomena. Michelle, for example, in her Normal Affect Period, clearly apprehended words and had little difficulty providing perceptual details about how they were experienced: as Inner Speech with most of the same characteristics as her normal external speech. However, during her Dysphoric Period, she lost this perceptual clarity and could not say precisely whether words were present or not. Something "passed through the balloon"; it seemed as if they were words, but she could not be sure.

It may well be that Unsymbolized Thinking is the extreme form of this lack of clarity of perceptual detail. Some of our subjects who are describing moments of Unsymbolized Thinking say that it "was almost as if there were a hint of words," while others say "perhaps there was a very, very faint visual image."[1] If that is the case, then we have marked the continuum of clarity of inner visual experience with the points: Images, Indeterminate Visual Experience, Imageless Seeing, and Unsymbolized Thinking, and the continuum of clarity of inner verbal experience with the points: Inner Speech, Words Present, Wordless Speech, and Unsymbolized Thinking. We need more subjects to fully substantiate the details of these two continua.

DISCRIMINATING PERCEPTION FROM CONCEPTION IN DEPRESSION

The third outstanding observation of our affective subjects is that *our depressed subjects had difficulty in discriminating perceptual description from conceptual description.* All three of our depressed subjects at least occasionally described their inner experience as "seeing" an inner image, when careful probing revealed that the experience was not actually a visual seeing at all. Perhaps the most dramatic example of this was Michelle's struggle to describe the "balloon" during her Dysphoric Period. It required several hours-long sessions of careful clarifying conversation to determine that the balloon was apparently not a visually-seen image as it was originally described, and even then we were never absolutely sure of this conclusion. The point here is not so much to determine whether the balloon was a perception or a metaphor or some other conceptual experience; rather, we wish to emphasize how difficult it was for Michelle to make those distinctions about her own experience, even though she could easily differentiate such characteristics in exter-

---

[1]Discriminating between subjects who report that Unsymbolized Thinking is almost visual and those who report that it is almost verbal is an interesting area for further research; at the moment we can simply state that both such reports exist. We might note further that it seems to be precisely here that the controversy over imageless thought developed in the early 1900s (see Chapter 2). Are there in fact very faint verbal or visual images in *all* Unsymbolized Thinking? Titchener and the sensationalists would say Yes, while the Würzburgers would say No. Our own reply would be to say that the attempt to answer such a question is likely to be unproductive. Titchener might have preferred that we call this phenomenon *Almost-imperceptibly*-symbolized Thinking rather than *Un*-symbolized Thinking, and we would have no quarrel with that except that it is long and awkward. Whichever label we choose, the phenomenon seems to be much more prevalent in depression, and that is the only point we are trying to make.

nal descriptions (such as when metaphor was used in a short story she was reading). She could use the terms perception, metaphor, and conception accurately and easily about everything *except* her own inner experience.

The lack of ability to distinguish perception from conception may well be related to the continuum of clarity of inner experience that we described in the previous section. For example, Susan said she was seeing a picture of her therapist on the wall, but when we carefully requested the details of this apparently visual experience, she could not describe them. Perhaps this was an Indeterminate Inner Visual Experience as described above, but it seemed instead that Susan was using the word "seeing" to describe something that was more a cognitive experience than a perceptual one. That is, she was using the sentence "I see" to describe a cognition (thereby meaning 'I understand') rather than to describe a perception (thereby meaning 'I perceive with my eyes)'.

We wish to reemphasize that the inability to discriminate perception from cognition is *not* readily recognized by the subjects themselves. Perhaps that is the result of an extreme form of perceptual unclarity as described above, or perhaps the two phenomena are unrelated. We should also note that some of our schizophrenics have also had difficulty discriminating perception from cognition (see, for example, Hurlburt, 1990, Chapter 12).

THE UNCONSTANCY OF THE PERCEIVER IN DEPRESSION

The fourth characteristics of these samples is a similarity between two of the three depressed individuals, Michelle and Diane. In Chapter 4, we described a phenomenon we called the unconstancy of the perceiver, where we noted that Michelle seemed to have distinctly different mental states associated with different thoughts. For example, a thought might "involve energy," be a "reaction," or be "setting a task for herself." Each of these were experienced to be qualitatively different from the others, and these differences seemed more a characteristic of the thinking process rather than of the thought itself. That is, the task setting, for example, was not a characteristic of the *content* of the thought, but seemed to be a characteristic of the thinking *process*. Furthermore, in her Dysphoric Period, Michelle was not consistent in the point of perspective she took on her own experiences. Sometimes, apparently, she adopted a from-the-inside-looking-forward perspective and other times a from-the-outside-looking-back perspective, with no awareness of the perspective shift. As you may recall, that led to a confusion of right and left as well as other inconsistencies, which resulted in our concluding that Michelle had no stable platform from which to view her own experience.

In Chapter 6 on Diane, we noted what in some ways seems to be a similar phenomenon: Diane's Inner Speech, similar to that of our typical subjects, was usually experienced as being located somewhere inside her head. However, occasionally she experienced Inner Speech to take place in her stomach or in other parts of her body rather than inside her head. Here again, we are noting that it was *not* the case that sometimes Diane was thinking *about* her stomach, but instead the thinking process itself seemed to be *in* her stomach.

Our conclusion, then, is that individuals when depressed may not have a clear, stable platform from which to view their own experience. Here again, this may be a separate phenomenon or just another aspect of the same phenomenon we have already been describing. For example, perhaps Unsymbolized Thinking is simply the result of having *no perspective at all* on a visual or a verbal phenomenon; samples where the unconstancy phenomenon can be identified may then be transition states between perception of images or words and Unsymbolized Thinking. If that is true, that would explain why Susan did not have the unconstancy of the perceiver phenomenon in her Depressed Period: *all* those samples included some Unsymbolized Thinking, and so transitional states would not be noted.

THESE OBSERVATIONS APPLY BOTH BETWEEN AND WITHIN SUBJECTS

It is striking that the observations we have described so far apply both within subjects as well as between subjects. If person A is more depressed than person B, then we have found that A will have, for example, more Unsymbolized Thinking than B. It is also true in our sample that if person C is more depressed at time 1 than that same person was at time 2, then there will be more Unsymbolized Thinking at time 1 than at time 2. These same conclusions apply to other depressed individuals I have sampled but whose cases are not described here. If these observations are replicated by other investigators, then the experience sampling technique should emerge as a powerful technique not only for diagnosing individuals but for making repeated measurements on single individuals, for example, when assessing the effectiveness of antidepressant medication before and after administration, or charting the progress of psychotherapy.

THE PERCEPTUAL/COGNITIVE CHANGES ARE
NOT APPARENT TO THE INDIVIDUAL

We have discussed three cases (John, Michelle, and Susan) where the subject's level of affect differed rather dramatically from one sampling period to another. We have seen that each subject's cognition changed (toward more Unsymbolized Thinking, etc.) when these subjects became more depressed. It is noteworthy that while *all* the subjects recognized that their *affect* had changed, *none* recognized that their *cognition*, their way of thinking or perceiving, had changed. Some of these changes in inner experience, as we have seen, were dramatic: Susan's huge differences in the relative frequencies of words and Unsymbolized Thinking; John's lessening of detail, clarity, and motion in Images; and Michelle's alteration of clarity of Inner Speech. However, these changes were simply not noted by the subjects themselves, even after we had explicitly examined many examples from different sampling periods together. Our interpretation is that people take for granted the way they think, and pay little attention to it.

EMOTIONAL PROCESSES OUTSIDE OF AWARENESS

Three of the four subjects in this section (John nearly always, Michelle in her Dysphoric Period, and Susan in both her Mildly Depressed/Upset Period and Brighter Affect Period) reported the relatively frequent existence of emotional processes ongoing in their physical bodies, but which were not recognized in awareness at the moment of the beep. That is, these individuals might be anxious or upset, and their bodies would be expressing this, but their awareness at the moment of the beep would be devoid of emotion.

My general impression, from these subjects as well as from others with whom I have sampled, is that as these individuals become more depressed, they report a higher incidence of Feelings (emotions present in awareness at the moment of the beep) and a lower incidence of emotional processes outside of awareness; furthermore, these Feelings are generally negative (depressed, anxious, angry, etc.) in times of increased depression. Such an observation, like others in this book, needs replication.

ON THE SMALL SAMPLE SIZE

The above observations are explicitly based on a sample of only four individuals, so any observations we make must be recognized as tentative. (I have partial sampling data from a handful of other depressed individuals, and the above generalizations apply to them also.) We need to consider many more cases to determine whether these kinds of effects are typical of some, most, or all depressed individuals. Perhaps further research will show that Unsymbolized Thinking is a characteristic not only of depressed individuals but also other non-depressed people; for example, my own incomplete observations of other subjects led me to speculate that Unsymbolized Thinking is also a frequent characteristic of non-depressed people for whom emotions are predominant factors in their lives. That is, my preliminary observation is that those people who "wear their feelings on their sleeves," so to speak, whether depressed or not, have Unsymbolized Thinking as a major component of their inner experience. We simply need further research to validate or invalidate this and other generalizations.

Furthermore, not only is our sample small, it is relatively homogeneous, being entirely white middle class. Three of our subjects are American, while one was Dutch. It is entirely possible that the observations we have tentatively made are applicable only to some subset of the population at large.

We might note, however, that while we are considering here directly only four subjects, they have provided eight sampling periods. Taken together with the normal subjects from the previous book as well as the handful of other depressed subjects I have sampled, these observations, while still tentative, can be regarded as based on more than four data points.

CAUSE AND EFFECT IN OUR RESULTS

We must be clearly aware that we cannot infer from our data that depression *causes* Unsymbolized Thinking or that Unsymbolized Thinking *causes* depression. The two are strongly related in our sample, but which one causes the other, or whether a third factor is responsible for both, is impossible to determine from our data. We might note in passing that most of our depressed subjects become somewhat less depressed as the sampling procedure progresses, and that their reports of inner experience become somewhat clearer. It is true that the sampling procedure itself can be regarded as a kind of "calisthenic" exercise for becoming clear in inner experience: we are constantly asking subjects to clarify their reports if possible, and we are sending them out into their natural environments with a beeper which will remind them to do just that. One might suspect, therefore, that our procedure is reactive in the sense that it *causes* individuals to become more clear in the way they apprehend their own inner experience, and therapeutic in the sense that such an increase in clarity leads to the lessening of symptoms. Whether or not such speculations are true needs further research.

COMPARING OUR OBSERVATIONS TO THOSE OF BECK

We have discussed the five most salient characteristics which we have found in our observations of depressed subjects. Are those the same characteristics other investigators have found when they studied inner experience in depression? Not at all! No author on depression that I know of has identified any of these characteristics as being important. This surprising fact merits some discussion along two lines. First, what *do* other authors describe as the salient cognitive characteristics of depression? Second, how can we account for the fact that our own observations are so dramatically different from those of other investigators? Our task here is not to review and/or criticize the depression literature; we are simply focused on what individuals' inner experience is like. We discuss how other investigators have describe cognition in depression primarily to highlight the differences between our findings, thus underscoring the fertility of the experience sampling method.

Since our aim is simply to describe our method, not to review (much less criticize) the depression literature, we will contrast our results with only one cognitive theory of depression, that of Aaron Beck. We chose Beck's theory as representative because it is perhaps the most influential cognitive theory of depression; the comparisons and contrasts we will make between our observations and Beck's theory could apply equally well to other cognitive theories of depression.

There are two ways of approaching the comparison of our results to those of Beck: first, did Beck describe in his writings about his depressed patients the characteristics of depression which we have identified? Second, did our subjects' samples show the features Beck had described?

We have identified the frequency of Unsymbolized Thinking, lack of perceptual clarity, difficulty in discriminating perception from conception, the unconstancy of the perceiver, and the presence of emotional processes outside awareness as being our major results from this study of depressed individuals. Has Beck described those characteristics as existing among his patients? Not that we can find. As far as we can tell, these observations about depressed individuals are now.

Did our subjects, then, show the characteristics that Beck identified

as being important? We will see that the answer to that question is also
No, but to consider that we will need to describe briefly Beck's results.

Beck (1967; Rush & Beck, 1978; etc.) described the characteristics of
cognitions in depression in two ways—the "primary triad" and the
"cognitive distortions." The primary triad includes cognitive characteristics relating to the negative construing of experiences, the negative viewing of self, and the negative viewing of the future:

> The disturbances in depression may be viewed in terms of the acti-
> vation of a set of three major cognitive patterns that force the indi-
> vidual to view himself, his world, and his future in an idiosyncratic
> way. The progressive dominance of these cognitive patterns leads to
> the other phenomena that are associated with the depressive state.
>
> The first component of the triad is the pattern of construing
> experiences in a negative way. The patient consistently interprets his
> interactions with his environment as representing defeat, depriva-
> tion, or disparagement. He sees his life as filled with a succession of
> burdens, obstacles, or traumatic situations, all of which detract from
> him in a significant way.
>
> The second component is the pattern of viewing himself in a
> negative way. He regards himself as deficient, inadequate, or un-
> worthy, and tends to attribute his unpleasant experiences to a physi-
> cal, mental, or moral defect in himself. Furthermore, he regards
> himself as undesirable and worthless because of his presumed de-
> fect, and tends to reject himself because of it.
>
> The third component consists of viewing the future in a nega-
> tive way. He anticipates that his current difficulties or suffering will
> continue indefinitely. As he looks ahead, he sees a life of unremit-
> ting hardship, frustration and deprivation. (Beck, 1967, p. 255)

The cognitive distortions are a series of logical or reasoning flaws, for
example:

> *Arbitrary inference* is defined as the process of drawing a conclu-
> sion from a situation, event, or experience, when there is no evi-
> dence to support the conclusion or when the conclusion is contrary
> to the evidence.
>
> A patient riding on an elevator had the thought, "He (the eleva-
> tor operator) thinks I'm a nobody." The patient then felt sad. On
> being questioned by the psychiatrist, he realized there was no factu-
> al basis for this thought. . . .
>
> *Selective abstraction* refers to the process of focusing on a detail
> taken out of context, ignoring other more salient features of the
> situation, and conceptualizing the whole experience on the basis of
> this element. . . .
>
> *Overgeneralization* is the patients' pattern of drawing a general

conclusion about their ability, their performance, or their worth on the basis of a single incident. . . .

Magnification and minimization refer to errors in evaluation so gross as to constitute distortions. . . . [For example,] a man reported that he had been upset because of damage to his house as the result of a storm. When he first discovered the damage, his thought sequence was, "The side of the house is wrecked. . . . It will cost a fortune to fix it." His immediate reaction was that his repair bill would be several thousand dollars. After the initial shock had dissipated, he realized that the damage was minor and that the repairs would cost around fifty dollars.

Inexact labelling often seems to contribute to this kind of distortion. The affective reaction is proportional to the descriptive labelling of the event, rather than to the actual intensity of a traumatic situation.

A man reported during his therapy hour that he was very upset because he had been "clobbered" by his superior. On further reflection, he realized that he had magnified the incident and that a more adequate description was that his supervisor "corrected an error" he had made. After reevaluating the event, he felt better. (Beck, 1967, pp. 234–235)

This is Beck and his colleagues' description of the cognitions of depressed individuals: the primary triad (negative construing of experiences, self, and future) and the cognitive distortions (arbitrary inference, selective abstraction, etc.). We did not find such cognitions in our samples from depressed individuals. The content of thinking of our depressed individuals was quite similar to that of our normal subjects, and neither group had large percentages of such thoughts.

Now that we have noted that our own observations are substantially different from those of Beck, we need to ask, How could Beck and his colleagues not have seen what is for us so clearly apparent? There are two distinctions to be made to answer this question: the distinction between the content and the process of thinking, and the distinction between observed and inferred thinking. We will examine each in turn.

When we examine Beck's characteristics of depressive cognition, we find that his primary triad and cognitive distortions are characteristics of the *content* of depressed individuals' thinking, and that he apparently took for granted that the thinking *process* of depressed individuals is basically the same as that of normal individuals. Thus the problem in depression is that this normal thinking processes focuses on the wrong details or exaggerates the importance of those details. Consider for example one of the features from the primary triad: when Beck described patients as "construing experiences in a negative way," he apparently understood that everyone, normals and depressives alike, construes experiences, and the construing process itself functions the same way for normals and depressed individuals. The difference is in the content: depressives construe *negatively*.

Consider also an example from Beck's cognitive distortions, the passage above on magnification and minimization, which also demonstrates that the depressive's cognitive process is intact while the content is abnormal. The man whose house was damaged was "upset," and this upset was understood as a normal reaction (that is, a normal cognitive process) to a magnification (that is, an abnormal cognitive content) of the damage ("The house is wrecked"). The therapeutic intervention was to correct the cognitive content (that is, to help the patient realize that the damage was in fact minor); the result was that the normal cognitive-affective process continued but the upset diminished.

Let us consider one more passage from Beck to ensure that we securely grasp this distinction. Rush and Beck (1978) gave some examples of attributing depression to maladaptive cognitive contents:

> The cognitive theory considers the other signs and symptoms of the depressive syndrome to be consequences of the activation of the negative cognitive patterns. For example, if the patient incorrectly *thinks* he is being rejected, he will react with the same negative affect (e.g., sadness, anger) that occurs with *actual* rejection. If he erroneously believes he is a social outcast, he will feel lonely. (p. 202, italics in original)

When Rush and Beck stated that "if the patient incorrectly *thinks* he is being rejected, he will react with the same negative affect . . . that occurs with *actual* rejection," they implied that the patient has his *facts* (cognitive contents) wrong (he is not in fact being rejected) but the cognitive *process* itself is normal: "the same negative affect" will follow normally from that mistaken fact).

The characteristics of depressed cognition are, then, according to Beck, mistaken characteristics of the *contents* of thinking (most, if not all, other cognitive theories of depression are also content oriented). One of the reasons our own observations are strikingly different from Beck's is that we found cognitive *processes* (Unsymbolized Thinking, unclarity of inner perception, difficulty in discriminating perception from conception, and unconstancy of the perceiver) to be the salient characteristics of depression, while we found that cognitive contents were quite normal. The normalcy of cognitive content was perhaps most striking in the samples we obtained from Susan while she was very depressed and soon before and after she had strong suicidal ideation (see Chapter 5).

The sample ten minutes before the suicidal ideation was an Unsymbolized wondering about what glossolalia (a term she had read) meant; two minutes after the suicidal ideation was an Unsymbolized Thinking about what to wear to her next psychotherapy appointment—flats or heels, etc. The content of these very-depressed-affect thoughts was quite typical of all of our subjects and was not in any way a cognitive distortion, etc.; the process, however, was Unsymbolized Thinking, which is, as we have speculated, a characteristic of depression. Thus one difference between Beck's (and other cognitive theorists') observations and our own is that Beck focused on content while we found process but not content differences.

The second distinction between Beck's observations and our own lies in the fact that the word "thinking" has at least two distinctly different meanings which we will call "observed thinking" and "inferred thinking." "Observed thinking" corresponds to the term "thinking" as used in this book. It is the usage which calls for a real-time, momentary examination of the contents of consciousness, as in response to the question, "What are you thinking about right now?" On the other hand, "inferred thinking" does not ask for an immediate observation of what one is thinking about right now, but instead requires the making of an inference about a cognitive process, going beyond direct observation to infer characteristics of structures or processes which are themselves not observed directly. It is my opinion that Beck (and other cognitive theorists as well) sometimes blurred this distinction between the two (observed and inferred) usages of the term "thinking."

Let us consider a few passages from Beck, first the portion of the extended quotation cited at the beginning of this section where Beck defined arbitrary inference (Beck, 1967). An example of arbitrary inference there was, "A patient riding on an elevator had the thought, 'He (the elevator operator) thinks I'm a nobody.'" Is this "thought" an observed or an inferred type of thinking? That is, are we to understand by this passage that the man in the elevator actually thought to himself, "He thinks I'm a nobody"? The way the passage is constructed, with "the elevator operator" in parentheses as if that were what was meant by the actually thought word "he," seems to imply that Beck did indeed mean that the man thought these words to himself. Thus, we conclude that Beck meant that this was an observed thought, but the passage itself does not make that fact explicit.

Reconsider also a portion of the passage from Rush and Beck (1978) cited above: "If the patient incorrectly *thinks* he is being rejected, he will react with the same affect that occurs with *actual* rejection." Here there is no explicit or implicit clue as to whether the word "thinks" is being used to imply an observed thinking (as if Beck had written, "the man thought, 'I am being rejected'") or an inferred thinking (as if Beck were inferring that there must be a cognitive process which holds that the man is being rejected).

Let us consider one more example, this one a continuation of the overgeneralization definition cited at the beginning of this section:

> A patient reported the following sequence of events occurring within a period of half an hour: His wife was upset because the children were slow in getting dressed. He thought, "I'm a poor father because the children are not better disciplined." He then noticed a leaky faucet, and thought that this showed he was also a poor husband. While driving to work, he thought, "I must be a poor driver or other cars would not be passing me." As he arrived at work, he noticed some other personnel had already arrived. He thought, "I can't be very dedicated or I would have come earlier." When he noticed folders and papers piled up on his desk, he concluded, "I'm a poor organizer because I have so much work to do." (Beck, 1967, p. 235)

The construction of this paragraph results in ambiguity as to whether Beck intended us to understand that the patient actually observed these thoughts ongoing in himself or not. This ambiguity is made salient by putting some of the thoughts in quotations ("I'm a poor father because the children are not better disciplined.") and some not ([he] thought that this showed he was also a poor husband). Why this change in style exists is not explicitly stated; my interpretation is that for Beck the distinction between observed and inferred thoughts was not important.

Thus, we conclude that Beck (and others) blurred the distinction between observed and inferred thinking. This is, I believe, a particularly important distinction precisely because, as we have seen, depressed people themselves have difficulty making this very distinction when they refer to their own inner experience. This is the difficulty of distinguishing between perception and conception: depressed people frequently cannot distinguish whether they are actually observing thoughts (perceptual events in inner experience) or whether they are inferring general characteristics about themselves (conceptual events).

Another reason that the distinction between observed and inferred thinking is so important to us is that the two forms of thinking are often dramatically different from each other. The present book is based on an effort to focus exclusively on the observed type of thinking, and we engaged in a systematic effort to train subjects to focus on the observed contents of awareness at the moment of the beep and to suspend reports about inferred cognition. The individual descriptive chapters which form the main body of this book therefore have not described the characteristics of our subjects' inferred-type thinking. However, our subjects did occasionally give reports about inferred cognition, particularly during their first or second sampling days, before they had been adequately trained to make clearly the observed-inferred thinking distinction. At some of those times, they gave an inferred-type thinking report first, but then gave an observed-type description when we asked questions about the observed characteristics of their thinking.

As an example of the difference between inferred and observed thinking, consider the following sample from John's first sampling day (Chapter 3). He wrote in his sampling notebook at the time of the beep: 1809 [6:09 p.m.]

Getting dressed to go to Farm Basket [a fried chicken fast-food restaurant] for food.
THOUGHT: What I am going to eat.
FEELING: Good, I just don't want to go out now but I also don't want to cook. I feel happy but a little tired.

During his sampling interview, he began his description of his thought by saying that turkey sandwiches were on sale at Farm Basket, and that he and his wife were looking forward to going to get them. This is an example of an inferred thought—a general inference about what was going on with him at that time. (Note that the inference is here made by the subject himself! An external observer would have even more difficulty.) However, when we pressed him for the (observed) details of his inner experience, he said that what he was actually observing in his experience at that moment was the seeing of an Image of a greasy piece of breaded turkey meat boiling in a deep-fryer basket. It was a clear, vibrant Image, in color and motion (the grease boiling, etc.) as if viewed from the perspective of the cook. The turkey meat in the Image was depicted unpleasantly (it was slightly green and very greasy) and the Image was accompanied by feelings of dislike and mild disgust, and of not wanting to go to Farm Basket. Note how different the actual observed experience (the Image of the greasy turkey meat along with dislike or disgust) is from the inferred-type thinking (looking forward to getting a turkey sandwich). In the inferred-type description, there was no mention of an image nor of a feeling of displeasure or disgust about going to Farm Basket, for example. The point here is that John's initial account is more an *inference* about what his own ongoing thinking process was than it was an *observation* of that process, and the two accounts are by no means in agreement.

The reader may agree that two different kinds of thinking are in fact being discriminated here, but wonder whether "observed" vs "inferred" are adequate terms to characterize this distinction. Perhaps it would have been better to contrast "specific" vs "generalized" kinds of thinking. If we used that terminology, then John's original account of looking forward to getting the turkey sandwiches would be called a "generalized" account of his thinking process, and the description of the turkey-meat image would be a "specific" account. While such usage has the advantage of simplicity, it has the disadvantage, I think, of taking for granted the mistaken view that individuals can adequately generalize about their thinking. The term "generalized" implies that the subject has an acquaintance with a series of specific instances from which a common characteristic is abstracted, but our research shows that that cannot be taken for granted. Our subjects are frequently very surprised by some major characteristics of their own inner experience (for example, it is not unusual for normal subjects prior to sampling to believe that they never have visual images, only to find that such images comprise 50% of their sample). In our example, John's sequence of individual observed thoughts seemed, under careful examination, to center around a negative evaluation of fast-food turkey's taste and nutritional characteristics; it would be impossible to "generalize" from that sequence to the positive looking-forward which he expressed in his initial report of his thinking. I therefore think it advisable to use the broader, more assumption-free term "inferred" rather than "generalized."

Most of our subjects initially give these inferred accounts of their inner processes, even though we had carefully instructed them to report only what they were thinking about at the *moment* of the beep. It apparently takes rather specialized, repetitive training for people to be able to observe their inner experience directly. Since Beck's patients did not receive this kind of specialized training, it seems likely that they were describing inferred-type cognitions, rather than observed moments of thinking.

When Beck's patient reported the sequence of thoughts, "I'm a poor father . . .," "I must be a poor driver . . .," and "I can't be very dedicated . . .," etc., were those reports accurate descriptions of actual observed thinking? I think not. We have just seen that depressed individuals' reports of their inner experience in general may be unreliable, and we have also noted that much of the inner experience of depressed individuals is Unsymbolized, in particular, nonverbal, so that the clear verbalness of Beck's patients' descriptions makes it unlikely that they were reporting actually-observed thoughts.

We have demonstrated that our own understanding of the inner experience of depressed individuals is apparently much different from that of Beck (and many, if not all, other cognitive theorists of depression). I must underscore that the existence of this difference does not mean that I believe that Beck is mistaken. On the contrary, I think that Beck's descriptions are quite accurate characterizations of what depressed individuals generally report about their thoughts. The difference is that I believe that depressed individuals' actual momentary inner experiences are much different from their (inferred) stated descriptions of their thinking.

It remains to be seen whether this difference is important. Beck has amassed an impressive array of data showing that attempts to change depressed individuals' cognitions (inferred thinkings in our terminology) have been successful in alleviating depression. An evaluation of the outcome of psychotherapy based on experience sampling has not been attempted, but we noted above in passing that all three depressed individuals whose cases are reported here both increased the clarity and symbolization of their inner experience over the course of sampling. We speculated that participation in the sampling study might serve as a sort of "calisthenic" for the clarity of moment-by-moment thinking, forcing patients to look as carefully as they can at their momentary experiences. The result of this effort might be that thinking in fact becomes clearer, and this increased clarity then allows constructive changes in affect. If we accept this hypothesis, we might explain the success of Beck's therapy by suggesting that when his patients perform their homework assignments to monitor and replace the content of their (inferred) cognitions, a by-product of this activity may be an increase in the clarity of their thinking as well, with the result being an alleviation of depression. Attractive though this hypothetical explanation might appear, there are, of course, many other explanations for why our three subjects' depression lifted while participating in the study (the passage of time, the attention they received from me, coincidence, etc.), and for the efficacy of Beck's therapy. Further research is clearly called for.

II

Bulimia

The first two chapters in this part present sketches of the inner experience of two individuals for whom bulimia was a serious problem. Both were successful professional people with eating patterns which met the DSM-III-R diagnosis of Bulimia, including frequent binge eating and purging (self-induced vomiting).

Chapter 9 describes one of five bulimics included as subjects in the Masters Thesis of Stephanie Doucette at the University of Nevada, Las Vegas. Chapter 10 makes some general observations about this sample of six bulimics.

A Bulimic Operating-Room Nurse

"Ashley Greene" was a 42-year-old married mother of three children who worked as an operating-room nurse. She volunteered to participate in the study after hearing it described in a hospital colloquium. She met the DSM-III-R criteria for Bulimia, being an episodic binge eater and purger; purging was usually triggered by feelings of physical or psychological fullness. Ashley would not vomit for perhaps a few days, and then would vomit daily, sometimes several times per day, for perhaps a week, followed by another few days of no vomiting, etc.

Ashley sampled for nine days, during which time 38 samples were adequately discussed. This time period was one of rather strong emotional turmoil for Ashley, and thus the samples reported below may or may not be typical for her. Ashley's inner experience, as we will see below, was constantly characterized by multiple simultaneous thoughts and feelings—sometimes as many as 10 or 30 at a time. Furthermore, we found it necessary with Ashley (and to a somewhat lesser extent with other bulimic subjects but not with any of our other subjects) to distinguish between "Experienced awareness" and "Sensed awareness." In Experienced awareness, Ashley was directly aware of a particular ongoing thought (or feeling) and its contents; by contrast, in Sensed awareness, Ashley knew that a thought (or feeling) was ongoing at the moment of the beep, and knew what the content of that thought was, but the thought (or feeling) itself was outside of awareness. That is, in Sensed awareness, the content of awareness was not the thought itself but was instead the knowledge that the thought was ongoing. We will return to this concept in a separate section below. Thereafter, we will describe the following salient characteristics of her inner experience: Multiple Experienced Unsymbolized Thinkings; Multiple Sensed Unsymbolized Thinkings; Multiple Experienced Feelings which were felt to be either in Ashley's body or her head (or which had no bodily location); Multiple Sensed Feelings (with the same location possibilities); and both Clear and Indeterminate Images. We note that there were 3 samples (of 38) which included Inner Speech as one aspect of inner experience; in each of those cases, the multiple processes listed above were also apparently simultaneously occurring.

MULTIPLICITY IN EXPERIENCE

Unlike some other subjects for whom only one or perhaps a few salient characteristics were experienced as occurring at each beep, Ashley consistently reported that many simultaneous thoughts and/or feelings were a feature of *each* sample, as many as 30 or more discrete thoughts and feelings in simultaneous awareness at a single beeped moment. There was *never* a beep where her experience had only one ongoing train of thought, etc.; much more common were beeps where Ashley reported 10 or 20 different thoughts and 5 or 10 separate feelings all occurring simultaneously.

For example, at Sample #19, Ashley was talking to another nurse about a diagnostic procedure that Ashley had administered to a patient. She was saying aloud, "One of his responses was quicker." These words were not "coming out" fluently, and it seemed as if the ideas she was trying to express (about using clinical judgment in diagnosis, using the results of the whole diagnostic procedure to make decisions about whether that particular response was unusual) were not yet sufficiently verbal to be expressed in words. At the same time that Ashley was saying this, she was rocking her left hand back and forth in imitation of what the patient had done during the procedure. She was simultaneously thinking in awareness what seemed to be about 15 nonverbal thoughts, each of which was a separate Unsymbolized Thinking. These thoughts might be represented (rather inadequately because of their nonverbal nature) in words as follows: just try and explain it to her (the other nurse); don't try and explain it because she might think I hadn't administered the procedure in accordance with the established procedures; I had a reason for what I did (for the way the procedure was administered); Ashley, you're OK—you've just lost the reason you did it for the moment; I've got to get back to checking the patient in the next room; etc.

At the same time there were five separate, simultaneous Feelings all present to Ashley's experience: feeling bad, self-doubt, ambivalence, frustration, and time pressure. These were Experienced Feelings, not merely Sensed (a distinction we will make clearer below), and seemed to be mostly in or around her head, all churning up together in a way that seemed as if she "couldn't get through" the feelings. It seemed as if she had "to get these feelings to settle" before she could get the words to come out.

Thus, at this beep Ashley was talking aloud and simultaneously thinking 15 different Unsymbolized Thoughts and experiencing 5 separate feelings. This was *not* an unusually complicated beep for Ashley, but instead rather typically represents the experienced multiplicity of each of her momentary awarenesses during the sampling period.

EXPERIENCED VS. SENSED AWARENESS

Ashley described her thoughts and feelings as existing in her awareness in two different ways, which we will call "Experienced" and "Sensed" (Ashley herself had no term for this differentiation; in fact, until she participated in this sampling study, she had no clear awareness that such a differentiation existed for her). An Experienced thought or feeling is one which is directly and explicitly a part of awareness; thus all the types of thoughts we have described in the previous book (e.g., Inner Speech, Unsymbolized Thinking, etc.) and until now in this book are Experienced thoughts. A Sensed thought or feeling is one where the *knowledge of the ongoing existence* of the thought or feeling is present to awareness, but the thought or feeling itself is outside awareness, even though it is known to be ongoing.

Ashley used the metaphor of an aquarium to describe this aspect of her inner experience. Thoughts and feelings were "fish" in her awareness "aquarium." Many fish could be swimming around simultaneously in the aquarium (this is her metaphor for Multiplicity in Experience); each of these directly observed fish were one of Ashley's simultaneous Experienced awarenesses. However, some of the fish in the aquarium were "under the rocks with only their tails exposed (that is, with only their "tails" in Ashley's awareness at the moment of the beep). These were the Sensed thoughts or feelings: the "tail" that was visible from under the rock was the knowledge present in awareness that the particular thought or feeling was ongoing. The fish itself was the thought or feeling that was known to be known in immediate awareness to be occurring outside of awareness (but not experienced in awareness directly).

We should note that while we have described the Experienced/Sensed distinction as an either/or dichotomy, Ashley experienced thoughts and feelings at intermediate points between Experiencing and Sensing. Metaphorically, it was possible for fish to be "partially under a rock," "almost entirely under a rock," or "just going under a rock," etc.

MULTIPLE (EXPERIENCED) UNSYMBOLIZED THOUGHTS

Almost all (at least 31 [82%] of 38) of Ashley's samples included Unsymbolized Thinking, the process where thinking is experienced to occur without words, images, or other symbols, and is simply known to be ongoing. Approximately two-thirds (21) of these samples included Multiple (Experienced) Unsymbolized Thoughts, where Ashley's awareness was divided between 10 to 30 separate (but usually related) simultaneous Unsymbolized Thought processes, and where these thoughts were directly apprehended in awareness (rather than just Sensed to be ongoing; see below).

We should emphasize that the phenomena that we are now calling "(Experienced)" Unsymbolized Thoughts or "(Experienced)" Feelings are simply called Unsymbolized Thoughts or Feelings for our non-bulimic subjects, since it is only with our bulimics that we have needed to make that distinction. To emphasize that connection, and yet still to allow us to contrast Experienced with Sensed phenomena, we place the word "Experienced" in parenthesis in the title of this section.

We have given one example of Multiple (Experienced) Unsymbolized Thinking above, the diagnostic procedure sample (#19) described in the section on Multiplicity in Experience. Another example was at Sample #15, where Ashley was sitting in a tavern talking with friends. At the moment of the beep, her friend Jill was saying to a third friend, "I can tell you something about how to do that," that is, how to arrange a meeting of doctors in the hospital. At the moment of this sample, Ashley was aware of about 20 Unsymbolized Thoughts which were all occurring simultaneously in her awareness. It is impossible to translate these thoughts accurately into words, since they are not verbal, but some of them approximated: 'Jill is helping Alicia (a mutual friend)'; 'Jill didn't do what she said she would do'; 'Am I crazy?'; 'Did I hear her right?'; 'Is it my fault?'; and 'Jerry heard her the way I did.' There were perhaps 10 other Unsymbolized thoughts present simultaneously in awareness and all on the same theme, but Ashley found it impossible to remember them long enough to write them down after the beep. None of these thoughts were verbal at the time of the beep, but each was nonetheless there in awareness, with an energy seemingly attached to it that made it "swim around" in awareness.

Also present at the moment of the beep was a group of Feelings, the strongest of which was a Feeling of inadequacy. This inadequacy seemed to be felt diffusely spread throughout Ashley's body, although Ashley was not absolutely sure of that. The Feeling was described to be "yucky, slimy, and hurting." This Feeling of inadequacy was "so strong as to be almost a thought"; that is, a nonverbal thought 'Ashley is inadequate' was almost Sensed to be present along with the other Experienced thoughts at this beep. Anxiety and irritation were also Feelings Sensed to be present at this beep, but they were not as strong or as explicitly felt as was the feeling of inadequacy. Rather, they were simply Feelings Sensed to be present at the dim edge of awareness, available to be made explicit if Ashley so chose.

MULTIPLE SENSED UNSYMBOLIZED THOUGHTS

Nine (24%) of Ashley's samples included multiple thoughts which were Sensed to be ongoing, rather than Experienced directly in awareness. That is, at these beeps Ashley was aware of many thought processes, each existing outside of her awareness. Thus she was aware at the moment of the beep that the thoughts existed, rather than being directly aware of the thoughts themselves.

For example, at Sample #12 Ashley was sitting in a tavern talking with friends. At the moment of the beep, her friend Jill was saying, "I think he (Alan) got told" not to go to Newport Beach, a nearby resort. Ashley was hearing Jill say this, and also was aware that she was thinking perhaps 10 or 20 simultaneous nonverbal thoughts, all of which related to Alan. If put into words, some of these thoughts might be: 'Alan is not making his own choices'; 'Alan is choosing to let others make his choices'; 'Judy (Alan's wife) is making Alan's choices'; etc. These thoughts were all Sensed to be present, as if they were being thought just at the edge of awareness rather than in awareness itself. Ashley could not completely describe this sensing except to say that all the thoughts were somehow known to be present, and although none of them were explicitly in awareness at the moment of the beep, any of them could be made explicit and elaborated if she so chose.

Ashley said that there was also present at the moment of the beep a hazy image of Judy and their friend Jennifer telling Alan not to go to Newport Beach. Ashley could not say definitively that this image was clearly present at the moment of the beep, but she again had a "sense" that the image was present. She described this image as seeming to exist about a foot in front of her, and it seemed to be an accurate representation of the two women telling Alan not to go to Newport Beach. Although she could not be sure of the visual details of the image at the moment of the beep, she sensed that a visual image was present, and could create upon questioning an image which seemed to represent the image which had been sensed to be present at the moment of the beep. However, she could not confidently give an explicit description of the image as it had actually existed. Thus this seems to be an example of what we are calling Indeterminate Inner Visual Experience, although it might also be more correctly called Sensed Visual Experience.

Ashley was also aware of Sensing Feelings at the moment of the beep. Irritation, anger, tolerance, and a feeling that she shouldn't have the irritated and angry feelings were all Sensed to be separately present. These Feelings were not being felt in awareness at the moment of the beep; rather, only the Sense that those Feelings were ongoing was present as a part of awareness. She had a vague sense that these Feelings were present bodily; for example, irritation was felt somewhat in her shoulders, but she was not at all confident of that aspect of her description. It was as if these were all separate Feeling processes, present just at the dim edge of awareness, and each could be explicitly felt if she so chose.

MULTIPLE (EXPERIENCED) FEELINGS

Ashley reported Feelings as ongoing parts of awareness at nearly every sample (35 [92%] of 38; the 3 samples where Feelings were not reported were, I believe, due to my failure to inquire about emotions during the interviews rather than Feelings not having been present). Just as with the thinking processes described above, Ashley's Feelings could be either directly Experienced in awareness (28 [74%] of her 38 samples) or Sensed to be ongoing outside of awareness (14 [37%] of her samples). As was the case in the thinking processes, both Experienced and Sensed Feelings were occasionally reported as occurring at the same moment. Feelings were always reported multiply, usually 3 to 7 different Feelings, such as: "irritated, angry, tolerant, and self-critical;" "curious, interested, enjoying myself, amazed, and envious;" "anxious, inadequate, and irritated;" "bored, uneasy, sad, and depressed;" "tense, indecisive, angry, bitter, resistant, in pain, and grieving." Sometimes these Feelings were reported to be mixed together, but more often they were experienced as separate Feelings ongoing simultaneously.

While Feelings were thus an important part of Ashley's experience, and while she could easily differentiate them so that each of the Feelings in the above lists were known to be distinct, she found it very difficult to describe how Feelings were present to her. Sometimes Feelings seemed to be located somewhere in her body (18 samples); at other times they seemed to be located inside or near her head (8 samples); or they seemed to be neither in her body nor her head (14 samples). She was *rarely* confident of the experiential details of Feelings (location, sensory characteristics such as pressure or warmth, etc.); this was in marked contrast to the fact that she was *always* extremely confident in reporting the existence of and distinctions between Feelings themselves (for example, anger but not jealousy, anxiety but not tension, etc.). Her reports of the experiential perception of Feelings were almost always marked by indecision, hesitation, qualification, and contradiction. For example, she might say, "I feel them (anger, frustration, hatred, and indignation) in my body—in my chest mostly, but I have a hard time recollecting my body. I believe it was all over my body, but I'm not sure." Even with the practice of 9 days of repeated interview questioning, Ashley was rarely able to give confident descriptions of the physical concomitants of her Feelings, remaining for the most part indecisive regarding them (while at the same time extremely clear about the kind of Feeling which was ongoing). When she *was* confident of physical referents, Feelings were located in the region within and just outside her head, in her chest, on the surface of her skin, and in her knees.

The examples which we have given in previous sections have all included descriptions of ongoing Feelings. We give now an additional example which includes one of Ashley's strongest Feelings, the so-called "slug" Feeling. At Sample #22 Ashley was thinking about her friends Walter and his wife Kim and a conversation she and they had had a few days earlier. Earlier that same day she had talked with her husband Winston about that conversation, and was still thinking about it. At the moment of the beep she heard Kim's voice saying, "He's (Walter is) mine." Kim had said these same words twice, once several months earlier in a telephone conversation with Ashley, and once several days earlier while riding in a car. The present experience was complex: she clearly heard Kim's voice, which was apparently identical to the way it had sounded in the car. This voice was experienced as being inside Ashley's head, a clear recollection of what her friend had said earlier. At the same time, however, Ashley experienced herself as *being* back in the car hearing Kim say those words. This phenomenon was not easy to describe, but Ashley was confident that she directly experienced herself as being in the car hearing Kim say those words. Furthermore, in a phenomenon which seemed simultaneous, Ashley also *Sensed* that she was sitting on her bed hearing Kim say those words over the telephone. It seemed that Kim's voice stayed the same, while Ashley herself seemed to change locations.

There also seemed to be a hint of an image of the inside of the car, viewed from the perspective of where Ashley had actually sat the night of the conversation she was thinking about. Ashley thought she was seeing this image at the moment of the beep, as if it were a quick flash or maybe a hint of a quick flash; she could not be sure of the details; this is another example of Indeterminate Inner Visual Experience. Furthermore, there seemed to be an Indeterminate image of Ashley sitting on her bed talking on the telephone, but this image was even less confidently described than the image of inside the car.

There were, simultaneously, also Multiple (Experienced) Unsymbolized Thoughts (again rendered rather inadequately in words): Remembering what Winston had said. 'I've lost something'; 'Everything is going on at once'; 'I don't care what Kim had meant—it was how I felt that was important'; 'I could only interpret what Kim had said in the same way I always had done'; 'Now I have "slugs" again—I hadn't had them with Walter'; 'The slugs came where I least expected them'; 'I've been bad'; 'I've been inappropriate and therefore I have the slugs.' All these thoughts were nonverbal but present to Ashley's awareness at the moment of the beep. It did seem, although Ashley was not sure, that the words, "appropriate," "slugs," and "Walter" were somehow present as words, flashing in and out of awareness very quickly at the moment of the beep.

Feelings were also present in Ashley's awareness at this beep, all Experienced directly in awareness. Grief, a feeling that "all her experiences were bullshit," anger, pain, self-pity, disgust and the "slug" Feeling were all part of Ashley's awareness at the moment of the beep. These Feelings were experienced as being in her body; all except the slug Feeling seemed to be mixed together and yet separate: her knees were weak, her hands were shaking, and she was aware of her stomach. The slug Feeling was a strange yet familiar quivering Feeling in the skin of her arms and hands.

This slug Feeling deserves some additional description. It was described by Ashley as being the worst possible feeling. While she consistently used the words "slugs" and "slimy" to describe this feeling, it developed that the slimy wetness connoted by these words was metaphorical, and what Ashley was directly experiencing was a bodily *avoidance*, an experiential tendency for the skin to withdraw, as if to withdraw from a slimy slug. It was as if her skin quivered in an attempt to avoid a slimy, dirty presence (which was not itself experienced). Thus there is nothing experientially slimy about the slug Feeling; rather, there is a very strong experienced avoidance.

Ashley said that all these Feelings were in awareness simultaneously, and that she was more *aware* of the anger and the slug Feeling than of the others. And yet, surprisingly, it seemed that the grief and pain were more *pervasive* than the other Feelings.

MULTIPLE SENSED FEELINGS

Just as Unsymbolized Thoughts were both Experienced in awareness and Sensed to be ongoing outside of awareness, Feelings were also both Experienced and Sensed. In 14 samples (37%), Ashley knew, as a feature of awareness, that multiple Feelings were present for her even though those Feelings themselves were not being directly experienced at the moment of the beep. She would typically refer to these experiences as "feelings under the rocks," or "tails" of feelings, her metaphor for the direct awareness of their existence rather than the awareness of the Feelings themselves. Sample #12 was one example of Multiple Sensed Feelings (described above in the section on Multiple Sensed Unsymbolized Thoughts). There, Ashley knew that irritation, anger, tolerance, and a feeling that she shouldn't have those irritated and angry feelings were all ongoing processes, and she Sensed that they were somehow present in her body, but at the moment of the beep she was *not* directly aware of these feelings themselves; she was just aware of a Sense that these Feelings were ongoing. Furthermore, irritation, anger, tolerance, and the "shouldn't-have" feeling were Sensed separately, not mixed together into one feeling which had those four attributes.

Sample #15, described above in the section on Multiple (Experienced) Unsymbolized Thoughts, also contained examples of Multiple Sensed Feelings: anxiety and irritation were known to be present at the edge of awareness, but not actually present to awareness itself. Sample #15 is also an example of Experienced and Sensed Feelings occurring simultaneously.

As with Multiple Unsymbolized Thoughts, this Experiencing/

Sensing phenomenon was not a dichotomy; Feelings could be more or less "out from under the rocks"—more or less directly Experienced.

INDETERMINATE INNER VISUAL EXPERIENCE

In more than half of Ashley's samples (24 [63%] of 38), she described visual images as being part of the experience at the moment of the beep. Most of these reported images (19 of 24) were described with hesitation and uncertainty, as if Ashley were not sure whether an image was actually present in her awareness at the moment of the beep. Visual details could not generally be described for this kind of experience; for example, if the reported image were of a particular person, Ashley could not say whether the person was seen from the side or full face, or whether the image was in color and if so, what colors, etc. She sometimes described the images as being quick or fleeting, but we were never sure whether this was actually a characteristic of the images themselves or simply an explanation of why they were so hard to describe. We are calling this phenomenon Indeterminate Inner Visual Experience.

We have given two examples of Indeterminate Inner Visual Experience above, Samples #12 (described in the section on Multiple Sensed Unsymbolized Thought and discussed further in the section on Multiple Sensed Feelings) and #22 (described in the section on Multiple [Experienced] Feelings), and will amplify the visual aspects of these samples here. Sample #12 involved thinking about whether Alan was making his own choices. Ashley thought she had an image of Alan's wife and another woman telling him not to go to the Newport Beach resort. She thought the image was clear, and could confidently say it seemed to exist about a foot in front of her (which was true of all her images), but she could not provide any further details. Was Alan in the middle or to the right or left of the two women? From what perspective was the view of the three people? She couldn't say. This lack of perceptual detail leads us to infer that the phenomenon was Indeterminate.

Sample #22 involved a replay of a conversation which took place in the car and also earlier on the telephone. Ashley said she saw an image of her view (from the back seat of the car) on the night of the conversation, but she couldn't give any visual details of that view; we therefore concluded it was an Indeterminate Inner Visual Experience. Furthermore, there seemed to be an even more Indeterminate Inner Visual Experience of Ashley herself sitting on the bed talking on the telephone, but Ashley was even less confident in describing that image.

Sometimes, these Indeterminate Inner Visual Experiences occurred in sequence. For example, at Sample #13 Ashley was sitting in a tavern listening to her friend Alicia tell a story about when her father, who had had both his legs amputated, had taken some money across the border into Mexico. As Alicia told this story, Ashley created a series of visual scenes, all of which included Alicia's father. These scenes were relatively (but not perfectly) clear, judged to be Indeterminate Inner Visual Experiences at the clear end of the continuum; each scene passed rapidly from one to the next, each lasting only a second or so. The passing from one scene to the next was felt to be a smooth transition, and the scenes seemed to change faster than could be simulated with the real visual projection of a movie. The scene present at the moment of the beep was of an old man with no legs sitting in a chair. Ashley provided some additional descriptive details, but she was not sure that these details belonged to the inner scene present at the moment of the beep. Perhaps they were part of a scene which occurred seconds before or after the one in question, or perhaps they were added in the process of attempting to recall what was occurring at the moment of the beep. The details were that the old man was dressed in a suit, and his girlfriend was also hazily present in the scene, a voluptuous, earthy-appearing woman. Ashley was not sure, for example, in which direction the old man was looking, or whether the girlfriend was to the right or left of the old man.

Ashley attempted to describe the sequence of Indeterminate Inner Visual Experiences that occurred surrounding this beep, although she was not at all confident that she could give them in the correct sequence or that she was not omitting any. The scenes were experienced to occur so quickly that a complete description would have been impossible. The kind of scenes which were present close to the time of this beep were: Alicia's father by himself in the house; Alicia's father with his girlfriend in the house; Alicia's father with his girlfriend and the money in the house; Alicia's father driving the car; Alicia's father driving the car with the money; Alicia's father in the back seat while his girlfriend drove the car; Alicia's father in the back seat with the money while his girlfriend drove the car; etc. Each visual experience was relatively clear, and Ashley also experienced a sense of choice with respect to these scenes, as if there were many other Sensed images which could have been seen for a second or more, and Ashley was choosing which ones were being made explicit in this sequence.

There were also Multiple Sensed Feelings at the time of this beep; Ashley did not explicitly feel them but was aware of their presence. She said she had felt at least some of these Feelings explicitly just a moment before the present beep, and these Feelings were experienced as lingering: there was a sense that the feelings had been present. The Feelings themselves were curiosity, interest, enjoyment, amazement, a Feeling of how healthy Alicia's relationship with her father is, and envy. Ashley's impression was that these feelings were in her body, but she did not have any direct bodily experience of them.

IMAGES

On 6 occasions (16%), Ashley experienced Images at the moment of the beep about which she could give visual details. About half of these involved a series of quick flashes of Images, all related but each different from the others. In these experiences, Ashley *could* give confident descriptions of the visual details.

For example, at Sample #18, Ashley was talking with her friend Karen about their mutual friend Janet. They had been discussing Janet's clothing and how everything went together. Ashley had just been describing Janet's shoes, which had miniature artificial fruit on them. At the moment of the beep, Karen was asking "Were her (Janet's) earrings fruit too?" and Ashley was experiencing a sequence of Images, each of which followed the other in rapid succession: Janet's shoes; the whole Janet; Janet's face with fruit earrings. At the moment of the beep, the focus seemed to be on the fruit–bananas and red strawberries, etc. Janet's face in the Image was not clear, but the earrings themselves were quite detailed and clear. The Image seemed to exist about a foot in front of Ashley, at eye level, as had her other Image experiences. There were no other thoughts that Ashley could identify as present in her awareness, except perhaps an almost worded "No," but Ashley was not sure about this. The Feeling of amusement was present as an Experienced Feeling (her whole body and head felt light), and also perhaps some discomfort and relief, but Ashley was not sure about these last two Feelings.

It might be observed that this was a relatively simple, uncomplicated inner experience for Ashley, at least in contrast to the multiple thoughts and feelings which were her norm. It was generally true that if a sample included a visual Image, there were fewer thoughts and feelings occurring at the same time, and that the more clear the Image, the fewer the other elements of inner experience. There are other possible interpretations, so we should not be too confident about this observation.

EXPERIENCE DURING THE URGE TO VOMIT

Ashley was a relatively frequent purger, vomiting perhaps daily for a period of a week, followed by several days without throwing up. I asked her to sample at times when she thought that vomiting was relatively likely, and she complied on the last day of her sampling period.

Vomiting for Ashley was most frequent in the late afternoon or early evening, and was usually preceded by a feeling which Ashley described as "fullness." The following three samples occurred during such a time, in fact, when the urge to vomit was extremely strong. Ashley said that she had never had an urge to throw up which was this strong and which was not followed by actually vomiting.

The first of these was Sample #35, which occurred at 7:45 P.M. while Ashley was watching a rerun of Masterpiece Theater on television, in which a man was talking about a scar. She was hearing the man talk, but was mainly paying attention to a "funnel" of thoughts which had to do with throwing up, in particular with having a choice as to whether to throw up or not. These Multiple (Experienced) Unsymbolized Thoughts were all nonverbal except for a sense that she may have been saying the word "choice" silently to herself, although she wasn't sure of this or that it was in fact in awareness at all. There were perhaps 20 thoughts, all apparently simultaneous, each demanding its own share of Ashley's attention. If put into words, the thoughts were: 'I have a choice whether to do this'; 'You have a choice'; 'Should I eat a hot dog?'; 'Will I eat one or two hot dogs?'; 'I should hurry up and do this before [husband] Winston comes home'; 'I know I won't throw up if I eat one hot dog but I will if I eat two'; 'It wouldn't matter if Winston came home— he'd just sit there and wouldn't know or care'; 'Winston wouldn't say or do anything'; 'Whenever I express anger I lose something'; 'I didn't get to play with Kim Friday night'; 'See what happens when I express anger!'; 'Don't throw up because you will fuck your throat up more'; 'If you have a choice, don't throw up'; and 'Throwing up wouldn't be a good idea now.' These thoughts were all simultaneously being experienced in awareness, each separately being thought and understood.

Also part of this moment were two "tails," that is, two Sensed Unsymbolized Thoughts which had been the explicit focus of attention a moment before. One of these had been about Ashley's husband Winston and her anger toward him. That thought process had now moved from the center of attention, but was still Sensed to be ongoing. If Ashley had so chosen, she felt she could have again focused her attention on this thought and resumed it exactly where she had left off. The other thought process which had been explicit but now was present just as a "tail" was about the pain in the throat and the possibility that her vomiting had caused it or made it worse. Ashley was aware at the moment of the beep that this train of thought was present just outside of awareness.

Also perhaps present to awareness was an Indeterminate Inner Visual Experience of a hot dog. This image, if present as an image at all, was so dim that Ashley was not sure that it was being seen at the moment of the beep. The image was clearly there when Ashley later described the moment, but she could not be sure whether the image seen at the time of reporting was actually present at the time of the beep.

Feelings were a strong characteristic of this moment. There was a strong awareness of Feeling driven to throw up, as well as Feelings of being alone, lonely, and empty. These Feelings were a part of awareness at the moment of the beep, but Ashley was not able to describe how she felt them. It was also a fact that her throat hurt, but she had just a Sense of that pain's existence rather than an explicit awareness at the moment of the beep.

All these thoughts, "tails" of thoughts, and feelings were present simultaneously to Ashley's awareness in a way which she described as a "funnel." This whirlwind of thoughts and feelings were all directed toward a single thing: throwing up.

The next sample (#36) occurred a few minutes after Sample #35 (she had not thrown up even though the urge had been very strong), and Ashley had gone into her bedroom to "brood" (lay on her bed and think about what was going on with her). At the moment of the beep she was thinking about the "games" she plays with other people, and was saying to herself in Inner Speech, "What games I play!" These words were said with a bemused feeling and inflection, but it was as if the words were being spoken into a tape machine—she was speaking the words to herself, but not hearing herself speak them.

These inner-spoken words did not occupy the center of Ashley's attention; instead, most of her attention was divided between many individual, simultaneous, Multiple (Experienced) Unsymbolized Thoughts. If these thoughts were translated into words, they might resemble the following (but again it should be noted that these thoughts did not have the linear form of verbal thoughts, thus a verbal rendering is in many ways inadequate): "How lonely I am"; "How much I would like to be held or touched"; "How often I would like to be held or touched"; "I wouldn't let Winston touch me"; "I'm making Winston like my father"; "What I want most from Winston I won't allow"; "I allow sex as long as there's no affection"; "I allow affection as long as there's no sex"; "How outrageous I am at work—bawdy"; "How I imply at work that I'm sexy at home"; "How I project an image of earthy sensuality"; "How I know I'm lying when I do that"; "I know I want to be touched"; and "I know I won't let myself be touched."

There was also perhaps an Indeterminate Inner Visual Experience; if it was present, it was quite dim or hazy, but Ashley was not sure. It seemed to be an image of Jack, a fellow worker, and included a knowledge of a few recent interchanges with him where Ashley had jokingly told him that he was "cranky because he hadn't been getting any" (sex) at home. Part of this interchange had been Ashley's awareness of her untrue implication that *she* had been sexually satisfied.

Also present in Ashley's awareness were Multiple Experienced Feelings: lonely, depressed, abandoned, hypocritical, sensing her own mystery, curiosity, and emptiness. These Feelings were all present in awareness, not merely sensed, but Ashley could not describe how their presence was known to her.

The third sample in this sequence (#37) occurred a few minutes later. Ashley was replaying in her mind a conversation she had had with me two days earlier. She remembered herself saying after the previous sampling discussion, "This week has been like throwing up without throwing up." This replay involved a clear Image, seen as if from an elevated perspective about fifteen feet away, and Ashley felt as if she were actually there in the scene saying the words. The scene as viewed from the external perspective was quite clear, with me being seen more clearly than Ashley herself: both of us could be seen in profile, me from the right and Ashley from the left, and seemed to be an accurate reconstruction of the scene as it had actually taken place. While the Image was clearly seen and the Feelings experienced, the focus of Ashley's attention was on the words themselves, which were experienced as being said by Ashley in her own voice with normal inflection, just as if she were saying them aloud although no sound or lip motion was experienced. Ashley was replaying this conversation over and over, repeatedly inner speaking her own words and hearing my response, concentrating most of her attention on the words that both of us spoke and the intonation and feeling which they carried; she was trying to "get it," that is, trying to fix in her mind her understanding of the whole of the conversation. In order to "get" the whole, it seemed she had to replay its parts over and over.

There were other thoughts coexisting with this repetition of our conversation, all nonverbal Multiple (Experienced) Unsymbolized Thoughts apparently present simultaneously to awareness. If put into words, these thoughts might be: "I haven't thrown up yet"; "I'm kind of amazed that I haven't thrown up"; "Wondering whether the sampling process has altered that"; "Wondering whether simply writing down the beeps would do the same thing as also talking about them"; "It's been an hour and a half since I put the beeper on when I had an incredible urge to throw up and I haven't"; and "About the impact of the throw-up stuff on Dr. Hurlburt—not wanting him to be involved but happy he was."

There were also several Sensed Thoughts present at this beep, processes close to the dim edge of awareness: a sense that she would throw up if she took the beeper off; a sense that she didn't want me to get too deeply involved with her vomiting; and a sense that she wasn't hungry.

There were also Feelings Experienced in awareness: anxiety, curiosity, and appreciation. Ashley was also a bit satisfied, proud and pleased that she had not thrown up for an hour and a half, and that the drive had lessened. There was also an "under the rock" Sensed worry about the ramifications of talking about these beeps with me.

Ashley did not vomit this day; this was the first time in Ashley's recollection that she had such a strong urge to vomit and didn't do so.

DISCUSSION

We have seen in our other subjects occasional examples of multiple simultaneous thoughts and feelings, but not nearly to the extent that Ashley reported. We questioned Ashley thoroughly on this phenomenon over the nine sampling days, and she was confident and unshakable: these thoughts and feelings *were* perceived to be simultaneous. She allowed for the possibility that they actually were rapidly sequential, but was adamant that that was *not* how they were experienced. We will see that some of our other bulimic subjects also have multiple simultaneous thoughts, more so than our other subjects but not so many as Ashley.

The distinction between Experienced and Sensed Awareness was also one about which Ashley was confident and unswerving. Yes, thoughts did continue to exist for her even when she was aware of only a small part of the particular thought. No, it was not merely that she came back to a similar thought later on; it was the *same* thought which had been waiting, as if frozen, to be continued. Some of our other bulimic subjects have reported a similar phenomenon, but not with the clarity of Ashley's experience. Christine (Chapter 9) referred, for example, to the "string" of a thought which was present in awareness while the thought itself was outside of awareness; this was a similar metaphor to Ashley's "tails" of thoughts. But the references by the other subject were not as frequent or as confident as Ashley's.

We might note that Ashley was the oldest of our bulimic subjects; what effect age has on the patterns of inner experience in general and of bulimics in particular is not known.

A Bulimic Junior High School Teacher

Stephanie Doucette and RTH

Christine (not her real name) was a 30-year-old junior high school science teacher at the time the samples of her inner experience were obtained. Christine satisfied the DSM-III-R criteria for bulimia and considered herself bulimic, although she had never been formally diagnosed. She had, however, enrolled herself in weekly therapy sessions with a group of individuals suffering from anorexia and/or bulimia. With the help and support of her therapy group, Christine was working on restraining her bulimic tendencies; at the time of sampling, she was successfully refraining from episodic binge eating and purging. She stated that she had been able to control her bulimia for considerable periods in the past and was confident she could do so again at this time.

Christine volunteered as a subject in the present study after hearing about it from another group member. She wore the beeper on 7 days over the course of a 3-week period. We discussed 29 (about 90%) of those samples in depth; this report is based on those samples.

We will provide in the next few paragraphs a brief overview of Christine's inner experience as observed in these samples, and then return to describe each salient characteristic in detail. Nearly all (86%) of Christine's samples were complex, many-faceted phenomena which we call Multiple Inner Experience. The elements which were intertwined with each other included, most frequently, Unsymbolized Thinkings,

This chapter and Chapter 10 are part of the first author's Masters Thesis in the Department of Psychology, University of Nevada, Las Vegas.

but Feelings were also multiply experienced, including simultaneous paradoxical Feelings.

The single most salient characteristic of Christine's sampled moments was the phenomenon of Multiple Unsymbolized Inner Experience, usually several concurrent Unsymbolized Thinkings all perceived as ongoing at the moment of the beep, yet all perceived as separate events on which Christine was able to focus sequentially, one at a time. In most of her samples, Christine described the multiplicity of thoughts as being "interwoven" in her inner experience. However, in two samples, she reported the phenomenon she called "string" thinking (which we are calling Sensed Unsymbolized Thinking) where there was a hint of the thought—a "string" of it—in her awareness; the whole thought existed somewhere in her mind but was "parked," not actually being thought at that moment. Christine reported that such thinking was quite familiar to her.

Thus, Unsymbolized Thinking could be divided into two categories: (a) (Experienced) Unsymbolized Thinking, with or without a visual or verbal orientation but in the absence of words or images; and (b) Sensed Unsymbolized Thinking, where there was an awareness of the content of a thought that was not actually present in inner experience.

Another feature of Christine's inner experience was Feeling, which possessed two main characteristics: (1) Somatically Oriented Feelings, which had a bodily location and a physical quality, in that Christine was aware of a distinct bodily manifestation. Among these somatically Oriented Feelings were (1) anxiety, (which occasionally incorporated a slight feeling of depression), frustration, tension/stress, and "good" Feelings, and (2) Thought/feelings, which had an emotional as well as a cognitive component.

Christine reported experiencing Multiple Feelings in 34% of her samples; many of them seemed contradictory or paradoxical. In two of her samples, Christine reported that she was conscious of an awareness of her current physical state which did not correspond to the actual state of her body, a phenomenon we call Incongruent Bodily Awareness.

Christine reported only one sample which included a visual Image. However, four samples included the phenomenon we have called Indeterminate Inner Visual Experience, in which the inner experience seemed to be visual but in which visual perceptual details were not convincingly present. We turn now to discuss these characteristics in detail.

MULTIPLE (EXPERIENCED) UNSYMBOLIZED THINKING

Christine reported Unsymbolized Thinking in 21 (72%) of her 29 samples, most of which included multiple simultaneous thinkings. She described the majority of these occurrences of Unsymbolized Thinking to be "just there," with no perceptual mode of experience, but in 3 of the 21 samples, she experienced perceptions that were on the threshold of Wordless Inner Hearing, where words were not actually present to Christine, but where the experience seemed to be more like hearing than simply knowing the existence of the meaning. Two other samples verged on Wordless Inner Speech, where again, words were not actually present to Christine, yet something was perceived as almost having been "spoken."

For example, in Sample #13 Christine experienced multiple incidences of Unsymbolized Thinking at the moment of the beep; all were perceived to be in her awareness at the same time and yet also seemed to be somehow sequential. She had been standing in line outside the Department of Motor Vehicles, talking to a woman who was concerned because her driver's license expired that day. Christine was saying aloud, "In fact, I think you have a grace period after it expires," and the beep sounded in the middle of the sentence. At that moment, Christine was aware of trying, in Unsymbolized Thinking, to resolve a particular characteristic of the situation: Either the woman had not had much experience in the process of renewing her license or she was young and had not had to renew her license before. At the same time, Christine thought, again in Unsymbolized Thinking, that the woman did not look young enough for this to be the case. Also simultaneously, Christine was aware of thinking that although the woman was not beautiful, she was nevertheless appealing because of her high cheekbones and the shape of her eyes. All these occurrences of Unsymbolized Thinking were in her awareness at the same time. However, Christine observed that she also could have "pulled them up and looked at any one of them" in more detail if she had so desired.

Another example of Multiple (Experienced) Unsymbolized Thinking was Sample #21, where Christine was in a movie theater watching a preview for *Dick Tracy* when she was signalled by the beep. At that moment, she was wondering about the motivation behind the making of such movies starring comic book heroes. In Unsymbolized Thinking, she was wondering if the object was to get the characters back into kids' lives, or whether profit was the motive, with the relationship between children and comic book heroes being a collateral effect. Simultaneously, Christine was aware of making a distinction between the two motives and of hoping that profit was *not* the overriding motivation for making those types of movies. All aspects of the thought seemed to her to be "interwoven," as if they were all in her awareness at once, yet she was aware of being able to focus sequentially on first one part of a thought, then another.

Sample #30 was another example of Multiple (Experienced) Unsymbolized Thinking. Christine had just said, "Hi. How are you?" to one of her students who had just arrived carrying an exhibit for the class Science Fair. At the moment of the beep, Christine experienced several simultaneous occurrences of Unsymbolized Thinking which, if put into words, might be "It's small"; "What is it?"; "Where's her model?"; and "She's a good kid." As in Sample #21 above, she described these thoughts as being sequential, as if somehow "braided together," overlapping in time but also coming one after the other. Simultaneously with the Unsymbolized Thinking, Christine also experienced two separate Feelings: A fleeting, warm Feeling that might be expressed as "She's a good kid!" and a continuous anxious awareness, felt in the left side of her heart, of all the things Christine had to do that day.

MULTIPLE SENSED UNSYMBOLIZED THINKING

In one of her samples, Christine reported an experience we call Multiple Sensed Unsymbolized Thinking, the ongoing awareness that a thought was somehow present in consciousness, but was somehow "on hold" or "parked."

The example of Multiple Sensed Unsymbolized Thinking was Sample #24. Christine was sitting in her evening class at the university waiting for the lecture to begin. At the moment of the beep, she was leafing through a summer class schedule, searching for a particular registration policy and saying aloud to a classmate, "Why would they tell you in a catalog that you can register in advance when you can't?" At that moment, Christine was aware of three Unsymbolized Thinkings experienced simultaneously yet separately. Two of the three Thinkings were examples of (Experienced) Unsymbolized Thinkings, and each of these was composed of several "subthoughts." The third of the three simultaneous Thinkings was Sensed Unsymbolized Thinking.

The first Unsymbolized Thinking involved three simultaneous subthoughts. Christine was thinking (1) about showing her classmate the advance registration policy; (2) that she wanted to show her friend that the policy was indeed stated in the catalog; and (3) that she wanted to help her classmate. A questioning, confused Thought/Feeling (to be explored in the Feelings section below) accompanied these thoughts.

The second simultaneous Multiple Experienced Unsymbolized Thinking again involved three subthoughts. Christine was (1) thinking that the inclusion of the statement about advance registration in the schedule seemed pointless because no one would benefit, since students could not register early; (2) wondering how the statement would help anyone; and (3) wondering why the university bothered to put the information in the catalog when it did not seem to be helpful.

The third simultaneous thought was Sensed Unsymbolized Thinking, a wondering of why the university would handle their registration policy in such a manner. However, the whole of this thought was not present in her awareness explicitly; rather, there was just a hint of it, what Christine called a "string" of the thought. The thought itself existed as having "gone off," as being "suspended" or "on hold" somewhere in her mind, but she was still aware of the slight pull of it, which she called the "string." This string, which was somehow "attached" to the thought, was actually present in her awareness at the moment of the beep, but was only a small part of the whole thought about the university's handling of the registration policy. This thought existed as an entity, but was not itself in awareness. The string which was attached to it signalled its existence and its availability as something to which Christine could return.

We wish to make this rather difficult phenomenon explicitly clear. Christine's wondering about the university registration was, at the moment of the beep, a concretely existing thought, but it existed in a suspended, outside-of-awareness manner. It was *not* the case that Christine simply knew she should return to thinking about university registration at some later time: Instead the *thought about university registration itself* was somehow *there*, present in her mind but outside her direct awareness. Inside her direct awareness was the "string"—the awareness that the thought was awaiting her attention.

(EXPERIENCED) FEELINGS

Christine reported Feelings in 20 (60%) of her 29 samples. Christine's Feelings could be divided into two categories: Somatically Oriented Feelings (emotions, including anxiety, frustration, tension/stress, as well as "good" Feelings, which were experienced as located primarily in her body), and Thought/Feelings (experiences which involved an inextricable fusing of cognitive and emotional components). Most Feelings were directly experienced in Christine's awareness; one Feeling was Sensed to be existing outside awareness and will be described in a separate section.

Christine gave clear, simple descriptions of the Feelings she experienced at the moment of the beep, but the phenomena she was describing were often quite complex. It soon became evident that this complexity existed in two forms: Occasionally, a Feeling would itself be complex, for example, anxiety which included a depressed, sad, enervated aspect. On other occasions, the complexity came from two or many separate Feelings existing simultaneously, not as aspects of each other but as separate, distinct, concurrent awarenesses. We call this latter phenomenon Multiple Feelings, and wish to reemphasize that it involved separate simultaneous Feelings, not a complex single Feeling.

Somatically Oriented Feelings

Christine experienced Somatically oriented Feelings, where the phenomenon of emotion had a clear physical focus, in 14 (48%) of her 29 samples. She was fairly consistently able to localize these corporeal Feelings in specific areas of her body. Some emotions, such as anxiety, were felt to exist in precisely the same bodily location (left side of heart) each time they occurred; however, other emotions, such as frustration, were located in different parts of the body at different occurrences.

Christine reported Feeling anxious in 8 (28%) of her 29 samples. For her, anxiety was an active type of Feeling synonymous with feeling pulled or "harried." For Christine, the Feeling of anxiety always manifested itself as a physical sort of discomfort specifically located deep inside her chest, just left of the center, in the left side of her heart. On a few occasions, a slight depression was incorporated into the anxiety, which she described as a "sadness or lowness," a "lack of energy," or an unsettling "sunken feeling."

Multiple (Experienced) Feelings

In 10 (34%) of her 29 samples, Christine reported two or more separate, simultaneous Feelings, each of which she perceived as a distinct inner experience.

For example, in Sample #4, Christine was driving her car, mentally reviewing what she must do to make her classroom appear organized and effective for a visit from the principal of another school. At the moment of the beep, Christine was aware of a Feeling of tenseness inside her head; it seemed to Christine as if her brain were pressing against her skull. Simultaneously, she experienced an anxious Feeling inside her chest in the left side of her heart. Thus Christine was simultaneously aware of two separate Somatically Oriented Feelings, tension and anxiety, each of which seemed to exist in a separate location in her body (in her head and her chest). These Feelings seemed to Christine to spring from the situation with which she was concerned at the moment.

The principal from another school was scheduled to observe her teaching and Christine was concerned about the impression her classroom would make on this important visitor.

Additionally, at the moment of the beep, Christine was aware of an Image of her classroom seen from the perspective of standing at the classroom door at the opposite side of the room from her desk. This Image was a series of scenes of her classroom (chalkboard, bulletin board, her desk), all in color but not vivid.

At the same time, she had a sense of "hearing" a series of thoughts, all present simultaneously, which if put into words (although no words were actually heard) might be: 'I'll need to clean more'; 'I'll need to make sure the room looks organized'; and 'I wonder what she'll consider good enough.' There was some emphasis on *need* and *organized* even though it was not words themselves that were emphasized. Also simultaneously, Christine was aware of the isolated concepts "colorful" and "bulletin boards." She "heard" the thoughts and concepts spoken in what seemed to be a softer version of her own voice, yet she had no sense of her own voice speaking. Furthermore, she was not aware of actually hearing the particular words. Thus, these thoughts are examples of Multiple (Experienced) Unsymbolized Thinking which in some way verge on inner hearing.

Contradictory Feelings

In half of the cases of Multiple (Experienced) Feelings, the simultaneous Feelings were perceived to be in some way contradictory to each other. An example of this paradox was found in Sample #23, where Christine was driving her car, listening to a Joe Cocker song on the radio, and singing along ". . . Lift us up . . . " At the same time, she was reflecting on an earlier telephone conversation she'd had with the principal of another school, during which the principal had expressed a desire to have Christine teach at the other school.

As the beep sounded, Christine was experiencing three Contradictory Feelings: a "good" Feeling which contrasted with a Feeling of anxiety and another, separate Feeling of stress. The "good" Feeling felt "warm and bubbly," and was experienced primarily in the center of her heart, radiating outward within her chest. She understood this good Feeling as springing from two distinct sources, the job offer and the music.

Concurrently with the good, warm Feeling, Christine experienced a slight anxiety that manifested itself in the left side of her heart, and a stressful Feeling felt in her head. As she described it, the anxious and stressful Feelings seemed almost to be in competition with the warm, bubbly Feeling, although this warm Feeling, on which Christine was focused when signalled by the beep, was perceived to be the dominant one.

Simultaneous with these three Feelings, Christine had a Congruent Bodily Awareness of a slight headache, felt inside the front of her skull as a pushing, throbbing feeling. Also simultaneously, Christine was aware of having a knot in her stomach, the result of having bolted down her lunch. She perceived this Bodily Awareness to be in the background of her inner experience; accompanying this Bodily Awareness was an Unsymbolized Thought, which, if put into words, might be, "Oh, it's still there!"

Another example of Contradictory Feelings was Sample #29. Christine was walking in the hallway at her school, playfully arm wrestling with her son, and smiling at something he had said. Another teacher passed by and observed, "Your morning's starting off tough!" As the beep sounded, Christine was wondering (in Unsymbolized Thinking) if she had been rude in not responding to the teacher. Also simultaneously at the moment of the beep, Christine was aware of a fragment of the teacher's comment remaining in her mind, reverberating as though Christine "heard" the words being repeated, one word at a time, although she was not actually "hearing" the words *per se*. Thus this is an example of Unsymbolized Thinking verging on inner hearing.

Christine simultaneously experienced two separate and Contradictory Feelings: a Somatically Oriented Feeling of slight anxiety, felt in the left side of her heart, and at the same time another Somatically Oriented "good" Feeling, murmuring and bubbling through the middle of her chest, as well as in front of her face. She experienced both Feelings in the same general area in her chest, but the anxiety seemed to be to the left of the "good" Feeling.

Thought/Feelings

Christine reported phenomena we call Thought/Feelings in 11 of her 29 samples (38%). She described Thought/Feelings as events that are an inextricable merging of both emotional and cognitive aspects. From the Feeling standpoint, Thought/Feelings were emotional events which were not as physical as Somatically Oriented Feelings, but often did possess some physical component, such as a bodily sense of distress or urgency. From a cognitive standpoint, Thought/Feelings were "fuddled," or otherwise cloudy thinking processes. Christine's Thought/Feelings often appeared to incorporate an underlying sense of urgency, a need to get something done.

Thus Thought/Feelings seemed to share experiential aspects both of Unsymbolized Thinkings and of Feelings, and it may seem that we could have concluded that the process we call Thought/Feeling was actually two parallel processes, one Unsymbolized Thinking and one Feeling. However, Christine was clear in describing this kind of experience as one phenomenon with two aspects, *not* two experienced processes occurring in parallel.

One illustration of Thought/Feeling was Sample #26. Christine was in an evening class watching a film about teenage suicide. In the film, a father was saying to his adolescent child, "I've decided I'm going to spend a lot less time telling you how to live your life." At the moment of the beep, in Unsymbolized Thinking, Christine was aware that, even though she had often given her own son some leeway, she ought to do so more often. Simultaneously, Christine had the Thought/Feeling sense of admitting to having made a mistake, which she experienced as a "right" kind of feeling of relief in the center of her body, in the chest area. The cognitive aspect of this experience (that she had made a mistake and was right to admit it) and the feeling aspect (relief in her chest) were not at all separate. It was as if she were thinking the thought in her chest.

Sample #14 provides another example of a Thought/Feeling. Christine had been searching through the contents of her purse, trying to locate some object, when she came upon her address book. As the beep sounded, Christine was Unsymbolized Thinking that since she had not heard from her aunt in a week, it might mean that all was well with her grandmother, who had been ill. At the same time, she had a Thought/Feeling that it was urgent that she telephone her aunt, a feeling that was perceived by Christine to be located in her chest area. Here again, the cognitive aspect of the Thought/Feeling experience (the need to telephone) was not separable from the feeling aspect (urgency felt in her chest).

SENSED FEELINGS

In Chapter 8, and in the Unsymbolized Thinking sections of this chapter, we have distinguished between Experienced and Sensed phenomena. All the Feelings which we have described so far in this chapter have been "experienced" Feelings—emotions whose content and bodily aspects were directly present in Christine's awareness. Christine also had one sample of "sensed" Thought/Feeling, where the knowledge that an emotional experience was occurring within her occupied a piece of awareness, but where the cognitive/emotional experience itself was not part of awareness.

In Sample #27, Christine was in her evening university class where the professor was going over the test the class had taken the previous week. The primary focus of Christine's inner experience was an Experienced Feeling of frustration, directly experienced as tension in the middle of her upper body (a Somatically Oriented Feeling). At the moment of the beep, she understood that the frustration was the result of having gotten a question wrong because the professor had given incorrect information to answer Christine's request for clarification during the test. This understanding was expressed as an Unsymbolized Thinking which, while nonverbal, might be expressed as, 'This was the question I asked you about, and you answered a certain way, and now I got it wrong.' Also present at the moment of the beep was a Sensed Thought/Feeling of confusion, a muddled Thought/Feeling which, if put into words, might be 'What is it that I missed?'; 'Now, wait a minute!'; or 'Have I misinterpreted?' However, these Thought/Feelings of confusion were themselves *not* being directly experienced. Instead, only the "string" of this awareness was currently in Christine's consciousness. The whole confused awareness was temporarily set aside and not currently focused on, but was waiting for her to get back to and address it. The "string" of this awareness was a part of Christine's ongoing experience: A small piece of this confusion was present in her awareness, along with the Unsymbolized Thinking, reminding her that the unfinished confusion awaited her attention. Additionally, Christine had a related Sensed Unsymbolized Thinking that she could take care of the problem later, and that she would speak to the professor about it after class.

BODILY AWARENESS

Christine was aware in 6 (21%) of her 29 samples of bodily sensations that had no particular emotional significance. We call this phenomenon Bodily Awareness to differentiate it from Feelings, which, as we have seen, also often possess a physical quality but which include an emotional content. Christine's Bodily Awareness was either Congruent, where her awareness of her body accurately reflected her actual physical state at the time, or Incongruent, where her awareness of her body did not accurately correspond to her actual physical state.

Congruent Bodily Awareness

An example of Congruent Bodily Awareness was Sample #8. Christine was removing clothes from her dryer and came upon a T-shirt imprinted with the words "South Wind," the name of her softball team's sponsor. In Unsymbolized Thinking, she was reiterating this phrase in her head and articulating it, although there were no words *per se* in her awareness. At the same moment, seeing the name on the shirt triggered the awareness of a bodily soreness resulting from her first softball practice of the season; this was strictly a Bodily Awareness with no emotion attached to it. We call such an experience Congruent because the awareness accurately represented the actual soreness in her body.

Incongruent Bodily Awareness

Christine had two instances of Incongruent Bodily Awareness, which did not accurately reflect her bodily state. Both were sensations of "puffiness." Although she experienced this awareness in only two of the 29 samples discussed in depth, Christine indicated that she experiences this puffiness periodically in her everyday life, and stated that such sensations, which she called "feeling being fat," were more common when she was actively bingeing and purging (which was not the case at the time of sampling).

In Sample #1, Christine described puffiness as "a feeling of feeling the weight," a perception involving feeling her body expanding against her skin, almost as if her inner body were growing larger, moving outward in her upper arms, hips, and face, the areas with which she is the least satisfied. For Christine, it was a sense of her body inflating at its peripheries, a "growing" that did not include expansion of her inner organs. As the puffiness set in, Christine was cognizant of an awareness of "feeling being fat," which was to emerge again in Sample #28.

In Sample #28, Christine was in her car driving to school. At the moment of the beep, she was reexperiencing how it felt for her to be thin, aware of a joyous Somatically Oriented Feeling of lightness—a "rush" in her face and chest. Simultaneously, she was aware of an Incongruent Bodily Awareness of the heavy, boneless puffiness she was experiencing in her body now. The heaviness was perceived to be located primarily in Christine's thighs and chin area, and was accompanied by a Feeling like being in mourning, sad and wistful. The ponderous, puffy sensation had the effect of making Christine seem somehow "extra." Also at the same moment, Christine was cognizant of actively and cognitively comparing her reexperienced "joyously thin" Feeling with the Incongruent Bodily Awareness of puffiness.

INNER VISUAL EXPERIENCE

Christine reported one relatively clear Image and four samples (14%) where her experience was of inner visualization but where characteristics of the image were difficult to specify. We call this phenomenon Indeterminate Inner Visual Experience.

Images

The sole Image Christine reported was in Sample #4, described earlier in the section on Multiple (Experienced) Feelings. At the time of this sample, she had been thinking about preparing her classroom for a visiting principal's visit. At the moment of the beep, Christine was aware of an Image of her classroom, in color, although the Image was not a vivid Image. The experience was the seeing of a series of scenes of her classroom. All were present in her awareness simultaneously, yet she focused separately on each scene, a process she referred to as "scanning." At the moment of the beep, Christine was scanning the Image clockwise, from the perspective of standing at the classroom door at the opposite side of the room from her desk (as it is situated in reality). She started her visual scanning at her desk, which seemed to Christine to be more distant than it would be from that vantage point in reality. At first the desk was out of focus, but as she imaginally scanned it, the desk became "pretty crisp." Next she scanned past the chalkboard to the bulletin board, picking out various displays and focusing on them. At the time of these scanned images, Christine was aware of Unsymbolized Thinking concerning getting the classroom ready for the visiting principal—needing to clean, to make sure the room looked organized. Also at the same time, she was aware of the concepts "colorful" and "bulletin boards," although not the words *per se*.

Indeterminate Inner Visual Experience

At Sample #27 (discussed above in the section on Sensed Feelings), Christine was remembering how she had consulted with the professor of her evening class about an item on the test she was taking. Christine was visually aware of herself walking up to the professor's table in the front of the room, "seen" from the perspective of her seat in the classroom. She "saw" herself from the side, leaning over the table, pencil in hand. She was cognizant of both her own and the professor's upper bodies leaning over the table, but had no sense of the clothes they were wearing, only the knowledge that her forearm was bare. However, these seeings were not as clear as those in the classroom described above; for example, she was not sure whether she "saw" the pencil or just knew it was there. The only portion of the scene which she was confident of actually seeing was her bare forearm. This lack of clarity of the distinction between seeing in inner experience and simply knowing the visual details of the scene is the feature which leads us to call such an experience Indeterminate.

Sample #28 (described in the section on Incongruent Bodily Awareness) also included an example of Indeterminate Inner Visual Experience. Christine was reexperiencing being thin, and was at the same time imagining herself in a conversation with her husband, "seeing" herself acting in a light, spontaneous manner—the way she remembered acting when she was thin. She "saw" herself full-face, but had little access to the visual details of the image. For example, she could say that only her face, not her whole body, was being "seen," but could not be more explicit. Furthermore, her husband was known to be in the scene but was not being visualized; Christine simply sensed an awareness of his presence.

DISCUSSION

Multiple inner experience was the rule for Christine, rather than the exception. In the majority of her reported samples, Christine was aware of Feelings, often two or more, as well as several Unsymbolized Experienced or Sensed Thinkings. She perceived all such inner experiences to be occurring both concurrently and consecutively, in a pattern she described as "interwoven" or "braided together."

Christine's samples require that we make the distinction between Experienced and Sensed processes. Christine referred to Sensed processes as having a "string," where the process itself was intact but suspended outside of immediate awareness, with only a "string" present in awareness which was somehow connected to the process itself. The similarity of metaphor between Christine's "strings" and Ashley's "tails" (see Chapter 8) was striking; we shall return to discuss this in more detail in the next chapter.

Christine reported experiencing Feelings almost as often as Unsymbolized Thinking. For her, Feelings were Somatically Oriented, possessing bodily locations and a physical quality, perceived as either active or passive, and included anxiety, frustration, tension/stress, and "good" Feelings. Christine often experienced more than one Feeling in a given sample, and many of her samples contained Contradictory Feelings.

Much of the time, Christine's emotional awarenesses included undifferentiated affect and cognition, leading us to create the salient characteristic we called Thought/Feelings. We shall see in the next chapter that this pattern was characteristic of other bulimic subjects as well.

Christine's Incongruent Bodily Awarenesses, experiences where there is an awareness of bodily position or state that does not correspond to the body's actual condition, are quite unusual in our sampling experience, although as we shall see in the next chapter, such awarenesses occur in other bulimic subjects as well.

Christine reported only one Image in her samples. That Image had qualities similar to her Multiple Unsymbolized Experience and her Multiple Feelings, in that, rather than one Image, it was more a series of images all present in awareness simultaneously, yet Christine was able to focus separately on any of them. Additionally, Christine experienced several occurrences of Indeterminate Inner Visual Experience that, while not clearly images, nonetheless had an unequivocally visual component and provided the sensation of "seeing."

Inner Experience in Bulimia

Stephanie Doucette and RTH

There have been a total of seven individuals who meet the DSM-III-R diagnostic criteria for bulimia who have been sampled using the descriptive techniques described in this book. Ashley (Chapter 8) was sampled by this book's author; Christine (Chapter 9) and four other bulimic subjects were sampled as part of Stephanie Doucette's Master's Thesis at the University of Nevada, Las Vegas (sampling interviews for these five subjects were most frequently performed by Doucette and Hurlburt together); and an additional (seventh) subject, who met both the criteria for anxiety disorder and for bulimia, was sampled by Hebert (1991), again with Hurlburt's participation. All seven of these subjects were female; one of the subjects also met the diagnostic criteria for anorexia nervosa. The seven subjects ranged from those able to control their bulimic tendencies at the time of sampling to active binge eating and purging on a daily basis.

We should note that—although they are usually female (Crisp, 1982)—bulimics constitute a large and diverse group of individuals. Our subjects, however, constitute a small, diverse, nonrandom sample from this population. No attempt was made in this study to sample bulimics in any particular stage of bulimia or post-bulimia; the fact that our bulimics displayed a range of bulimic behaviors was a coincidence.

There were four salient characteristics (Multiple Inner Experience, Sensed Awareness, Thought/Feelings, and Incongruent Bodily Awareness) that emerged from our study of these seven bulimics that seem to set the bulimics apart from the nonbulimic subjects described by Hurlburt (1990), Monson (1989), Hebert (1991), Shamanek (1992), and other unpublished reports collected by Hurlburt. It should be remembered that these four characteristics are based on only seven bulimic subjects, and so are not intended to be definitive descriptions of the characteristics of bulimics in general. These characteristics are offered as an invitation for further, more conclusive study of the inner experiences of the bulimic population.

MULTIPLE INNER EXPERIENCE

Multiple Inner Experience is the simultaneous occurrence of a few or many separable, identifiable inner happenings, all taking place in inner experience at the moment of the beep. One of the most striking findings in our study of bulimics was that Multiple Inner Experience was a frequent characteristic of the inner experience of *all* our bulimic subjects. This is in sharp contrast to the findings of other researchers sampling nonbulimic populations, where the phenomenon of Multiple Inner Experience occurs occasionally but is rare (an exception is the example of Borderline Personality described in Chapter 14). In contrast with other subjects, however, Multiple Inner Experience was the rule, rather than the exception, among our bulimics: the frequency ranged from 40% to 100% within our individual bulimic subjects.

It was also the case that, for our bulimic subjects, the presence of Multiple Inner Experience was directly related to the degree of bulimic symptoms: the more actively bulimic the subject, the more multiple the inner experience. This was true both when considering the percentage of a subject's samples containing Multiple Inner Experience (the more actively bulimic, the higher the percentage) and also when considering the multiplicity of experience at any given sample (the more actively bulimic, the higher the number of separate experiences which were reported to be simultaneously occurring at any one beep).

The bulimic subjects experienced Multiple Inner Experience in various inner modalities. That is, many characteristics of inner experience, such as Feelings, Unsymbolized Thinkings, etc., may have been represented in a single sampled moment. It was not unusual for the subjects in Doucette's thesis to report a sample which included two simultaneous (Experienced) Unsymbolized Thoughts, a two-part Sensed Unsymbolized Thought, and two distinct Experienced Feelings, all occurring at the moment of one beep. Sometimes, as with Ashley (Chapter 8) and Christine (Chapter 9), much of the Multiple Inner Experience was in the form of Multiple Unsymbolized Thoughts. Ashley, for example, was aware of 10 to 20 separate (but usually related) simultaneous Unsymbolized Thought processes.

Multiple Feelings were reported by all our subjects. Ashley, for example, reported Multiple Feelings, usually three to seven separate, simultaneous Feelings, in almost all her samples.

SENSED AWARENESS

Another characteristic unique to our bulimic subjects was the phenomenon of Sensed Awareness. Four of our seven bulimic subjects, including Ashley and Christine, reported Sensed Unsymbolized Thinking or Sensed Feelings occurring at the moment of the beep, with frequencies ranging from 6% to 50%. As we have seen, Sensed Unsymbolized Thinking is the unsymbolized knowledge in current awareness that a thought is occurring, but the thought itself is not directly being experienced at the moment of the beep. Sometimes the thought itself seems to exist as if "parked," waiting to be "brought back out" and continued; sometimes the thought itself seems to be currently ongoing but is occurring outside of direct awareness. In either case, in current awareness there is an active, ongoing knowledge of the existence of the outside-of-awareness thought. Feelings could also be experienced as Sensed, in which case there was in awareness a knowledge at the moment of the beep that a Feeling was somehow occurring, but that Feeling itself was not part of that momentary awareness. Ashley also reported instances where visual phenomena were Sensed to be occurring. We group all forms together under the heading Sensed Awareness. The phenomenon of Sensed Awareness is, to our knowledge, unique to bulimics.

It was striking that our subjects spontaneously used similar descriptive metaphors to describe this process. Ashley referred to the "tails" of thoughts (or the tails of feelings), which were present in awareness, and were attached to the body of the thought which existed "under the rocks," that is, outside of awareness. Christine referred to "strings" that were attached to thoughts or feelings, which were in awareness while the thoughts or feelings themselves were outside of awareness.

This may give the reader a glimpse into the process of the descriptive sampling method. Our procedure is to allow each subject to describe her inner experience using her own vocabulary. We did not, for example, inquire of Christine (with whom we sampled after the study of Ashley had been completed) whether she experienced "tails" of thoughts; her description of "strings" emerged in her own attempts to explain her private experience to us. It was the authors, not the subjects, who created the term "Sensed Awareness" and applied it to those cases our subjects called tails or strings. We believe that this kind of confluence of similar, yet different, metaphors to describe a phenomenon can be taken as evidence that our interrogatory procedure does not unduly "lead the witness" into reporting a phenomenon which does not exist.

The occurrence of Sensed Awareness seemed to be related to the degree of bulimia: the four most actively bulimic subjects experienced Sensed Awareness, while the others did not. All subjects who experienced any Sensed Awareness reported both Sensed Unsymbolized Thinking and Sensed Feelings.

THOUGHT/FEELINGS

A third characteristic experienced by our bulimic subjects was the relatively blurred distinction between thought and feeling. Our bulimics frequently seemed to "think their feelings" or "feel their thoughts." By contrast, most normal subjects in our sampling were very clear about the distinction between thinking and feeling. Even on those occasions where they have difficulty providing the experiential details of a thought (as in Unsymbolized Thinking, for example), most nonbulimic subjects have no doubt that the thought is a "cognitive" or "mental" experience; the same is true for affective experiences. An exception is our anxious subjects (see Chapter 13), who also at times had difficulty distinguishing between affect and cognition.

This phenomenon led to our creating the Thought/Feeling category, describing moments where cognition and affect were experientially inseparable aspects of the same moment. Thought/Feelings were experienced by all our bulimic subjects, with frequencies ranging from 19% to 77% (median 40%).

The fact that bulimics (in this study, at least) often "think" their feelings and "feel" their thoughts might explain why some of these subjects were somewhat hesitant at first to *describe* their Feelings, despite the fact that they all were unequivocal about *experiencing* Feelings. For example, the subject who reported the largest proportion of Thought/Feelings stated on her first day of sampling that thinking and feeling were not separate experiences for her. By the end of sampling, she almost never had reported a "pure" Feeling, that is, an emotional experience which was not somehow fused with cognition. Instead, all her Feelings could be arranged on a continuum of Thought/Feelings, as her

Feelings always possessed some degree of cognition. Another example was Christine (Chapter 9), who stated that when she experienced what we call a Thought/Feeling, her mind seemed a little "fuddled."

INCONGRUENT BODILY AWARENESS

Bodily Awareness is the awareness of bodily sensations that do not have a particular emotional significance, such as pressure, pain, itching, tingling, bodily position, etc. Bodily Awareness is to be distinguished from Feelings, which may also have a bodily component, in that Feelings have a clear emotional significance while Bodily Awarenesses do not. Incongruent Bodily Awarenesses, where the awareness of the body did not mirror the subject's current actual body position or condition, were reported by three of our bulimic subjects (including Christine, Chapter 8), but only rarely, if at all, by our other subjects.

Christine and one of our other bulimic subjects both experienced Incongruent Bodily Awareness that consisted of a sense of "puffing up" or expansion of the body, even though such an expansion was not actually occurring. Christine was aware of this sense of puffiness in two samples. In both of these, the expansion was perceived to be in the areas of her body with which she was dissatisfied: thighs, upper arms, hips, and face.

An example of Incongruent Bodily Awareness reported by another subject was the experience of sitting sideways in front of the television set and having to turn her head to view the TV screen; in actuality, she was sitting *facing* the set and did not have to turn her head at all.

The previous section described the difficulty bulimic subjects had in distinguishing thought from Feeling; a similar difficulty occurred occasionally between thought and Bodily Awareness. For example, one subject reported that at the moment of the beep she was uncomfortable in her own skin, having a sensation that she was trapped inside it, unable to escape. However, her sensation was not located in her body, but in her *head*, although it was perceived as a "pushing out" or expansion of her *body against the skin*.

OTHER CHARACTERISTICS OF THE INNER EXPERIENCE OF THE BULIMIC SUBJECTS

The previous four sections described characteristics of our bulimics which were strikingly different from those of other groups we have sampled with. We note here additional characteristics which, while not unique to our bulimics, occurred at noteworthy frequencies.

Unsymbolized Thinking

Our bulimic subjects had very high frequencies of Unsymbolized Thinking, ranging from 36% to 92% of all of a subject's samples (median 76%). There was a strong relationship between the severity of bulimic symptoms and the frequency of Unsymbolized Thinking: the 36% frequency was from a subject who was not actively bingeing or purging during the sampling period; the remaining frequencies were all greater than 72%, with the highest two frequencies occurring in the individuals with the most severe bulimic symptoms.

There is considerable variability in the frequency of Unsymbolized Thinking in the normal subjects with whom we have sampled, ranging from 0% to more than 50%. As we have seen, depressed subjects report as much as 75% Unsymbolized Thinking. Anxious subjects reported Unsymbolized Thinking in about half of their samples, as we shall see in Chapter 13, and it was found in 36% of the samples of learning disabled subjects (Shamanek, 1991). The bulimic subjects therefore reported Unsymbolized Thinking about as often as our depressed subjects and more often than any of our other groups.

Inner Speech

Inner Speech was a relative rarity for our bulimic subjects, with the median only 6%. In comparison, Inner Speech occurs relatively frequently in normal subjects, but there are large individual differences, ranging from nearly 0% to nearly 100%; 21% of a group of adolescent subjects' samples included Inner Speech (Monson, 1989); anxious subjects' samples included 31% (see Chapter 13), and learning disabled subjects reported Inner Speech in 10% of their samples (Shamanek, 1991). Thus, bulimics have the lowest frequency of Inner Speech among any of the groups with whom we have sampled.

Most of our bulimic subjects reported the experience of Unsymbolized Thinking that "verged on" wordless Inner Speech, that is, which seemed almost to have some of the characteristics associated with speaking (e.g., a sense of rhythm, a sense of linearity, one bit after another, or a sense of voicing) but which did not include words *per se*. Furthermore, our healthiest bulimic subject, who was not actively bingeing or purging during the sampling period, had a relatively high frequency of Inner Speech (66%) but a relatively low (for our bulimic subjects) frequency of

Unsymbolized Thinking (38%), leading to the speculation that Inner Speech may transform into Unsymbolized Thinking as the symptoms of bulimia become more severe.

Feelings

Feelings, the experiencing of emotion with or without a bodily manifestation, were reported by all our bulimic subjects, and almost all our bulimic subjects at times experienced multiple Feelings. Our bulimic subjects reported Feelings extremely frequently; the median frequency was 71% for our bulimics. In contrast, Feelings are moderately infrequent in normal subjects, occurring in perhaps a quarter or less of samples, although there are large individual differences in this regard. Monson (1989) reported a 50% frequency of Feelings in her adolescent subjects; anxious subjects experienced Feelings in an average 55% of their samples (see Chapter 13); and learning disabled subjects experienced Feelings in about 70% of their samples (Shamanek, 1991). Thus, the experience of Feelings was more frequent for our bulimics than for any group sampled to date except the learning disabled group.

Normal subjects experience Feelings as differentiated phenomena that are generally understood to take place in the body, particularly in the chest. All our bulimic subjects, too, experienced Feelings that manifested themselves in their bodies, most often in the head and upper torso, but they also experienced Feelings as taking place in their arms, in the stomach, and other bodily areas.

It should be recalled that our bulimic subjects also frequently reported a fusion or confusion between cognition and affect, which has been described above in the section called Thought/Feelings.

Inner Visual Experience

All our bulimic subjects reported some instances of Inner Visual Experience. Such experiences ranged in color and clarity from clear, colorful Images, complete with detail, to blurry, indistinct Images that may or may not have been in color and where only some of the visual components could be described, to Indeterminate Visual Experiences, which were understood to be inner visualizations, but where, nonetheless, no visual characteristics of the Image were possible to specify.

At a median frequency of 34% across our bulimic subjects, the occurrence of Inner Visual experience seems to be somewhat higher than might be expected of normal subjects. However, our bulimic subjects reported more Indeterminate Visual Experience than they did Images, which sets them apart from normal subjects, who have very little Indeterminate Visual Experience. We shall see in Chapter 13 that anxious subjects also reported a high frequency of Indeterminate Inner Visual Experience, but other groups have reported low or zero frequencies of this phenomenon.

There are individual differences among our bulimics in this regard. Two of our bulimic subjects reported frequent Images and *no* Indeterminate Inner Visual Experience, while the other subjects reported at least as many Indeterminate Inner Visual Experiences as Images.

Four of our bulimics (including Ashley, Chapter 8, and Christine, Chapter 9) reported inner visual experiences where they were "scanning" a series of inner scenes as if to retrieve certain information. All the scenes were present in their awareness simultaneously, yet they were able to focus separately on each scene. Most of the normal subjects' Inner Visual Experience is quite simple by contrast, comprised of just one scene at any given sample.

Thoughts Relating to Bulimia

Bulimia is an eating disorder in which individuals are obsessed with food and their weight. How often did our subjects think about food, weight, eating, or purging?

All our subjects reported one or more thoughts about food at the moment of the beep; the median frequency of such thoughts was about 5%, and the highest frequency was 16%. Thus the actual frequency of thoughts related to bulimia was relatively low. It should be noted that across all our subjects in all our subject groups, the frequency of *any* content category is usually very low—in fact, 16% is a quite high content category frequency in our studies.

When our subjects did think about food, such thoughts were often accompanied by Feelings so strong that we were led to call them "Drives" for one of our subjects. For example, one of these Drives incorporated a strong need to taste the cake the subject was Imaging, complete with an Incongruent Bodily Awareness of salivating (which was not actually taking place).

Christine (Chapter 9) was the only bulimic subject who had thoughts about her weight at the moment of the beep. Two of her samples involved a perception of "puffing up," discussed earlier in the section on Incongruent Bodily Awareness.

Ashley (Chapter 8) was asked specifically to sample on a day when she thought that she was likely to purge. On that day, Ashley experienced Multiple (Experienced) Unsymbolized Thoughts—she called it a "funnel" of thoughts—that incorporated the possibility of choice over whether to vomit. Also present to her awareness were two Sensed thoughts, vestiges of thoughts that had been the explicit focus of her attention a moment before, as well as an Indeterminate Visual Experience of a hot dog. A number of Feelings, including a drive to throw up, loneliness, and emptiness were strong characteristics of Ashley's sampled moment. Thus the intensity of the urge to purge seemed more related to the heightened multiplicity of thoughts and feelings than to the content of food or weight.

DISCUSSION

Bulimia was not introduced as a separate nosological entity until 1980, when it was classified in DSM-III-R. In 1987, the American Psychiatric Association renamed the disorder "bulimia nervosa" and, for the first time, provided clear-cut, unambiguous diagnostic criteria.

To date, there are very few studies which investigate directly the inner experience of bulimics. We can, however, compare our results with those other existing reports.

Brouwers (1988) used a rationalistic cognitive approach to identify typical thought content among bulimic female college students. She found that, because many women with bulimia engage in an "all or nothing" type of circular thinking (Lacey, 1982; Russell, 1979), their thoughts often become jumbled, leading to chronic indecision. Our own research corroborates this observation if we can accept the premise that the Multiple thoughts reported by our subjects at many samples correspond to the phenomenon Brouwers called "jumbled" thinking. Most of our own subjects described, before sampling began, their own thinking as being in some way jumbled, and a few had some awareness that there were simultaneous processes populating their inner experience. It was only after sampling and discussing repeated samples that our subjects became confident of the extent of the multiplicity of their inner experience. Thus we are led to conclude that Brouwers' "jumbled" thinking is the way bulimics view their thinking retrospectively, and that this phenomenon becomes refined into Multiple experience when viewed one moment at a time by our sampling technique.

Observers (Garner et al., 1985; Gordon, 1990) have noted that bulimics are emotionally turbulent, and our observations about Feelings support this report. Our bulimics experienced Feelings far more often than did the normal population, and all the bulimic subjects reported Multiple Feelings. Furthermore, our bulimic subjects appeared to be somewhat confused about their Feelings: they often confused thinking and Feeling, sometimes thinking their Feelings or feeling their thoughts. It could be speculated that bulimics are not easily able to separate their emotions from their cognitions and thus, they find their emotions unduly distressing, which in turn cues them to binge.

Casper, Eckert, et al. (1980), among others, reported that bulimics do not overeat just to ease hunger sensations, but also to relieve distressing emotions (Elmore & de Castro, 1990), which generally agrees with Brouwers' (1988) observation that bulimics are often unable to express intense, painful emotions, and binge to numb themselves from feeling. Our subjects did not actually have a high frequency of thoughts about food, and it did seem to be the case, especially with Ashley, that the urge to purge was more associated with a "funnel" of thoughts and emotions than with hunger *per se*.

Bulimics are reported to hold a more negative view of themselves and others; to possess a more helpless, hopeless world view; and to have a generally bleaker outlook on life than nonbulimic individuals (Butterfield & Leclair, 1988), as well as to have a depressogenic style of cognitive processing (Dritschel, Williams, & Cooper, 1991). Our study supported this view: our subjects reported a considerably greater proportion of negative Feelings than of positive ones.

Many researchers have concluded that bulimic individuals tend to be depressed (e.g., Garfinkel et al., 1980). My impression was that our bulimics were not particularly depressed during the sampling period, but they did have a very high frequency of Unsymbolized Thinking, as do depressed subjects (see Chapter 7). Rather than depression, our bulimic subjects were more likely to report active emotions, such as anger, frustration, tension, stress and anxiety as Feelings in their inner experience.

Casper and her associates (1980) and Brouwers (1988) reported that bulimics are more aware of bodily functions and have more somatic complaints than does the general population. Indeed, our own bulimic subjects reported experiencing more Bodily Awareness than do other populations sampled using this method. Perhaps this was because they were more aware of their physical selves than they were of their psychological selves.

Many researchers (see, for example, Farley, 1986; Hsu & Sobkiewicz, 1991) have reported that bulimics have a body image distortion, and our research supports this to some extent. Our subjects reported several Incongruent Bodily Awarenesses, imaginal awarenesses of body and bodily processes that do not reflect the body's actual condition. The sample in Chapter 8 from our subject Christine, where she reported a "puffing up" bodily sensation, seems strikingly like that of Gordon's

(1990) patient who felt victimized by a "pumping mechanism" that made her "balloon up." However, the Incongruent Body Awareness phenomenon was far from widespread in our subjects.

It has often been observed that eating-disordered individuals (and their families) do not know how to explore and share their inner experience (Gordon, 1990). Our sampling confirmed that observation. Most of our subjects were initially unaware of and then had difficulty describing their multiple experiences, and they were often initially reluctant to describe Feelings because of the unclear distinction between thinking and feeling.

Thus it may be said that our own observations generally support those of researchers who used other methods (primarily clinical observation and retrospective reports). Our own research must be acknowledged to be preliminary, based as it is on a sample of only seven bulimics, who were not chosen randomly. However, the promise of this method for illuminating our understanding of bulimia seems great. For example, that all our subjects shared the characteristic of multiplicity of inner experience at high frequencies leaves little room for doubt that this is an important characteristic of many, if not all, bulimic individuals, and this feature alone provides an important insight into the bulimic's inner world. The persistence of multiple thoughts and feelings, as many as 10 or 20 at a time, all simultaneously present in awareness seems to be a major refinement of Brouwers' (1988) retrospective observation that bulimics experience "jumbled" thinking. The Multiplicity observation seems to be an explanation for this jumbled thinking, and gives some hints as to the direction therapy might take. More research is clearly needed.

III

Anxiety

The two chapters that follow present sketches of the inner experience of two individuals for whom anxiety was a serious problem. These two individuals were included among the five subjects in the Masters Thesis of Judith Hebert at the University of Nevada, Las Vegas. Chapter 13 makes some general observations about this sample of five individuals. We should note that there are many different kinds of anxiety disorders, ranging from generalized anxiety to phobias to panic; we have as yet made no attempt to select systematically subjects from within this large range. We merely provide some glimpses into it.

A Biology Student with Panic Attacks

Judith Hebert and RTH

"Nancy" was a 36-year-old female biology student who had a history of anxiety attacks for which she had no explanation. These attacks were sufficiently severe that her husband had had to call paramedics to their home in the middle of the night because she believed she was going into cardiac arrest. She had seen several physicians and psychologists for these attacks, but had never been seen on an inpatient basis.

Nancy sampled on 5 separate days over a 3-week period, collecting and discussing 28 samples. We will describe five major characteristics of her inner experience during these samples.

UNSYMBOLIZED THINKING

The experience of Unsymbolized Thinking occurred for Nancy in 15 (54%) of her 28 samples. Nancy's Unsymbolized Thoughts were quite similar to the other Unsymbolized Thoughts described in this book: discrete, differentiated thoughts whose meanings and content were easily understood but which did not include words, images, or any other symbols.

For example, in Sample #25 Nancy was sitting at the table drinking coffee. She had been reading an article on Gathris, the biologist, and at

This and the following two chapters are part of the first author's Masters Thesis in the Department of Psychology, University of Nevada, Las Vegas.

the moment of the beep she was looking directly at his picture above the article in front of her on the table. As she looked at the picture she was Unsymbolized Thinking that he had a kind face. This was clearly a thought, an inner comment on the picture (as opposed to a mere recognition of a kindly face, for example), but there were no words which carried this meaning. She was not sure how the thought was processed in her inner experience, only that she "knew" the meaning. The Unsymbolized Thinking just seemed to occur while she was looking at the picture, and was her main focus at the moment of the beep. A secondary focus of attention at this beep was on a sensation of warmth in her mouth and tongue from the coffee she had just swallowed. She described this warmth as a "glowy" sensation.

Occasionally, Unsymbolized Thinking occurred as part of a complex, multiple-level inner experience, as in Sample #27. Nancy was watching the TV news and had just heard the words, "Are you worried about becoming a victim of crime?" At the moment of the beep she was muttering to herself in a barely audible out-loud voice, "Definitely!" She was aware that three newscasters were still talking on TV at the moment of the beep, but she was not listening to them and had shut out the sound of their voices from her inner experience. Furthermore, she was not really paying attention to the details of the picture on the TV screen, although she was staring at it. Her attention was focused on a quick series of "jumbled" Unsymbolized Thoughts about the high percentage of crime, the different types of crime in the United States, the number of people assaulted each year, and the percentages of each type of crime reported annually. She was not sure whether these thoughts were indeed simultaneous or whether they were sequential and overlapping, but she was confident that a jumble of discrete, separate thoughts were occurring. Simultaneous with this jumble of Unsymbolized Thoughts was an Indeterminate Inner Visual Experience (see below), a brief, incomplete seeing of a table of percentages. This was experienced as a "quick flash" of a chart showing percentages in blocks or groups on a royal blue background, but with no visual detail available to awareness. She was not sure if the blue background was part of her inner visual experience or if it was part of the background from the TV screen; however, she was sure the percentages and blocks were a part of the seeing in her inner experience.

FEELINGS

Nancy was aware of emotional experience in 17 (61%) of the 28 samples collected. She experienced such Feelings as excitement, anxiety, discomfort, confusion, and panic. At times she was able to describe these experiences in detail, but more frequently she was unable to differ- entiate clearly the aspects of her experience.

For example, in Sample #14 Nancy was reading her lecture notes, looking directly at the term "Ambyptin," a species of salamanders. In the center of her awareness was a Feeling of confusion, but even though it was the main aspect of her awareness she had difficulty describing this Feeling. It was quite clearly *not* a thought, either in words or Unsym- bolized, but it was also not clearly a bodily process either. She resorted to metaphors to describe this experience: she wanted to "pull down the shutters and not deal with the confusion"; it was as if she "could see a light or whiteness on the paper in front of her"; it was "as though there was a blank there, as if a blank page had been substituted for the real page," but she was unsure if this was an actual inner seeing. It was an awareness that what she was seeing in her notes did not correspond with the information she had gotten from the class lecture. She was also mildly aware of having cold feet. They were somewhat numb, but this was clearly a secondary focus to the confused Feeling.

The Feeling of relief was experienced by Nancy as a "lack of sensa- tion" in Sample #5. Nancy was listening to her husband who was telling her that he had visited the doctor and his blood pressure was OK. She was Feeling concern for him, which was experienced as a calmness in her body. She described this Feeling as a recognition of relief in that there was a lack of tension in her body as she listened to him. Thus this Feeling was not the direct awareness of calmness (or any other direct bodily aspect), but was rather the recognition of the *absence* of any bodily process. At the same time as he was speaking and she was recognizing her relief, she was also actively trying to attend to the meaning of what he was saying, purposefully concentrating on his talking but not focus- ing on his exact words or hearing exactly what he was saying. She was not aware of the exact words he was speaking but was actively trying to understand (an example of the "Doing" of Understanding which we will describe below). During this beep, Nancy was sitting sideways at the table facing her husband, who occupied her visual field, but her focus was not on his visual presence. The TV was on and although she was aware of this, she was not really taking in the sound of the TV.

Thought/Feelings

In the two examples of Feelings which we have just described, Nancy's Feelings had a distinctly "unbodily" presence which was char- acteristic of most of her Feeling experiences. By contrast, when Nancy felt panic, which she did on 7 (25%) occasions, it involved a clearly

Somatically-oriented awareness of her stomach, which was "flipping," "churning," or had "butterflies."[2] Furthermore, there was a mental aspect to this panic, a cognitive awareness directly tied to the bodily awareness, not experienced as a specific mental event such as Unsymbolized Thinking. Thus we refer to the anxiety experiences as Thought/Feelings (similar to those experienced by Christine in Chapter 9).

For example, in Sample #13, Nancy was studying, and having a Thought/Feeling of panic which took place in part as a "fresh flip" of her stomach, that is, her stomach seemed to have "just turned over." This flip had started in her stomach and went down both her legs on the outside, as far as midthigh. There was no constant sensation of churning; in fact, the flip had passed, but she still felt weak in some way as the panicky sensation quickly passed down her body. This panicky Thought/Feeling also took place as a mental awareness that she was not getting through the material she was studying. This awareness was a mental process which was not a thought but was more like a recognition that went along with the bodily panic. She was unaware of anything she was doing at the beep as the panicky Thought/Feeling was her entire focus at that moment.

Another panic Thought/Feeling was at Sample #9 where Nancy was studying and was aware of a "fluctuating feeling of panic" whose bodily aspect was in her stomach near her rib cage. Her stomach was churning, and there was again a "freshly flipped over" sensation. This sensation occurred in one big, quick wave inside her stomach, which was similar to sample #13 (described in the previous paragraph). However, in other samples panic was experienced as a more constant, "butterfly-like" sensation. At the same time she had a mental sense of not learning the material. This mental sense was not a thought, not even an Unsymbolized Thought, but was a fast and automatic recognition, parallel with the bodily panic. The panicky bodily awareness and the awareness of not getting through the material were equal, simultaneous, but separate components of this single Thought/Feeling. At the same time, she was looking at the names on the page in front of her, not really reading the words as a unit but taking them into her awareness very

---

[2]Because stomach flips occurred so frequently (7 of 28 samples) during Nancy's sampling, we asked Nancy, after the sampling research was completed, to wear the beeper again and, instead of writing down her experience at the moment of the beep, simply to note whether or not she was experiencing a stomach flip at that moment. She responded to 48 beeps in this way, and reported experiencing a stomach flip during 9 of them (19% compared to 25% in the original sampling period). This corroborated the fact that stomach flips were a frequent aspect of her experience.

quickly, individually, as though "reaching out" in an attempt to make the categories more concrete in her mind.

Thus, even when emotions had a clearly bodily focus, there was still a portion of the Thought/Feeling process which seemed to be mental, but which *was not* experienced as a thought. This blurring of the distinction between feeling and cognition was also apparent in Sample #10, where Nancy was reading her biology text, and was aware of an excited, uneasy sensation in her stomach. This physical sensation was not as unpleasant as the churning described in Sample #9 above, but was instead a very slight "rush" in the same area. Simultaneous with this bodily awareness, Nancy was also cognitively aware of a sense of achievement, an excited recognition that she was finally getting the content of her studies and was taking in the information more easily. She was reading the material on the page, and although she was reading word for word, it was as though she were reaching out and trying to take into her awareness the full meaning of the text all at once. This reading process then was an example of the "Doing" of Understanding described below.

INNER VISUAL EXPERIENCE

Nancy was aware of inner visual experience in 10 (36%) of the 28 samples collected. There was a continuum of clarity of these visual experiences, ranging from clear and colorful Images (3 of the 10 visual experiences) to the phenomenon we are calling Indeterminate Inner Visual Experience (7 of the 10). Images were inner seeings which were detailed and immediately available to Nancy, and which could be described quite easily. At the other end of the continuum, Indeterminate Inner Visual Experiences were inner perceptions which were in some way visual but in which the inner seeing itself was not clear: objects were "sensed" or "known" to be visually present; colors were "known" to exist in a visual way but were not actually seen in inner experience, etc.

Images

Images were present as clear, vivid, and colorful flashes of visual experience which were very easy for Nancy to describe. The details were available to her and she was aware of the presence of a snapshot-like picture. One of the most vivid Images Nancy experienced was at Sample #19. At the moment of the beep Nancy was reading a psychology text about facial expressions that denote anger in humans and animals. The beep took place just as her eyes were looking directly at the word "angry." At the same time she saw in inner experience a distinct, colorful, three-dimensional Image of a chimpanzee. The Image was of the chimpanzee's face, neck, and shoulders, with no background or border around the Image. The chimpanzee was baring its teeth as though anger were being displayed. The color in the Image was realistic, black with pink on the face and white teeth. The focus of the Image was on the chimpanzee's face, very close up, in particular on the mouth which was moving. The background of the Image was dark and fuzzy; she could not see beyond the head and shoulders, and she described the Image as being "constrained" in some way, as if the visual field had only a limited extent despite the lack of definite edges. The experience of this Image took place as though the Image of the chimpanzee were just behind Nancy's forehead, being viewed from a point higher in her head, near the top between her temples, looking forward and down at the forehead-image area. The experience took place inside her forehead, but somehow the Image seemed to be outside her physical body. In describing this experience, Nancy was struck by the clarity of the Image.

Another clear Image was accompanied by Unsymbolized Thinking. In Sample #26, Nancy was watching the local TV news and was seeing a man from the fire department talking about the hazards of above-ground fuel tanks. Nancy was attentively listening and watching the man on the TV screen. As she watched and listened, she had an Unsymbolized Thought that his hair looked like indoor-outdoor carpet. This thought was not in specific words, but was "just there in her mind." At the same moment she was aware of an Image of her glass reptile tanks which in fact had indoor-outdoor carpet on their floors. She could see the broad side of the empty tanks, the clear glass walls, and the green carpet on the bottom. Prior to the beep she was aware of experiencing a smile crossing her face as the indoor-outdoor carpet/hair idea had begun, and at the moment of the beep she was aware that the smile was still there. It was as if she had no control over the smile; it was happening all by itself. Thus, at the moment of the beep, Nancy was aware of four experiences simultaneously: (1) the visual seeing in reality of the man on TV; (2) the Unsymbolized Thinking that his hair looked like indoor-outdoor carpet; (3) the Image of the reptile tanks and the carpet inside them; and (4) the awareness of the smile on her face.

Indeterminate Inner Visual Experience

Six of Nancy's 10 visual experiences were less concrete and vivid; these experiences were understood to be visualizations but the things seen lacked detail and clarity. Thus these were Indeterminate Inner Visual Experiences. In Sample #8 Nancy was studying, looking at a textbook page showing charts of species of frogs. However, her awareness was divided between an uneasiness in her stomach (like butterflies or a tight knot around her stomach area, directly above the abdomen near her rib cage, and close to the surface), and thinking about how many pages she had left to read. This thought involved saying out loud to herself the words, "Am I finally getting to the end of this?" and an Indeterminate Inner Visual Experience of the number "2" or "3." The speaking aloud was experienced as if the words just came out automatically, with no real thought or direction; this is part of the phenomenon we will describe as the "Happening" of speaking below. The Indeterminate Inner Visual Experience involved a visual apprehending of the numeral "2," or possibly "3," visually apprehended to be in her own handwriting in black on lined white paper. However, she was not confident of the visual details, even to the extent that she was not sure whether the number seen was "2" or "3." She was, she said, somehow visually aware of the numbers, as if she were seeing-but-not-really-seeing them, but instead just knowing their visual characteristics. Perhaps the blackness of the letters and the lines on the paper were just known to be present rather than seen in inner experience. At the same time she was also aware of the sound of her husband scribbling on something. The sound was like a dull pencil on paper, a rubbing and scraping sound, and was more in the background of her experience.

THE "DOING" OF UNDERSTANDING

In 8 (29%) of the 28 samples collected, Nancy experienced an active grasping or reaching out for the meaning or content of what she was reading, hearing, or what was going on in the world around her. At times this involved a straining to attend to one type of information while actively attempting to block out other information that was distracting her.

We have encountered two examples already. In Sample #5, described above in the section on Feelings, Nancy was listening to her husband tell her about his doctor's visit and satisfactory blood pressure. The aspect we would like to highlight here is that this listening was *not* just a spontaneous receiving of her husband's meaning, but was instead a conscious, deliberate, active reaching out to grasp this meaning. We refer to this active reaching out as the "Doing" of Understanding to highlight the fact that this is not simply the receiving of information, but instead was an active, effortful "Doing" in a directed, purposeful attempt to grasp the meaning of her husband's words.

Most of our non-anxious subjects report that their understandings of conversation, reading, social situations, etc., are spontaneous phenomena which simply occur, unasked for and unaided; for example, the meaning of a friend's words in a conversation is immediately apparent without any effort on the listener's part. Nancy, by contrast, seemed to need to "try" to understand, to "work at" focusing her attention, to aim herself actively at the meaning of words she heard or read.

The second example we have already encountered was Sample #10, described in the Thought/Feelings section above. There, Nancy was reading her Biology text, and rather than simply absorbing the meaning of the sentence, she was actively reaching out toward the meaning, ignoring the individual words in her effortful aim at the meaning.

The experience of straining to attend actively to what she was hearing was also seen in Sample #7, where at the moment of the beep, Nancy was in the middle of feeding her reptiles in their cages and was listening to the TV news. This listening to the news involved an active concentration on attending as she strained to hear the sound of the TV from the other room. Her main awareness was in the straining and the effort necessary to attend to and recognize what she was hearing. She was also secondarily aware of the color of the pink food in which she had her hands placed. She was dividing the food onto plates, but her visual awareness was of taking in only the color of the food. The dividing of the food was automatic and required no thought.

The "Doing" of Understanding was unsuccessful at Sample #1. Nancy was sitting in bed studying, and her cat was walking across her stomach, directly between herself and the book she was studying. She was aware of actively trying to look at the book, and could see the photograph and writing underneath the photograph, just above the cat's body. At the same time she was aware of the consistent rattling sound of air blowing through the air conditioning vents, distracting her from concentrating on the reading. This awareness was like an annoyance, not felt in her body, but more an awareness that she could not tune out the rattling sound. She was aware of trying, unsuccessfully, to concentrate on the meaning of what she was reading while actively trying to exclude the cat's body and the rustling of the air.

Another example of the "Doing" of Understanding while reading was Sample #17. Nancy was reading an article which discussed using the parent as a therapeutic agent. She was engrossed in this and was rereading a sentence on psychotherapy, actively trying to take in the meaning of the sentence. She was aware of the print on the page, but was not focused on any one word. She was much more aware of actively analyzing and grasping the content of the sentence as she reread it.

There were also present a number of Unsymbolized Thinkings: Why were the authors giving parents psychotherapy? What was the parent's role? These Unsymbolized Thoughts were not clear, as if scrambled, and also seemed to include an Indeterminate Inner Visual Experience with no detail whatsoever. It was as if she were trying to figure out the meaning of the sentence through Unsymbolized Thoughts and Indeterminate Inner Visual Experience. The entire process was jumbled, and it was as if she were trying to unscramble something.

THE "HAPPENING" OF SPEAKING

Nancy had one example (Sample #8, described in the section on Indeterminate Inner Visual Experience) of the phenomenon we call the "Happening" of Speaking, where inner or spoken words just seem to roll out unguided. In that sample, Nancy was studying, feeling uneasy, and wondering how much studying she had left. Part of this complex experience involved her saying out loud to herself the words, "Am I finally getting to the end of this?" These words just seemed to occur, with no sense of being directed by her; the words just seemed to "Happen." This is in contrast to the way our more typical subjects experience speaking, whether aloud or in Inner Speech: people generally report that they sense that they control their speaking, not in a premeditated way, but that they are the active author of their own speech. In Nancy's Sample #8, however, the words just occurred, unbidden.

CRITICAL OF SELF/OTHERS

The characteristics of inner experience we have described in Hurlburt (1990) and elsewhere in the present book can for the most part be considered "process" characteristics, features of the *how* of inner experience. When we began this research years ago, we had no intention of focusing on process characteristics; it just so happened that the salient features which emerged from subjects' reports usually were aspects of process. A "content" category, describing the *about what* of inner experience, emerged for Nancy as well as for our other anxious subjects (see Chapters 12 and 13). This category, which we call Critical of Self/Others, includes moments in which Nancy was critical or judgmental about the way she was studying, her lack of ability to memorize, or of the material she was reading. Such content was characteristic of 6 (21%) of the 28 samples she collected.

One example of this characteristic occurred in Sample #18, where Nancy was reading her psychology homework assignment. At the moment of the beep, Nancy was aware of being confused about the information she was reading on inter-observer agreement. She was Unsymbolized Thinking about the parent and the observer not agreeing in a particular study. There were no specific words or images in this Unsymbolized Thought, but if it were to be put into words it might be something like, 'Either a person is speaking or he is not. That's stupid! Psychologists should be able to figure it out.' The "that's stupid" and "psychologists should be able . . ." content of this though is, of course, the portion we are calling Critical of Self/Others. She described this thought as being kind of "rolled up," where its entire content seemed to occur at one time and as one presence. This jumbled thought process seemed to take place at the top of her head, near the front. She was also aware of hearing her husband talking on the phone in the next room. She described this as being an irritant that she was trying (unsuccessfully) to shut out; thus this was an aspect of the "Doing" of Understanding of her homework—she was actively trying to concentrate and bring in its meaning while at the same time trying to exclude the extraneous sounds. She was also aware of a background Thought/Feeling of irritation caused by the sound. She described this irritation as being very mild and like a "small percentage of a thought"; that is, this Thought/Feeling was somehow present in her head, but not in her body.

Another example of the Critical of Self/Others content was in Sample #21, where Nancy was reading and was simultaneously cognizant of having misinterpreted a passage she had just read. This cognitive awareness was more a recognition than a thought. The point we are highlighting here is that this awareness involved an explicit cognitive judgment about herself. That is, rather than merely going back to the passage and rereading it, Nancy was cognitively *commenting* on her reading process. This judgment was accompanied by a mildly irritated Feeling which was secondary in her awareness. She was not sure how this Feeling took place, only that she "knew" it was there. A more prominent Feeling at the moment of the beep was a slight Feeling of panic—a tickling, irritating, unpleasant butterfly-like sensation in her abdomen near the rib cage. The doorbell had startled her a few minutes before the beep and her stomach had strongly "flipped over"; now this flip was "coming down" or subsiding.

These samples indicate how strongly the irritation and annoyance was experienced during the Critical of Self/Others experience. All of the samples which included stomach flips also included some kind of Criticism.

DISCUSSION

Nancy reported the occurrence of Inner Speech during one of her samples. This single observation assures us that she was quite capable of reporting Inner Speech if it occurred, so we can be confident that Inner Speech was *not* a frequent phenomenon for her.

We shall see in Chapter 13 that Nancy's descriptions of Feelings, Indeterminate Inner Visual Experience, and the "Doing" of Understanding and "Happening" of Speaking were quite similar to those of our other anxious subjects.

A Graduate Student with Test Anxiety

RTH and Judith Hebert

"Jean" was a 40-year-old graduate student who described herself as having frequent, severe test anxiety, and who could be observed in class becoming breathless and flushed, talking rapidly and incessantly about upcoming tests. Jean also experienced difficulty when presenting talks in class, reading her reports word for word rather than presenting the material more informally, due to performance anxiety and her fear of being embarrassed if she lost her place during the presentation. She reported having experienced test anxiety since graduating from high school, worried continuously about getting through her undergraduate program, and sometimes panicked when thinking about the amount of work and testing she had to encounter during the graduate program.

Jean was a subject for a training seminar in the descriptive experience sampling method, where three graduate students who were learning the sampling techniques, along with the senior author, conducted the sampling interviews as a group.

Eight salient characteristics of Jean's inner experience emerged from the sampling, and we will describe each in turn: Inner Speech, Worded Thinking, Unsymbolized Thinking, Feelings, Indeterminate Inner Visual Experience, Rumination, the "Doing" of Understanding and the "Happening" of Speaking, and Critical of Self/Others.

INNER SPEECH

Jean described herself as "talking to herself" in 9 (36%) of her 25 samples. This experience was as though she were speaking words aloud in her own voice, complete with her own natural inflection and rhythm, although no sound or movement was experienced. She was unequivocal about this Inner Speech in most cases and could describe it in detail.

For instance, in Sample #11, Jean was thinking, "Oh, this beeper isn't working," at the moment of the beep. These inner words were spoken naturally in her own inner voice, and Jean was also aware of listening to herself speak these words. There seemed to be an effort involved in listening to the words, although there did *not* seem to be effort involved in the *speaking* of them—it was as though the words spoken "just happened" (see the section on The Doing of Understanding and the Happening of Speaking below).

Sometimes Jean was mulling over the words she was saying in Inner Speech, a phenomenon she called "Ruminating" (described below). For instance, in Sample #3, Jean was driving and had stopped at a
→ traffic light. She was saying over and over to herself in Inner Speech, in her own naturally inflected voice, "Do I want WordPerfect or is Mac-Write good enough? . . . Do I want WordPerfect or is MacWrite good enough?" This Inner Speaking was mentally exhausting for Jean, requiring deliberate strenuous mental effort to attach meaning to the words as they were being heard as well as spoken. This was in contrast to the Inner Speaking in Sample #11, where the words were effortless and seemed to "just happen" with no mental energy spent in Inner Speech.

WORDED THINKING

There were 6 times (24%) where Jean was thinking in words at the moment of the beep, but these words were not being spoken, heard, or "voiced" in any way. She described this as having an "essence of a perception" in that the words were "just there" in her mind, clearly noticeable, but as verbal presences devoid of production or perception; we call this phenomenon Worded Thinking.

In Sample #6, for example, Jean was writing a sentence in longhand and experiencing the word "emphasis" while writing that word. The word was "in her brain" at the time of the beep, not spoken, heard or seen; it was "just there." The experience of the word was not creative or active, but seemed to be located across the front of Jean's head, inside her brain.

Worded Thinking was also one part of Jean's experience at Sample #23, where Jean apprehended three separate thinking experiences all apparently occurring simultaneously. Jean was driving to pick up her children after school. She saw a basketball hoop on a house she was passing, and was Worded Thinking "basketball hoop" as the beep signalled. Those words were "just there" as two distinct words, not being said or heard. At the same time, Jean was Unsymbolized Thinking a thought that, while nonverbal, might be expressed by the words, "I wonder if Rob feels shafted because he never got a basketball hoop installed at this new house; it was promised to him two different times." Also at the same time was another Unsymbolized Thinking, which if put into words might be, "He'll probably have one installed as soon as his son is born—probably while he's still in the hospital."

Jean described these seemingly separate inner experiences as occurring at the same time, but also as quickly coming close together, one after the other. It was impossible for her to rule out the possibility of these thoughts being rapidly sequential, even though they seemed simultaneous. Each of the three thoughts was present as a whole in its entirety, not as sequential strings of words. The "It was promised to him" Unsymbolized Thought was experienced to be different from the others; it required some effort and it somehow seemed to "come inward" more than the others. Accompanying the Unsymbolized Thinking of "He'll probably have one installed . . ." Jean Felt anger, which she described as "like a tension" in her jaw, which at the same time she understood to be anger at Rob's father for not installing the basketball hoop.

Sometimes Worded Thinking was described as "verging on visual" thinking. For example, in Sample #12, Jean was looking at the word "Ditropan" on the label of an old pill bottle. She was looking at the word and actually trying to memorize it, as she wanted to go downstairs and look the drug up in her textbook. At the moment of the beep, Jean was looking at the actual word, "Ditropan," written on the pill bottle, and was also aware of the separate presence of the word inside her head, "just there," behind her forehead. Jean did not see the word in her inner experience, but it seemed to have some visual characteristics. Thus she was aware of the configuration of the in-her-head word: Capital D, lower case i, lower case t, etc. Although Jean did not see the inner word, she was aware of what it looked like. She knew the visual details of the letters without actually seeing or imaging them. Thus this experience could almost be called an Indeterminate Inner Visual Experience (see below) at the most indeterminate end of that continuum.

Just as there were times when Worded Thinking seemed to be almost visual, there also were times when Worded Thinking was almost Inner Speech. She described these experiences as a "saying" of the words, but was not sure whether or not she actually produced or heard inner words. For example, at Sample #16, Jean was reading a scientific report when the beeper signalled. At the moment of the beep, she was saying the words "literacy scores" to herself as she read them. Although she was clearly "saying" the words at the moment of the beep, she could not unequivocally say that she had the sense of creating those words, which is the hallmark of Inner Speech. At the same time as she was saying these words to herself, Jean was also saying to herself, "I'm confused. Is it my fault, or is it poorly written?" Again, this "saying" seemed to lack the clear sense of articulation that characterized Jean's other occurrences of Inner Speech although she could not say that the sense of articulation was clearly absent, either. These "sayings" seemed to be somewhere in between Worded Thinking and Inner Speech.

These two "sayings" appeared to occur simultaneously, but Jean experienced them quite differently since they seemed to involve an unequal amount of Effort. The speaking of "I'm confused . . ." seemed somewhat more central to Jean's awareness than the speaking of "literacy scores," and it took less effort to say those words. Paradoxically, the "I'm confused", while taking less effort, also seemed to consume more energy. Jean said that the Inner Speaking of "I'm confused . . ." was exhausting, because it had meaning attached to it, requiring her attention, whereas "literacy scores" did not. Jean was certain that she was having these seemingly separate inner experiences at precisely the same time. She described it as having her brain full of both thoughts.

UNSYMBOLIZED THINKING

Jean was engaged in Unsymbolized Thinking, where she experienced detailed thoughts with no words or images involved, in 6 (24%) of her 25 samples. In these samples, Jean knew what she was thinking, and could describe the specific details of the momentary thought even though she could not describe how that thought took place. Despite her lack of ability to describe how she knew the contents of her inner experience at the moment of the beep, these experiences were nevertheless "concrete" for Jean. That is, Unsymbolized Thoughts were equally as "real" to her as those inner experiences which had definite inner perceptual characteristics. These Unsymbolized Thoughts were described as being "just there," "in my brain," or "just thoughts."

We have described two examples of Unsymbolized Thinking above, the "it was promised to him" and "he'll probably have one installed" simultaneous thoughts from the basketball hoop Sample #23 (see the section on Worded Thinking above). Sample #21 was a simpler example. Jean was reading the words "instantly go back," and possibly (she was not sure) saying them in Inner Speech as she read them. At the same moment she was Unsymbolized Thinking about what she referred to as "old tapes," recurrent unpleasant memories from childhood or background. This Unsymbolized Thinking consisted of wondering what was going to happen to her own "old tapes" as well as her thinking about those tapes themselves. This Unsymbolized Thinking seemed to occur quickly, and its entire meaning was available all at once, rather than sequentially or word for word. All these aspects of the thoughts were "just there" at the same time. The Unsymbolized Thinking seemed to take away her concentration from reading the words "instantly go back," and the process was somewhat exhausting to Jean (although not as exhausting as in other samples).

FEELINGS

Jean was aware of emotional experience in 9 (36%) of the 25 samples. She was usually unable to give many details of her perception of Feelings, and frequently experienced Thought/Feelings, where she was uncertain about the distinction between feeling and thinking.

A rather typical example of Jean's Feeling was the anger in the basketball hoop sample (#23), described above in the section on Worded Thinking. Her anger over the basketball hoop included the experience of tension in the region of her jaw, but additional details could not be supplied.

An example of her Thought/Feelings was Sample #7, where Jean was saying to herself in Inner Speech, "Today is not a good day," words which seemed to be occurring in her own voice in a region inside the entire area of her forehead. At the same time, she was Unsymbolized Thinking a Self-Critical thought that she was not performing the sampling research adequately. This Unsymbolized Thinking repeated itself over and over, an exhausting example of Rumination as described below. Also present at this beep was a Thought/Feeling of frustration, which, like the ongoing thoughts, seemed to be deep inside her head, inside the entire space of her forehead. Jean stated that she was angry and disappointed that she could not do the task properly, and the frustrated Thought/Feeling was as much a knowing that she was frustrated as it was an actual emotion of frustration. Jean could not give additional details of how this frustration was experienced, and became rather unsure of herself when we asked her for those details. Maybe it was just a thought about being frustrated, rather than a feeling, she said, but she could not supply the content of such a thought.

While this phenomenon was difficult for her to describe, we note that it was distinctly *unlike* Jean's (and other subjects') Unsymbolized Thinking, where the content was clear even though the perceptual details were absent, and also different from the fact that most subjects experience Feelings as existing somewhere in the trunk of the body.

We might note in passing that Jean said both before and at the conclusion of her participation in the sampling study that she was *never* angry. She made this claim quite emphatically despite having described to us in detail during the sampling interviews several samples in which anger was a prominent feature. This general denial of the presence of anger was also seen in several of our other anxious subjects.[1]

INDETERMINATE INNER VISUAL EXPERIENCE

Jean experienced no clear visual Images in any of the 25 samples. There were 5 occasions (20% of the 25 samples) where Jean's inner experience seemed to be somehow visual even though she was not sure that there was either a visual image or a clear sense of seeing. This phenomenon involved an apprehension or knowledge about the visual characteristics of an object, even though that object itself was not unequivocally visually present to inner experience. These are Indeterminate Inner Visual Experiences: She "thought she saw" an image, but she was not sure, and could not provide details.

We have seen one example already, in the "Ditropan" Sample #12 described above in the Worded Thinking section. A similar example occurred at Sample #10. Jean was studying, and had just read the name "Meichenbaum" on a typewritten set of notes. She was about to look that name up in a journal article, and was now "remembering how the word looked" (an Indeterminate Inner Visual Experience), so she could find it in the article. Jean did not see an inner image of the word "Meichenbaum," but somehow apprehended it in a visual way, as a whole word, with no other words around it. Although she was not "seeing" the word, she said it existed in her inner experience as if typed,

---

[1]This observation highlights one of the major contributions of the sampling studies to the understanding of processes often called "defensive." Without the benefit of sampling, it would be observed that Jean "denied her anger," and the understanding (after Freud) would be that angry thoughts were defended against, that is, never allowed to become conscious. As Jean's sampling shows, this is not a correct understanding, since angry thoughts did in fact frequently penetrate her awareness at the moments of many beeps. The "denial" comes only when she characterizes herself retrospectively: she does not *remember* that she has frequent angry thoughts, even though those thoughts themselves are easily available to consciousness at the moment of the beep.

present to her in black ink. She said it was *as if* she were looking at the word and picturing its appearance. But this "as-if" looking and picturing was not really a visual experience. She did not experience herself to be looking at something; she simply knew the visual characteristics of the word.

There was apparently some variation in the degree of visual detail present in this kind of experience. Samples #10 and #12 (described above) were at the least-visual end of this range. By contrast, Sample #5 was at the most-visual end of this continuum. Jean was thinking about what her children were eating, and had just said to herself, "It was better than donuts." At the moment of the beep, she was thinking about a package of donuts which was on her kitchen counter, and was particularly involved with the visual characteristics of the donuts. This inner representation of the donuts "looked like" the actual donuts on the counter: they were arranged in the same fashion, viewed from the same perspective, had the same shape, etc. This sample was more visually detailed than either the "Ditropan" or "Meichenbaum" samples; here Jean was sure that she was "seeing" something like an image, with some visual detail, but with no vividness or color. However, she could not be certain that she was actually seeing the donuts in her inner experience; perhaps she instead simply "knew" their complex visual characteristics.

RUMINATION

Jean described "Rumination" as being a thought process which occurred over and over in a seemingly interminable, uncontrolled, mentally exhausting manner. This repetitive thinking could be in Inner Speech, Worded Thinking, or Unsymbolized Thinking, and occurred in 6 (24%) of her 25 samples.

For example, in Sample #3 (described under Inner Speech) Jean was Inner Speaking repeatedly, "Do I want WordPerfect or is MacWrite good enough?" It seemed as if this question was occurring over and over without seeming to stop. She described this Ruminating question as being mentally exhausting, with no progress being made toward answering the question. The exhaustion associated with this thinking was entirely mental; that is, it did not seem to affect her physical energy.

Another example of Ruminating was described above in the section on Unsymbolized Thinking (Sample #23), where Jean was Ruminating about what was going to happen to her "old tapes." This Ruminative Unsymbolized Thinking seemed to occur as one quick and complete idea, all parts of which were present simultaneously, rather than word for word; the complete thought seemed to occur over and over without ending. She felt as if she had no control over this sequence.

THE "DOING" OF UNDERSTANDING AND THE "HAPPENING" OF SPEAKING

When Jean listened to others who were speaking, her listening was experienced to be an active, conscious, purposeful, effortful focusing of attention which was mentally (but not physically) exhausting. In fact, the amount of effort expended in a particular inner process was a prominent characteristic of Jean's inner experience. She had great difficulty in describing exactly what she meant by "mental effort," but she was insistent that the amount of mental effort required was a distinct characteristic of her inner life: some thoughts unquestionably required much effort while others required less.

In the samples where Jean was listening to others speak, or was reading, her inner processing was active and much effort of concentration was required. She did not simply relax and allow the other's meaning to unfold itself to her, but instead she actively concentrated on grasping the meaning and content of what was being spoken, as if she were reaching out to meet each word as it was spoken. In such cases, she found herself becoming mentally exhausted and was occasionally aware that her jaws were clenched as she listened.

For example, at Sample #9 Jean was driving a group of children home from school. One of the children, Cindy, was saying, "Julie won't come because she doesn't like birthday parties"; the beep seemed to occur as Cindy said the word "come." Jean was actively listening to these words, deliberately focusing on Cindy's words in an attempt to understand them. Cindy's statement was part of the rather idle chit-chat occurring between the children; thus it was not the case that Cindy's statement had any particular significance for Jean. Despite that, Jean was actively blocking out the other extraneous noises, inner processes, etc., and was purposefully bringing in each word to ascertain its meaning. Jean also said that she may have been annoyed at the moment of the beep, but she was not sure. She said she generally feels some annoyance when Cindy speaks, but could not be sure that this annoyance was actually ongoing at the moment of the beep.

In contrast, in samples where Jean was herself speaking, she experienced her inner process to be passive and relaxed, requiring minimal or no effort. Her words "came out" apparently automatically, expressing her meaning and content seemingly at the same instant that she understood the meaning herself, and without any sense of self-creation or direction—the words simply flowed without effort. Sample #11 (described above in the section on Inner Speech) was a striking example of both the activeness of listening and the passiveness of speaking. At the moment of the beep, Jean was saying to herself in naturally inflected Inner Speech, "Oh, this beeper isn't working." These words were experienced both as being said and heard in inner experience. The hearing of these words required an effortful concentration, despite the fact that she herself was saying (in Inner Speech) the words. By contrast, the Inner Speaking of those words did not require effort—it was as though they "just happened." The speaking seemed to flow naturally and easily, but hearing herself speak required effort!

CRITICAL OF SELF/OTHERS

Jean was critical, judgmental, or evaluative of herself or others in 10 (40%) of her 25 samples. For example, in Sample #13, Jean was saying to herself in her own, naturally inflected Inner Speech, "Oh, I don't know this stuff for tonight," reflecting self-doubt about her class preparation. Accompanying this Inner Speech was a hint of bodily tension, although Jean was not confident about the nature or extent of that tension.

We have seen several examples of this Criticalness in previous sections. In Sample #7 (described in the Feelings section) she was self-critical: "This is not a good day." In Sample #5 (described in the Indeterminate Inner Visual Experience section), she was critical of others: her children's snack was "better than donuts." And there was an implied criticism or judging of objects in Sample #3: "Is MacWrite good enough?" This Criticalness always included some Feeling of tension, annoyance, or irritation.

DISCUSSION

We have seen that Jean had relatively high frequencies of Worded Thinking, Unsymbolized Thinking, Indeterminate Inner Visual Experience, and Criticalness of Self/Others; had relative difficulty in apprehending the bodily aspects of Feelings; and seemed to reverse the sense of agency in communication, a phenomenon we called the "Doing" of Understanding and the "Happening" of Speaking. We shall see in the next chapter that she shared these characteristics with other anxious subjects.

Inner Experience in Anxiety

Judith Hebert and RTH

Nancy (Chapter 11) and Jean (Chapter 12) were two out of a group of five anxious subjects who formed part of the first author's Master's Thesis at the University of Nevada, Las Vegas. These five anxious individuals were not selected to represent any particular kind of anxiety disorder, but instead included a relatively wide variety of anxious disturbance including test anxiety, generalized anxiety disorder, agoraphobia, and panic attacks. The present chapter is based primarily on these five individuals and secondarily on additional anxious patients with whom the senior author has sampled in a clinical environment.

We remind ourselves that our task is to get a glimpse of some of the characteristics of inner experience which emerge when we sample individuals with disturbed affect, *not* to provide a complete catalog of such characteristics nor to provide a theory of anxiety. Such intentions would require larger numbers of subjects chosen to specifically represent particular anxiety disorders.

Nonetheless, we did observe some characteristics of our anxious subjects which deserve some comment, attributes which we found in at least several of our anxious individuals which do not characterize our other subjects.

VISUAL EXPERIENCES

Our five anxious subjects had an extremely low frequency of clear and/or colorful Images, ranging from 0% to 11% of their samples. Three of the five subjects had only one Image. The presence of one Image indicates that our anxious subjects can recognize and report a clear visual experience if and when one happens; the fact was that they did not happen often, despite *all* our anxious subjects' *wanting* to see inner Images, and spontaneously talking about this desire frequently in their interviews with us (even though this desire was irrelevant to our study). Most of our anxious subjects predicted before sampling that they would have highly visual inner experiences and were disappointed at what seemed to them as the "failure" to produce clear images.

Our subjects did have a relatively high frequency (between 8% and 25% of their samples) of what we are calling Indeterminate Inner Visual Experiences—a much higher frequency than our normal subjects have reported (but a somewhat lower frequency than our bulimics; see Chapter 10). Recall that Indeterminate Inner Visual Experience is the awareness of some kind of inner visual processing which occurs with little or no clarity, color, or detail. Our subjects sometimes refer to this phenomenon as "almost seeing," rather than the clear seeing of an image. Anxious subjects in general had some difficulty distinguishing between the *knowing* of the visual characteristics of an object present to inner experience, and the inner *seeing* of those characteristics. It is this difficulty which we sought to express with the term "Indeterminate."

Only very rarely have our normal subjects experienced this difficulty. Normal subjects usually either see images or they don't. A possible exception to this is a phenomenon we have called Imageless Seeing in the previous book (Hurlburt, 1990), where subjects reported having a visual experience but without an image being present. While we need further research to clarify this issue, our current understanding is that Imageless Seeing and Indeterminate Inner Visual Experience are two separate phenomena. Imageless Seeing involves a clear sense of seeing even though there is nothing being seen. Indeterminate Inner Visual Experience, by contrast, involves a lack of ability conclusively to distinguish "seeing" from "knowing about." In Imageless Seeing, subjects *see*, but see nothing. In Indeterminate Inner Visual Experience, subjects perhaps see, perhaps not.

WORDED THINKING

Our anxious subjects experienced a wide range of frequency of inner verbal thinking, ranging from Nancy's 4% (Chapter 11) to almost 70%. Much of that verbal experience was Inner Speech; in fact, all subjects had at least one Inner Speech experience. Our anxious subjects had no difficulty in describing Inner Speech when it occurred, describing clearly the tone, inflection, and rate of speed, pitch, etc. of the inner voice they were producing. These subjects could also describe how their Inner Speech had different tones of voice and inflection when, for example, they were arguing with themselves (as though in a debate) in comparison to when the Inner Speech was simply commenting.

The most striking characteristic of our anxious subjects' inner verbal experience was the presence of Worded Thinking, which was an aspect of between 0% and 24% of our anxious subjects' experiences. Words which are somehow present to awareness without being spoken or heard was an occasional but rare occurrence in our previous samples; Sonja Smith (Hurlburt, 1990, p. 111), for example, described the existence of Word Repetitions, which were words which had been spoken or thought previously and which were at the moment of the beep still existing in awareness (perhaps in corrupted form) even though they were no longer being spoken.

For four out of our five anxious subjects, new, original thoughts (not merely repetitions) took place in words which were not spoken—words which were "just there" in awareness, and for two of our anxious subjects, this phenomenon was a characteristic of nearly 25% of their samples. There was no doubt by any of the anxious subjects that specific words were clearly present in this kind of thinking, and the exact words could be and were reported to us. Thus, all of our subjects made a clear distinction between Worded Thinking and Unsymbolized Thinking. They also reported frequent Unsymbolized Thoughts, so the presence of Worded Thinking cannot be discounted as being simply the failure to communicate adequately about Unsymbolized Thinking.

Likewise, these subjects were equally as confident that the words present in the Worded Thinking samples had no voice, no vocal characteristics, no sense of production of the words, and no imaging of the words; that is, the Worded Thinking phenomenon was described to be much different from Inner Speech. Since all of these subjects also had samples where Inner Speech was present, that is, where inner words *did* have vocal characteristics, the absence of such characteristics in the Worded Thinking samples cannot be discounted as a failure to communicate adequately about Inner Speech.

THE "DOING" OF UNDERSTANDING AND THE "HAPPENING" OF SPEAKING

Normal subjects, when they are seeing or hearing the external world, usually do so in a relaxed, automatic, passively-receptive way:

characteristics, features, and objects of the environment present themselves without the subject's being aware of doing anything to aid, shape, or alter the process of perception. Objects simply appear, unbidden, so to speak, from the exterior.

Furthermore, normal subjects also have a sense of guiding their speech: they are aware of choosing the words, directing the inflection, holding back or rushing the speech, etc. (This does *not* imply that normal subjects experience a split between what they want to say and how they say it; on the contrary, the experience is unitary, with the normal subject the agent, controller, and experiencer of speech.) In sum, normal subjects have a sense that speaking is something they *do*, while hearing and seeing is something that *happens*.

For four out of our five anxious subjects, by contrast, these characteristics were at least occasionally and to some degree reversed.

The anxious subjects had the sense that listening and seeing were something that they had to *do* in an active, directive way. For example, while in a conversation, listening to the friend speak required a purposeful, effortful focusing of concentration. Every word seemed to have to be "reached out for," actively grasped and examined to ascertain its meaning. It seemed that they feared they would "miss something" if they didn't ensure that their attention was raptly focused. Typically, the anxious subjects reported this experience matter-of-factly, as if they took for granted that all people listen in the same active fashion.

By contrast, at times when our anxious subjects were speaking, they experienced that the production of words was something that simply happened, undirected, effortlessly. The words simply appeared, flowing in a stream which was not under the subjects' own direct control. In fact, sometimes those words expressed a meaning which was rather a surprise to the speaker, occasionally causing embarrassment or awkward social situations.

One of our anxious subjects (Jean, Chapter 12) experienced Inner Speech as a phenomenon which was both spoken and heard. In those samples, the speaking had the effortless, taken-by-surprise characteristic we have just been describing, and the hearing had the active, reaching-out quality of external listening, even though it was her own words which were being grasped. This same reaching-out effort was present when Jean listened to others speak.

UNSYMBOLIZED THINKING

We have seen in previous chapters that Unsymbolized Thinking is the experience of knowing the meaning and content of a differentiated thought with no simultaneous experience of words or images which might carry that meaning. Many of our normal subjects *never* experience Unsymbolized Thinking, and we have seen that it can occur with extremely high frequency in individuals who are depressed.

For our anxious subjects the frequency of Unsymbolized Thinking was moderately high; the range in frequency for the five anxious subjects was from 24% to 72%, higher than for most of our normal subjects but lower than for our depressed subjects (see Chapter 7) or bulimics (see Chapter 10).

RUMINATION

Rumination, as our subjects described it, was the experience of thinking, either in Inner Speech, Worded Thinking, or Unsymbolized Thinking, one thought over and over, or two alternating thoughts, over and over. This alternation or repetition of thoughts usually occurred at a rapid rate, and seemed to require much mental effort. We have not seen this Rumination phenomenon in any of our normal subjects, but it occurred in two of the anxious subjects, including Jean (Chapter 12).

The experience of Rumination appeared to be somewhat different for the two subjects who reported it. Jean's rumination (see Chapter 12) involved the simple repetition of thoughts as we described it in the last paragraph. Gina's experience (see Hebert, 1991) was much more acute. Her Ruminative Inner Speech and Unsymbolized Thinking were extremely rapid and intense, with no pauses; the thoughts occurred over and over with one thought overlapping another and going back and forth time and time again. Jean's Rumination (Chapter 12) involved no experience of the thoughts overlapping or going back and forth. The same thought was repeated over and over continuously at a rapid rate of speed.

FEELINGS

Our anxious subjects typically could not describe Feelings in detail; that is, they did not seem to have access to nuances of emotional experience. They reported the presence of emotional experience quite frequently (between 32% and 52% of their samples), but the affect being described was usually rather undifferentiated. Where a non-anxious subject might say that he was, for example, frustrated with a bit of anger at himself and a slight sense of futility, our anxious subjects might merely say, "I was frustrated." This seemed not to be a language or reporting difference, but a characteristic of the undifferentiated Feelings themselves.

Furthermore, our anxious subjects' Feelings usually were devoid of bodily awareness unless the Feeling was anxiety, leading our anxious subjects frequently to have some difficulty distinguishing between a Feeling and a thought. That is, an anxious subject might begin a description of a sample by saying she had been feeling angry at the moment of the beep, but during the course of the questioning as to how that experience manifested itself, she might begin to doubt that she had had an angry emotion at all, saying instead that she had been *thinking* that she was angry. This is considerably different from our experience with non-anxious subjects, who frequently have difficulty expressing how an emotion manifests itself, but are adamant that an emotion did in fact exist at the moment of the beep.

Our anxious subjects also had relatively frequent occurrences of Thought/Feelings, experiences which had both a cognitive and an affective component inextricably fused together. This phenomenon was also reported by our bulimic subjects (see Chapter 10), but not by others.

Our anxious subjects *were*, by contrast, clear about the experience of anxiety when it occurred. Anxiety had clear bodily locations, usually focused in the stomach (stomach tension, stomach flips, butterflies, etc.) or in the face (tension in the jaw). Anxious subjects never experienced any confusion about the presence of anxiety when it occurred, although it must be noted that several of our anxious subjects *never* had a sample which included the Feeling of anxiety.

We might also observe that most Feelings experienced by our anxious subjects were negative (e.g., frustration, anger, annoyance, or irritation).

CRITICAL OF SELF/OTHERS

The characteristics of anxious subjects' inner experience which we have been describing have all been aspects of the *process*, or the "how," of inner experience. In fact, nearly all the salient characteristics of inner experience which the descriptive sampling method has discovered have been process characteristics. However, a characteristic of the *content*, or the "about-what," of thinking emerged as a salient feature of anxious individuals: all our anxious individuals were frequently critical or judgmental of themselves or others. The frequency of Criticisms of Self/Others ranged from 21% to 40% across our five anxious subjects, much higher percentages than we had seen in our other subjects.

Our anxious subjects made a great many explicit judgments, and their thoughts were frequently characterized by "good/bad," "should/shouldn't," or "OK/not OK." Each of the anxious subjects' samples contained frequent self-criticism, criticism of others, judgments, etc. The anxious client described by Hurlburt and Sipprelle (1978, the only other sampling-based study of anxious individuals of which we are aware) also had frequent critical thoughts of himself and others. This client was unaware of his frequent inner criticisms, and shortly after the sampling results made this content category explicit (and after supportive and didactic therapy helped him to handle aggression), his anxiety lessened dramatically.

DISCUSSION

The anxious subjects described above were not chosen to be representative of the general population of anxious individuals since our group was a small, nonrandom sample. Perhaps future replication with larger, more representative groups of anxious subjects will demonstrate that some of these characteristics are the chance results of sampling with a small group of subjects; however, it does not seem likely that *all* of the aspects of inner experience which we have described will be dismissed by such replications.

Our aim in sampling with anxious individuals has not been to provide a theory of anxiety, but simply to show, as part of the attempt to explore the method, that the descriptive experience sampling method distinguishes between individuals of different diagnostic categories. In the process, we have discovered some characteristics which seem to reveal some provocative aspects of anxiety, discoveries which now call for replication.

IV

Borderline Personality

Our goal in this book has been to provide glimpses into the inner experience of individuals for whom affective disturbance is an issue, and our final case study is no exception to that general rule. We will present an individual who had been diagnosed as having borderline personality, a disorder characterized by an unstable self-image; sudden, unexplainable mood shifts; stormy, ambivalent interpersonal relationships with preoccupation over abandonment; and self-destructive behavior. Unlike the previous chapters, however, I have not sampled with a group of borderline patients. Fran is the only borderline patient with whom I have sampled. But her inner experience was so dramatically different from any which we have encountered previously, that I felt compelled to include her case in this book regardless of whether her characteristics are shared by *any* other individuals who have the borderline personality diagnosis. The case deserves serious consideration on its own merits as a means of broadening our understanding of the possibilities of human experience.

A Bank Teller with No Figure/Ground Phenomena in Perception

Fran Iverson (not her real name) was a 44-year-old divorced mother of a 16-year-old daughter who was living with her. She had been hospitalized three months earlier following a suicide attempt, and prior to that had been hospitalized several times, the first time being a year and a half before sampling began. Between hospitalizations she had been receiving outpatient psychotherapy regularly, which had stabilized her situation and provided effective crisis intervention. During some of her hospitalizations she had been diagnosed as depressed, but mental health professionals working with her also had other diagnostic impressions such as borderline disorder. In short, Fran had a relatively long-term disorder which was difficult to classify. The diagnosis which seemed most apt to me (and to her current psychotherapist) was Borderline Personality.[1]

Fran worked as a bank teller, holding the same job steadily for seven years except during hospitalizations. She described herself as functioning at her best at work, where the demands of the job structured her time effectively. At home, especially on weekends, she frequently "fell apart," resulting in a number of serious suicide attempts and frequent

---

[1]Disagreement about diagnosis is not at all uncommon in individuals diagnosed as Borderline Personality.

telephone calls of acute distress to her therapist. Fran described herself as being tormented by rapid, recurring self-destructive and derogatory ideas which were outside of her own control. As a result of these recurring ideas, Fran's experience was always extremely unpleasant, and occasionally so unbearable there was "no point in continuing to live."

She had taken antidepressant medication during and following some of her hospitalizations, but this medication had not seemed to ease her distress. A recently consulted psychiatrist had prescribed moderately small doses of the anti-psychotic Loxitane following reports that such dosage was therapeutic for individuals diagnosed as borderline. She had refused to take this medication because of fear of side effects and a belief that consenting to take the medication would demonstrate that she was psychotic.

Fran consented to participate in the experience-sampling research, and sampled for 9 days over a three-week period. She responded to 82 total beeps, of which 10 were not adequately discussed in our sampling meetings due to lack of time. Thus, this report is based on 72 samples.

During the first seven sampling days, Fran reported that she was in a relatively "bad" emotional state, which continued to worsen during this sampling period. After the seventh sampling discussion (which occurred on a Friday evening), Fran experienced a rather dramatic alleviation of her mental distress, saying that she had the most "peaceful" three-day weekend she had had in years—in fact, in as long as she could remember. She continued to sample for 3 days, during which time the thoughts which had tormented her for years remained absent. She was, however, troubled by some anxiety during this period. Thus there were two distinct sampling periods, which we will call the "Distressed" and the "Peaceful/anxious" Periods, respectively. We will describe each period in turn.

THE DISTRESSED PERIOD

Fran sampled 68 times during the Distressed Period, of which 58 samples were adequately discussed. Fran's experience during this period was characterized by vivid recurring Images, seen frequently two, three, or more at a time; multiple streams of attention in inner and exterior perception with an inability to differentiate figure from ground in perception; Inner Speech; Unsymbolized Thinking; and Feelings, almost without exception being distress, anxiety, and depression.

We shall see that Fran's reports of her inner experience were quite surprising, so we must raise the question of whether she was an accurate reporter of her inner experience.[2] While there never is unimpeachable evidence of the accuracy of reports of inner experience, I came to believe Fran's reports for three reasons. First, she made, early in sampling, the unusual claim that the same Image stayed in her awareness constantly for periods of days or weeks. Subsequent sampling did in fact show apparently identical Images being reported in samples separated from each other by several days. Fran's several reports of those Images, even when separated by as much as a week, were identical in detail (to the extent that my notes allowed comparing). Thus, it may be said that her reports were consistent. Second, Fran's reports occasionally included perceptions of external reality which could be checked for detail.[3] For example, she described an Image which was triggered by the real seeing of a newspaper advertisement (described more fully below). Her report included a description both of the Image and of the real advertisement, with comments on how the two differed. I secured a copy of the actual newspaper advertisement and found her description of it to be accurate. Thus it was clear that Fran could recall and report accurately about exterior perceptions. Third, other relatively nonspecific cues during the extended sampling conversations lent the impression of credibility to Fran's reports. For example, she was initially reluctant to describe the Multiple Images which occurred frequently because she was afraid I would not believe her. This reluctance lessened gradually, but reappeared when a new, emotionally charged aspect of her experience was about to be discussed. This pattern is consistent with my understanding of people who try to report accurately about something which is difficult and emotionally charged. These three factors, plus other nonspecific cues, led me to the conclusion that Fran was a credible reporter of her experience.

Multiple Images

The chief characteristic of Fran's inner experience during the Distressed Period was the presence of Multiple Images seen nearly continually, at least in 35 (60%) of the 58 samples;[4] since some of the Images

[2]Actually, we raise this exact same question with all our subjects, and use the same means to answer it in those cases as well.
[3]It is my practice with all subjects to unobtrusively check out the details of any externally observable event whenever possible, thus providing an external validity check of the subject's reports.
[4]This percentage underestimates the actual frequency of Images for Fran. During the first few days of sampling, Fran did not always report her Images, but I came to understand

were not reported, I estimate the actual percentage to be about 90%. These Images were generally experienced to be accurate reconstructions of scenes which Fran had in fact experienced in the past, usually viewed from the same perspective Fran had had during the original exterior perception. The Images were in color, and the color was usually accurate, but occasionally was more vivid or different from the same event in real life. When people occurred in the Images (which was usually the case), they were seen to be moving in apparently accurately recreated motion. They were frequently seen to be talking, yelling, or screaming, and the voices of these characters were most often accurately heard full of inflection and synchronized with the Image. These Images occurred multiply, with two, three, four, or more Images seen simultaneously, displayed as if occupying the same portion of the inner visual field, yet each Image itself was a coherent gestalt. Fran's attention was on all these simultaneous Images equally and at the same time; that is, she was *not* focused on one of the Images with the remaining Images seen in the background. They usually occurred without volitional control: while it was sometimes possible to initiate a pleasant Image, it was impossible for her to terminate ongoing Multiple unpleasant Images.

While we have not sampled adequate numbers of subjects to provide confident estimates of the relative frequencies of particular characteristics of inner experience, we are in a position to describe the manner in which Images are most frequently experienced by our normal subjects. Normal subjects typically experience single rather than multiple Images (although multiple Images have been occasionally reported by them). Typical Images of normal subjects are visual phenomena which occur *without* accompanying sounds (although there are frequent exceptions to this also).

A typical Image experience For Fran was Sample #34, which occurred at 8:30 one morning as she was preparing to leave for work. She was seeing the objects in her bedroom as she was getting ready, but her attention was focused on an inner reliving of two events, one an argument with her daughter from the night before, and the other a scene with her father which had occurred about two years previously. Both events involved vivid, colorful, moving visual Images which included

that Multiple Images were present at those beeps but absent in the reports. This lack of reporting was, I believe, due to two factors. First, she took the presence of the Multiple Images for granted; because they were constantly present, she did not realize that I also wanted her to report about them. Second, she was afraid I would not believe her reports about this phenomenon, and was reluctant to describe it. Early in sampling, these two factors together led to her failure to report Images which were in fact present at the moment of the beep.

hearing the voices of the people in the Images and reliving the emotional reactions. The first of these scenes was apparently an accurate reliving of a portion of the argument which Fran had had with her 16-year-old daughter. In the imagined event (as was the case in reality the previous night), Fran's daughter was standing in the bedroom shaking her finger at Fran and ridiculing her, saying, "I wish you had succeeded when you tried to kill yourself the first time!", and then throwing her hairbrush at Fran. The daughter's voice was heard (in Inner Hearing) to be loud, angry, abusive, and with the shrill tone of ridicule, just as it had been heard in reality the night before. The voice was experienced to have some of the same manner of speaking as Fran's father did when he was angry at Fran.

Fran's daughter was seen in the Image to be wearing white pants and a white sweatshirt; in reality, according to Fran's recollection, she had been wearing the same white pants but with a colored top. Fran experienced herself as looking straight ahead at her daughter, as if she were perhaps 6 or 8 feet in front of her, although the whole experience seemed to be more inside Fran's head than projected out into the surrounding space. Fran felt belittled, hopeless, helpless, and worthless in this relived experience, although it was impossible for her to describe exactly how those Feelings were represented to her.

Thus this appeared to be an exact reliving of a very unpleasant scene which had occurred the night before. The imagined scene was recreated accurately, both visually and in sound, with the exception of the daughter's blouse, which was imagined to be a different color from the one she actually had worn the previous night.

Simultaneous to this scene was a recreated reliving of a scene which had occurred about two years ago in Fran's parents' house. Fran was sitting at the dining room table, looking at her father who was sitting across the table from her. Her father was "telling her off," shaking his finger at her and saying, "You're no good—you're a failure!" His voice was accurately heard, with the same rate of speaking, pitch, and angry inflection as Fran recalled having heard that night two years ago. The scene was also accurate visually: her father was seen in accurate perspective, shaking his finger at her the same way he had in reality. Furthermore, her mother could be seen in the Image, off to the right, through the doorway in the kitchen standing at the stove. Thus, this scene was, as best Fran could recall, an entirely accurate reconstruction of the event of two years before.

Both these scenes, with all their visual and auditory detail, occurred simultaneously; this was not a case of alternation from one scene to the other. Both father and daughter were seen straight ahead, seemingly about the same distance ahead, as if superimposed on one another, except that there was no confusion of one Image with the other. Each scene existed as an integrated inner entity, internally consistent within its scene. Both scenes were present simultaneously, in the same visual space, and yet did not interfere with each other. Furthermore, the father's voice was easily identifiable as being part of the Image of her father, and the daughter's voice clearly was part of the Image of her daughter. This was apparently a case of two separate yet similar scenes being relived simultaneously, with neither scene disturbing the other.

Both scenes were experienced as occurring as a "flash," but it was difficult to be clear about the temporal duration of each scene. In some ways, the flash seemed to be quite quick, yet it also was true that the daughter and father were heard to be speaking rather long sentences at a normal rate of speed, which would require the scenes to have durations of at least a few seconds. Furthermore, it seemed to Fran that these two scenes were present constantly, uninterrupted, that particular morning, always there, seen and heard, unrelenting. This impression was corroborated by the samples which occurred during that four-hour period (Sample #35 through #41), all of which had these two Images present. These Images simply continued nonstop.

Sample #39, an example of how these Images persisted over time, occurred at about noon, three and a half hours after the first beep where the father and the daughter Images were reported. At Sample #39, Fran was at work talking to a coworker about an argument she had had with her daughter the evening before. At the moment of the beep, Fran was saying aloud to the coworker, "I'll probably come home to a very clean house—she's trying to make amends." At the same time as she was speaking these words, Fran was speaking to herself in Inner Speech the words "little turd," referring to her daughter and the way she tries to manipulate Fran. Also occurring at the same moment were the two Images of her daughter ridiculing and father shaking his finger which we described above at Sample #34. All four aspects of this experience (exterior speech, Inner Speech, and the two Images) were simultaneous, and the two Images appeared exactly as they had previously (father seated at table shaking his finger, mother standing off to the side of the Image in the kitchen at the stove, etc.), except that in the present sample, the Image of her daughter was seen to be in front of the father Image instead of superimposed as they were at all the other beeps of this particular morning.

The Image of her daughter was seen in front of the other Image, but we must be careful to note that this Image was not the "center of attention" in the way that Gestalt psychologists meant the "figure" as the center of attention. The other Image, and the inner and exterior speech, were in focus just as was the daughter Image; the daughter Image was simply in front.

The samples which we have been discussing took place on a Friday morning. Fran did not sample on Saturday (because we would not be meeting on Saturday or Sunday) and resumed sampling Sunday evening, responding to five beeps (#42 through #46) between 7:05 and 7:57. At all five of these samples, the Image of her father shaking his finger at her (but not the Image of her daughter ridiculing) was present as part of her inner experience. Fran said during the sampling conversations that the father Image had been present constantly throughout the weekend.

When sampling resumed the following (Monday) evening, the Image of her father shaking his finger was no longer present. Thus this extremely unpleasant Image was unrelentingly present to Fran for at least three (and possibly four) consecutive days.

Fran did not experience herself as having control over most of her Images. These Images haunted and preoccupied her, making her life generally miserable, and she was unable to stop their occurrence. She could predict when they might occur; for example, a conflict with her daughter might trigger a series of unpleasant Images. Furthermore, she could usually call to mind a pleasant Image when she desired, but the new Image would not replace the existing Images, being superimposed on them instead. The father and daughter Images of Sample #34 through #39 were examples of out-of-control Images.

Another example occurred at Sample #24. Fran was on her lunch break at work, crocheting, and was still angry about a telephone conversation she had had with her mother about an hour before. During this conversation, her mother had been "pushing her buttons," indicating her disappointment with Fran, and shortly after the conversation Fran had begun to see an inner Image of her mother in "sackcloth and ashes." This was a frequent Image for Fran over the past several years, and now for the last hour it was recurring vividly. At the moment of beep #24, Fran was crocheting and saying, in Inner Speech, "Stop!", trying to get the Image to disappear, without success.

The Image was of Fran's mother in her living room, kneeling on the living room floor with hands clasped and head and shoulders bowed as if praying. The Image was a realistic one, as if standing in the living room entrance looking into the room, and the furnishings in the room could be seen accurately. Her mother in the Image was wearing an ash-grey robe with a grey belt (in reality, her mother did not have such a robe, nor had Fran ever seen her in the praying position). The scene was seen vividly and three-dimensionally, and the mother was seen to be extremely humble and burdened.

This Image had been present in its exact same form since the telephone call, and was a frequent Image for Fran. There were, according to Fran, actually two variants of the same Image: one is as we have described it above; the second is the same as the first except Joan of Arc is seen to be kneeling next to Fran's mother, in the same type of sack-cloth robe, but wearing a white sash instead of grey belt. Furthermore, Joan of Arc is bent slightly more than Fran's mother, in a position that Fran interpreted to reflect somewhat more humility.

Multiple Images were present at almost all of her samples during the Distressed sampling period. There were a few occasions (perhaps about 10%) at which she believably stated that no Images were present, but those were the exceptions, rather than the rule.

Lack of Figure and Ground in Real and Imaginal Perception

Psychologists since the Gestalt psychologists at the turn of the century have accepted as fact that human perception has a relatively clear, distinct focus or figure, and that surrounding noncentral details are seen relatively indistinctly, usually behind the central figure. We will give an example to show why we believe that this was *not* true for Fran.

We have noted in the description of Images that Fran frequently saw several Images at one time, with no one of the Images any more prominent in her experience than the others. It was as if she did not have a focus of attention; instead, the Images were just inserted simultaneously into her awareness. This lack of focus of attention was also true within individual Images: Fran seemed to see both the central feature and all of the surrounding details of an Image at one time and at one level of awareness, rather than having her inner perception create an Image with a central figure and a relatively indistinct ground. This lack of perceptual centering was also a characteristic of her real external perception: she apparently did not and could not organize perception into figure and ground.

At Sample #17, Fran was sitting at the table with her daughter, who was reading the newspaper which was open to a Mervyns Department Store advertisement. Fran reported that the advertisement was a picture of a brown teddy bear surrounded by gold chains marked as being on sale for 50 percent off the usual price. Fran's eyes were aimed at and were taking in this newspaper advertisement, but her attention was focused on an inner Image of the same advertisement.

The Image had basically the same characteristics as the advertisement except that the Image was clearer and was more three-dimensional while the real newspaper ad appeared flat. Furthermore, the teddy bear in the Image was described to be reddish brown, while the bear in the advertisement was said to be more a chocolate brown.

Fran understood the Image to have the meaning, "What a come-on, using a teddy bear to advertise gold chains," but there were no words which conveyed this meaning; it was simply understood.

I inquired, since the Image was seen to be three-dimensional, whether the bear was in front of or behind the chains, and Fran's reply was that the bear was clearly, vividly in front of the chains. Is the focus of attention on the bear or the chains? I asked, and Fran answered that it was clearly the bear. Are the chains, then, slightly out of focus (because they are more distant and not the central figure)? At this question, Fran hesitated, as if unsure of herself. No, she replied, everything is in focus. Subsequent questioning did not shake her conviction that, while her attention was on the bear, the chains were also equally in focus, although not quite as detailed as the teddy bear.

I inquired about her experience when she was looking at the real newspaper advertisement: when she looked at the real picture of the bear, did the surrounding chains seem to get slightly out of focus? No, she said, everything stayed in focus. This seemed to violate the principles of the figure/ground characteristics of perception, and two alternative explanations appeared to me. First was the possibility that her recollection of her experience at the beep was inaccurate. As was described above, when we checked the real newspaper advertisement, we found Fran's recollected details to be absolutely accurate both in layout (bear surrounded by the gold chains) and in color (the bear a chocolate brown "about like my coat"), lending credence to her ability to recall and report accurately.

The second possible explanation of her failure to discern figure/ground relationships in her Images was that her perceptual awarenesses were somehow different from the figure/ground perception described by the Gestalt psychologists. To check this, I deviated from our usual task of conversing about individual beeps to explore her perception of current external reality. This series of meetings happened to take place in a McDonald's restaurant,[5] and I asked her to focus on the container of paper napkins which was perhaps 10 feet in front of her. Was the gentleman in the red sweater (seated also about 10 feet away but

[5]To interfere as little as possible in subjects' lives and activities, I usually scheduled interviews as close to the subjects' everyday locations as possible (rather than in my own office).

about 30 degrees to her right) slightly out of focus when her eyes were aimed at the napkins? No, he was equally in focus, but somewhat less detailed than the napkins.

I questioned Fran as to what she meant by "in focus but with less detail." When she turned her eyes from the napkins to the man, did she experience herself as "zeroing in" or "refocusing" on the man (phenomena which psychology takes for granted as being characteristic of attention shifts in perception)? No; the man just became more detailed. Wondering whether this was a characteristic of her perception in general or just her peripheral perception, I asked her to look at a chair which was perhaps 18 inches in front and just a few degrees to the left of the napkin container. Were the napkins in focus when she fixated the chair? Yes. Now fixate on the napkins; does that seem like a refocusing or a zeroing in? No; I'm just re-aiming my eyes. There was apparently no experience of creating a central figure in Fran's perception.

To further explore this apparent lack of central figure, I then sketched Rubin's well-known ambiguous figure of the two faces/vase. What do you see? I see two faces in profile, and a candlestick or vase or something in the middle. Do you see them both at the same time, or alternating, the faces and then the vase and then the faces, etc.? I see them both at the same time. Try to see the faces. Can you do that? Yes, but the vase is there also. Further questioning confirmed that she did not experience the alternation between faces and vase which psychologists assume this drawing always elicits.

I then turned my notepad, on which I had sketched the ambiguous figure for Fran, back towards me so that I could record my observations. The unintended result of this was that the faces/vase drawing was now turned obliquely on its side when Fran viewed it. "Oh," she said, "now I see what you meant! It's alternating now," which meant that she experienced herself as focusing first on the faces, then on the vase, etc. After that, she could easily comprehend my questions about change of focus. When the faces/vase drawing was viewed in its normal upright position, there was no alternation; both faces and vase were seen in focus simultaneously. Now that we had established effective communication about the experience of perception creating a figure and ground, we rechecked the real perceptions of objects in the restaurant. Fran was now very confident that objects in her visual periphery were in fact in focus, but simply not as detailed as objects in the center of her fixation, and that there was *not* a "zeroing in" experience as she shifted her gaze.

To explore further the figure/ground phenomenon, in a later interview I presented her with two additional commonly-used ambiguous figures: Jastrow's duck/rabbit and Boring's wife/mother-in-law (Kaufman, 1974, pp. 496–7). Her experience of the duck/rabbit figure was just like the faces/vase: She said she immediately saw the duck *and* the rabbit in Jastrow's drawing, simultaneously with no alternation.

Her way of dealing with Boring's wife/mother-in-law ambiguous figure provides another instance of why we came to accept her reports as being accurate. She initially stated she could see the old woman. When I explained that there was also a young woman in this figure, she said she could not see it. Even when I covered up the bottom portion of the picture (obscuring the old woman's lips, chin and feather boa) which left only the young woman, she couldn't see it. She asked whether she could take the ambiguous figures with her, explaining that she didn't really believe me when I said that most people experienced an alternation when these figures were viewed upright, and she wanted to try them out on her coworkers. She telephoned an hour later to report with some surprise that her coworkers had in fact reported the alternation experience, and she described to me what they had said the alternation experience was like, making it entirely clear that she did completely comprehend what was meant by the alternation phenomenon and that she had the verbal ability to put it adequately into words. By the way, she said, she could now see the young woman, present simultaneously with the old woman and with *no* experience of alternation.

Inner Speech

Nearly half of Fran's samples (28 [48%] of 58) in the Distressed Period included Inner Speech as part of her inner experience. Inner Speech never occurred alone, but was always accompanied by Images or other sorts of inner experience to be described below.

Fran experienced Inner Speech exactly as she did exterior speech except that there was no exterior movement or sound. That is, she experienced herself to be the creator of the words being uttered (not merely a passive listener to words); the words seemed to be spoken in her own voice with the same natural inflection that she would have used had she spoken the words aloud; the rate of speech production was usually the same as exterior speech, but occasionally was slightly faster; other than the occasionally accelerated rate, the remaining characteristics of her speaking (pitch, choice of words, pauses, etc.) seemed to be identical to exterior speech.

Sometimes Inner Speech was quite straightforward. For example, at Sample #6, Fran was at work putting money in the vault. At the moment of the beep, she was saying to herself, "I feel ugly, old, and sick." This sentence was experienced exactly as if she had said these words aloud except that no sound or movement was being produced. That is, it was as if she was creating the sentence, and it felt like it was her own production in her own voice at her own normal rate of speed and pitch, and was full of the inflection of despair and discouragement. At the same time, she was in fact Feeling old and sick, centered in her stomach (an upset feeling) and her lungs (the stuffiness of bronchitis).

In one sample (#62), the Inner Speech was accompanied by an Image of the word she was speaking. She was reading a pamphlet about the drug Loxitane which had been prescribed for her, but which she was not yet prepared to take. She had read the word "Loxitane" a few seconds before the beep as the title of the pamphlet, but was now a few lines down into the text. At the moment of the beep, she was reading the pamphlet and was saying in Inner Speech the word "Loxitane," as if it were a caption to her experience. Also, at the same moment, she was seeing a clear inner Image of the word "LOXITANE." This word appeared as if printed in black block letters, with the individual letters appearing as if printed in the kind of 3-dimensional perspective characters used in sign painting, but the letters themselves (as on a painted sign) were flat.

A group of other Images were also occurring at the moment of the beep. Most prominent was an Image of an old man at a psychiatric hospital begging not to be given Thorazine. This Image was a recreation of a scene which Fran had witnessed during her hospitalization three months before. There was also a group of Images which were scenes from a television program which Fran had watched the night before. The program had included a visit to a room where a group of people were using illegal drugs. In the program, the camera had panned the room, showing one person melting heroin in a spoon over a candle, another person giving himself an injection in his neck, etc. These scenes were recreated as accurate Images, but now Fran was seeing them all simultaneously instead of sequentially as they were on the television show. These Multiple Images were not directly superimposed on one another as were most of Fran's Images; instead, these Images seemed to be placed around a table in Fran's experience, one to the right, one straight ahead, one to the left, etc., as they had been in the actual room which had been videotaped.

Unsymbolized Thinking

Unsymbolized Thinking occurred occasionally (17 [29%] of 58 samples in the Distressed Period) in Fran's inner experience during this period, as "thinking" or "wondering" which did not involve words or images or any other kind of symbolic representation; Fran simply knew that she was thinking and exactly what she was thinking about. This Unsymbolized Thinking almost always occurred at the same time as Images, Inner Speech, or both. However, this is a characteristic of all aspects of Fran's inner experience because almost never did her experience focus on just one thing.

An example of Unsymbolized thinking occurred at Sample #56. She was standing in the cashiers' office and was thinking two separate thoughts and seeing a vivid Image simultaneously. The first of the thinkings was about how hectic it was at work that day. This thinking did not involve any images (of the workplace, etc.) nor any inner words (the word "hectic" did not appear, for example); Fran simply knew that she was thinking about how hectic it was at work. The second thought was that Mary, a coworker, was "making Fran crazy" by talking aloud to herself as she went about her business. This thought also did not involve images or words, and was experienced to occur simultaneously with the first thought. The Image was what Fran described as a "funny" image, the only playful Image reported in Fran's samples. It was an Image of a loaf of pumpkin bread wrapped in aluminum foil sitting on the shelf in Fran's freezer. The pumpkin bread had eyes and mouth, and was screaming, "Let me out! Let me out!" as if it were angry about being imprisoned in the freezer. As Fran watched the Image, the pumpkin bread jumped out of the freezer onto the floor and began to walk toward the front door on long, wooden, stilt-like legs.

This Image was seen more vividly, exaggeratedly so, than the real pumpkin bread which actually existed in her freezer. Except for the fantasy details, the remainder of the Image (refrigerator, floor, front door) were seen accurately as they in fact existed in real life. (Fran thought that this Image was a reaction to an event which had taken place a few days before. Fran had in reality put two loaves of pumpkin bread into the freezer. A few days later, she was surprised to find that only one remained. Fran asked her daughter where the missing loaf was, but her daughter denied knowing anything about its disappearance.)

One sample (#5) seemed about halfway between Inner Speech and Unsymbolized Thinking. She was talking to a coworker about this thought-sampling project, and at the same time was thinking about how down she was feeling. This thinking was in words, but the words went by so fast they were not clear. The experience was something like words in a blender, shooting by. As best she could reconstruct, the words were "Why am I doing this?", "Why?", "Why?", "Why bother?", "Why, why, why bother?" Fran was confident that these thoughts were in words, but not confident of exactly which words were being spoken.

Feelings

Most of the samples in Fran's Distressed Period included a report of Feelings which were present at the moment of the beep. These Feelings were almost always negatively toned: despair, distress, self-criticism, etc. These Feelings could be described accurately in the sense that despair could be easily differentiated from disgust, etc. Fran could not, however, describe how these Feelings were made known to her except by saying that they were generally felt all over her body.

Inner Experience When Fran was "Coming Unglued"

Fran was distressed throughout this sampling period, but the distress and pressure mounted as sampling continued, and Fran experienced herself as deteriorating, getting "wound up," or "coming unglued." Based on the sequence of samples, we can sketch the characteristics of Fran's experience as she became more and more "unglued." First, inner experience became more complex. Where early in the sampling, a typical sample might involve an Inner Speaking occurring simultaneously with 2 Images, when she was coming "unglued" there were 5 or 10 or an uncountable number of separate inner events all occurring simultaneously. Second, these events were perceived to be happening much more rapidly than before: flashes of thinkings, flashes of Images now raced through her experience. Third, she became less able to report the details of each aspect of her experience: they were too fast, too simultaneous, too crowded together to be able to report clearly. Fourth, Fran had even less of a sense of control over her inner process when she was wound up: the thoughts assaulted her and splintered her inner experience, as if she were in a crowded cocktail party and was being forced to listen to all the conversations in the room equally and simultaneously. Fifth, all the aspects of her multiple inner experiences were condemning or derogatory, and included suicidal images.

An example from this period is Sample #64. Fran was sitting in her room on her bed, which was what she generally did when she felt low. She was saying in Inner Speech, "I don't want to lose him," referring to her worry that her psychotherapist, who had recommended that she take an antipsychotic medication that she did not want to take, would desert her for failing to cooperate with him. Simultaneous to this Inner Speech, "There were so many thoughts that I'm not sure whether they were images or not." These thoughts came extremely rapidly, one after the next and overlapping, and Fran would dwell on one thought while others kept rushing by. At the moment of the beep the kinds of thoughts which were racing through her experience were: what a mess I've made/it's my fault/I mess up everything I touch/he's (my father) right, I'm worthless/I want to die/Yes, I want to die/No I don't/etc. Fran was not sure whether these meanings were carried by images or were inner hearings or Unsymbolized Thoughts: things were happening too fast.

The Suicide Image and the End of the Distressed Period

Sample #64, which we just described, took place at 8:35 on a Thursday evening. Shortly after that sample, Fran began to "calm down," and her sampled inner experience was less complex and more clearly in Images. The Images sampled later on Thursday evening and also Friday morning were clearer versions of the Image flashes which were part of Sample #64, and included the extremely negative content recurrent Images, some of which we have described before (the father shaking his finger, for example).

The sampling conversations for this series of beeps took place Friday evening, and was quite difficult for Fran (and for me) because of her reluctance to reexperience these Images in the retelling of them. This difficulty reached its peak in the discussion of Sample #65 which, like other samples after it (and also Sample #64, as one of the flashes) included a recurrent Image of Fran committing suicide.

Fran experienced the suicide Image as the most distressing of her Images. It had been a frequently-recurring Image for the past two months, at which time Fran had finally decided on the method she would use to end her life. It was extremely difficult for her to discuss this Image, and equally as difficult for me to encourage her to describe it. She agreed to discuss it only on the condition that I not divulge the contents of this Image to her psychotherapist, to which I reluctantly agreed.[6]

Sample #65 occurred while Fran was talking on the telephone to a friend who had called. There were many Images ongoing simultaneously: her father shaking his finger at her, her mother in "sackcloth and ashes," (descriptions of both these recurrent Images are found in the section on Images above) etc., but the most prominent (meaning seen to be closer to her than the other Images) was an Image in which she "relived" how she had decided to commit suicide. This had been a recurring Image which usually occurred by itself (an unusual charac-

---

[6]This is an example of the kind of ethical dilemma into which this sort of intensive, personal research can place its participants. I agreed to this condition only because I felt that I had a good relationship with this subject and also with her therapist, with whom I had collaborated on several previous projects.

teristic for her Images), but this time it was part of the collage of Images. The Image was experienced to be exactly the same each time it occurred.

The suicidal Image was really a series of Images held together by Unsymbolized "knowings." It began with an Unsymbolized knowing that Fran was home alone. The first Image was of Fran taking a pill bottle out of her purse. Only the pill bottle and the purse were seen in the Image; Fran's hand was (nonverbally) known to be the agent, but the pill bottle simply moved out of the purse. The next Image was of the pills being poured out of the bottle. Fran (nonverbally) knew that she was pouring the pills with her right hand into her left palm, but neither hand was actually seen in the Image. Then there was an Unsymbolized knowing that the pills had been consumed. Following that was an Image of walking into Fran's bathroom, seen just as if Fran actually were walking into the room: first the bathroom as seen from the door, sink and mirror on the right and tub and toilet on the left, etc; then Fran moved into the bathroom and turned to face the sink, seeing the sink and mirror ahead of her and the tub reflected in the mirror, just as she would were she actually standing in that position in the real bathroom. Then there was an Unsymbolized knowing that Fran had slit her wrists, and that the pills had made her too weak to call for help. Finally, there was an Image of Fran sitting on the floor of the bathroom, leaning her head against the sink cabinet, "asleep." While all of the previous Images in this sequence had been viewed as from Fran's own eyes, this last Image was viewed as if from the bathroom door, with Fran facing that door with legs outstretched in that direction.

THE PEACEFUL/ANXIOUS PERIOD

At the conclusion of the sampling conversation where Fran described her suicidal Image, she (and I) had been apprehensive that discussing, and thus in a sense reliving, this most sensitive of Images might cause her to have a very difficult next few days. However, the opposite occurred: the next days were the most peaceful she had had in years, in fact, in as long as she could remember. She was, for the first time, rid of her "gremlins," the recurring Images which had tormented her. The suicidal Image, which had been an almost constant phenomenon for the past two months, was gone: she occasionally thought of it over the weekend, but it would be a transient thought which would soon disappear. She felt that she had control over it, rather than the other way around. The father-shaking-his-finger Image, which had been a nearly constant aspect of her inner experience for years, was also gone. In fact, all of the recurrent Images had stopped.

She also felt that her experience in general, not just the Images, was more focused and under her own control. For example, during the Distressed Period, if five conversations were occurring in the room around her, she listened to all the conversations at once, whether she wanted to or not—they all forced themselves into her awareness. Now she could listen to several conversations at a time if she wished, but she could control her attention and focus on one or two at a time if she desired. In short, she could now concentrate. Being able to control her concentration "was an entirely different kind of feeling inside," and it made it much easier to function and to do the things which needed to be done.

Fran's control over Images was experienced as peaceful, but she began to experience strong anxiety on the second day after the recurrent Images had stopped. This anxiety became steadily more severe over the next few days. She sampled during three of these days, collecting and discussing 14 samples, almost all of which contained reports of anxiety, so we will refer to this as the Peaceful/anxious Period.

The sampled experiences in the Peaceful/anxious Period were markedly different from the samples during the Distressed Period, thus corroborating her general descriptions cited above. First, the recurrent Images which had plagued her during the Distressed period (father shaking his finger, suicide, etc.) were in fact not present during any of the Peaceful/anxious Period samples. She did have one Image which appeared on three consecutive samples (#79, #80, and #81) of herself sitting on her bed crying, "giving in" to the anxiety and pressure she was feeling, but these samples all occurred within a 15 minute span, and the Image was not present in Sample #78 (60 minutes prior to Sample #79) or in Sample #82 (25 minutes after #81). Thus, this Image was not of nearly as long duration as the Images of the Distressed Period.

Second, Fran's inner experience was much less multi-layered during the Peaceful/anxious Period than it was when she was Distressed. Nearly all of the Distressed Period samples had included Multiple Images, but in the Peaceful/anxious Period there were no examples of multiple Images. In fact, Images were present in only about one-third of the Peaceful/anxious Period samples, instead of almost always, as had been the case during the Distressed sample.

Third, almost all of Fran's Peaceful/anxious Period samples included Inner Speech as a prominent aspect of her experience. Inner Speech had been present during the Distressed Period, but had occurred in a little less than half the samples and had been only one aspect of a complex inner experience.

Fourth, Fran reported Unsymbolized Thinking during half the Peaceful/anxious Period samples. This kind of thinking, where Fran knew what she was thinking about but could not report any details about how she knew the contents of her thoughts, had been reported in about 30% of the samples during the Distressed Period. This lower frequency of reporting during the Distressed Period could have been due to a relative lack of Unsymbolized experience during that time, but it is also quite possible that Unsymbolized Thinking actually occurred frequently, but we failed to discuss it because it is difficult to describe and the remaining aspects of her experiences were so complex.

Fifth, Fran reported that a strong anxiety Feeling was present at all of her Peaceful/anxious Period samples except the first three. This anxiety was experienced as shakiness, uneasiness, both in her body and her mind. She felt like she was "going to crawl out of her skin," as though she had to move, run around, etc. At times it felt like she was "racing inside," like her mind was going at 100 miles per hour but her body was going slow, too slow because she did not want to be doing what she was doing. She was performing the activities that she felt she was expected to do, even though she did not want to be doing them.

A typical example of Fran's experiences during the Peaceful/anxious Period was Sample #79. Fran was getting ready for work, and was looking at her spools of thread, deciding which one to use to crochet a basket. She said to herself in Inner Speech, "What color?" At the same time she was seeing an Image of herself sitting on her bed crying. This Image was seen in full color, viewed from Fran's side so that Fran in the image was in profile. The Image was accurate in detail, color, etc., except that she was wearing a white blouse when in reality she didn't own a white blouse. Also at the same time Fran was feeling anxious, a shaky feeling in her body and her mind.

DISCUSSION

As we have seen, Fran did not experience perception as involving the formation of a relatively distinct figure against a relatively indistinct ground; she viewed all aspects of inner and outer experience with equal clarity (if not equal detail); and she experienced several or many aspects of her environment simultaneously. These are significant observations because they contradict what we took for granted about perceptual experience. We will need to integrate these observations into our understanding of perception.

Most psychologists take for granted that figure/ground is a basic organizational process of perception. In most introductory psychology texts, for example, one finds passages such as: "Geometric patterns are always perceived as figures against a background and thus appear to have contours and boundaries, just as objects do. Organizing stimuli into *figure* and *ground* is basic to stimulus patterning" (Atkinson, Atkinson, & Hilgard, 1983, p. 139; italics in original). Most of us hold this understanding as an unquestioned fact. For example, we believe that when observers view Rubin's ambiguous two faces/vase drawing (frequently seen in introductory psychology texts as an illustration of the figure/ground phenomenon), there unquestionably *is* an alternation between figure and ground. For example, Weintraub and Walker (1966) wrote "Either a vase or faces can be seen, but not both at the same time. If the vase is perceived, it becomes the figure, and the remainder of the picture becomes ground. If the faces are seen as figure, the body of the vase becomes a part of the ground" (p. 11). The present case attempts to show that for at least one subject, this figure/ground organization of perception did *not* exist, and that visual and auditory data were organized *without* the experience of a figure or ground.

The case of Fran lead us to question the adequacy of any theory of perception which posits figure/ground organization for all individuals. We are in no position to provide a new theory of perception, but this case shows that it can be productive to the science of perception, as well as to the understanding of psychopathology, to observe as carefully as we can individual moments of inner and external perceptual experience.

As we have seen, Fran's inner experience changed dramatically during the course of sampling, from being haunted by recurrent Multiple unpleasant Images to less complex inner experience characterized by Inner Speech and single Images. This simplification of her inner experience continued for at least a year following the end of her involvement in the sampling research. Was this change brought about by her experience-sampling participation, and if so, why?

That question is easier to ask than it is to answer, but we may offer some speculative comments. First, that her Multiple Images should disappear essentially immediately following our clarification of details of her darkest (suicidal, etc.) Images seems more than coincidental. There must have been something about either facing directly the worst that inner experience could offer or the emotionally charged interaction in so doing which facilitated her stopping creating those Images.

Second, it seems clear that an important ingredient in the experi-

ence sampling impact was her ongoing relationship with her psychotherapist, even though he was not a part of the experience sampling
itself. When, during the course of sampling, she would reach a new
level of clarity about some aspect of her inner experience, she would
comment that this new way of talking about herself would be helpful to
her therapy: she had been trying to explain that to her therapist for
months, but had not known how to express herself effectively. Fran
reiterated these impressions during our last interview, when she was
commenting on the impact that this experience had had on her. She and
her psychotherapist had reached a new, deeper level of understanding,
she said. He could now understand much better what she meant when
she said she "couldn't do" something he had requested of her, such as,
getting out of the house and engaging in some constructive activity
when she felt low. She did not mean this as an excuse for not performing, just that the burden of the multiple onslaught of the negative Images made things extremely difficult.

Third, Fran felt that the clarification of the way her inner experience
"worked" made it easier for her to control it. For example, before sampling began, an unpleasant event such as an argument with her daughter would trigger the series of self-derogatory Images which would then
remain with her for hours or days regardless of her attempts to curtail
them. Now, she seemed to be able to see that process at its very beginning, and at that point was able to effectively abort it.

Fourth, the experience sampling consisted for Fran not only of clarifying her inner experience, but also of intense, daily, 60 to 90 minute
interactions with a person (me) who was genuinely interested in the
details of inner experience. How much of the impact of experience sampling was due to the inner-experience clarification, and how much to the
interpersonal interaction? I can't see any way to answer that question
based on my experience in this case or the others that I have engaged in.
I would speculate that the nonspecific interpersonal aspect was not the
most important feature, because she had the ongoing relationship with
her psychotherapist who was also genuinely concerned about her and
whom she genuinely liked and respected, but more research with different personnel in both sampling roles is clearly required to separate these
two variables.

V

Postscript

Discussion

We have now completed the initial intent of these two books: that is, we have explored and presented the inner experience of a wide variety of individuals: normal and schizophrenic (in Hurlburt, 1990); and depressed, manic, anxious, bulimic, and borderline personality individuals here. It is now time to take stock of our findings.

Has the descriptive experience sampling method proven to be useful? It must be stated that none of the results described in these books can be considered proven until they have been replicated by other investigators. While I have been careful to describe phenomena as they exist in themselves, it is possible that my own unconscious processes have distorted my ability to perceive them accurately.

Assuming that I have been at least partially unbiased, however, the method can be said to be quite generative in its ability to elucidate the characteristics of inner experience. The method has revealed many phenomena of inner experience which either have never been described before or have never been portrayed at the present level of detail, including: "goofed-up," bent, or mutilated Images (in Hurlburt, 1990); Unsymbolized Thinking; multiplicity of inner experience; thoughts with "tails" (Sensed thinking); inner experience with no figure/ground; the "Doing" of Understanding; etc. Assuming that I am not completely biased, it seems clear that this method can bring our understanding of inner experience to a level of scrutiny unequalled in the western tradition.

Can the descriptive sampling method be applied to the range of disturbed individuals? Clearly it can. At least some people in all the diagnostic categories we have explored can and will respond to the sampling beep and attempt the sampling task. Some potential subjects refused to participate for one reason or another, and that has at times seemed related to the subject's psychiatric diagnosis (for example, it hardly seems surprising when a paranoid subject declines to participate). However, it must be noted that refusals have occurred in all our diagnostic categories (including the normals) and subjects willing to cooperate have been found in all of them as well (including, surprisingly, paranoid schizophrenic individuals). We have not systematically analyzed the patterns or reasons for these refusals, although that would be an interesting study in its own right.

Does the method discriminate between individuals in different diagnostic categories? The general characteristics of inner experience which we have described for each of the diagnostic classifications have been dramatically different from each other. For example, we found the "goofed-up" images and hyper-clear inner feelings in our schizophrenics but not in other individuals; we found the predomination of Unsymbolized Thinking in depressed bulimic individuals but not to the same extent in others; we found the "Doing" of Understanding and the high frequency of Criticalness of Self/Others only in our anxious subjects; we found that multiplicity of experience predominated only in bulimic and borderline individuals; we found Sensed awarenesses only in bulimics; we found the lack of figure/ground perception only in our borderline personality individual, etc. Clearly the method generates remarkably different pictures of different disorders.

These differences are based on such small samples. Doesn't that limit the validity of the results? The small sample sizes *do not* in the least diminish the fact that the method can be sensitive to widely disparate phenomena. However, the small sample sizes *do* make it necessary to consider characterizations of psychiatric groups such as those given in the preceding paragraph to be very tentative hypotheses which require further research. It is probably true that had we sampled with a different half dozen anxious individuals, for example, we might have advanced a different (or overlapping) set of phenomena characteristic of those anxious subjects. One of the next steps in the application of the sampling method is to apply it to larger, more carefully chosen, representative samples of psychiatric groups.

One might advance an analogy that the sampling method is to psychology what the microscope is to biology. These two books have established that the "microscope" works, that is, that the sampling method does allow us to examine psychological phenomena with a clarity of focus heretofore unavailable. It remains to be shown whether the first views we have had with that "microscope" are typical or atypical. When van Leeuwenhoek used his newly-developed microscope to explore unicellular life, he reached several incorrect conclusions; for example, he remained an animalculist, concluding that the sperm cells he could see for the first time with his new microscope contained a miniature but complete version of the entire adult organism. That opinion (as we now know) was erroneous, but it did not detract from the establishment of the microscope itself as a revolutionary tool in biology.

Is it possible that none of the tentative hypotheses about diagnostic groups will be supported, and if so, would that render the method worthless? That possibility exists, but it would not render the method useless. Consider for example the borderline personality individual from Chapter 14. It is quite possible that the long-term negative images which were characteristic of Fran are not characteristic of borderline personality individuals in general. If that turns out to be the case, then we will not have learned much about *borderline personality* from our explorations with Fran. However, we will have learned quite a lot about *Fran*. In the language which Allport popularized, perhaps we have not gained much "nomothetic" information about borderline personality, but regardless we have acquired an important "ideographic" perspective on Fran. That Fran had no figure/ground phenomena and had days-long harrowing images are of vital importance for understanding (and treating) Fran regardless of whether those phenomena are typical of borderline patients or any other group. Fran's psychotherapist, for example, prior to her being involved in the sampling study, responded to her complaints of being preoccupied with negative thoughts with the approach of trying to teach her to think about something else. This attempt was unsuccessful, apparently (as we can now see from our fresh perspective) because Fran could think the new thought the therapist was suggesting *without ceasing* to think the negative thoughts which were already ongoing. I know of no psychodiagnostic technique (interview, free association, questionnaire, or projective) other than descriptive sampling which could have provided this apparently important information about Fran.

We might note in passing that, despite 50 years of calls for ideographic psychological science by Allport and others, there never before has been a successful ideographic approach to psychology, even by Allport himself. There are doubtless many reasons for this which lie in the province of the social psychology of science and the individual psychology of scientists, but one reason that ideographic science is so difficult to perform is that there never has been a method for accumulating glimpses of real individuals in their natural environments. Interviews, even if repeated, and free association might be held to be the most promising sources of ideographic information, but they are much too strongly shaped by the inaccuracies of memory and the demand characteristics of the interview situation to be taken as descriptions of the actual moment-by-moment life of the individual.

Given that the characteristics of the particular psychiatric disorders should be regarded as tentative, what are the contributions of the method that should be regarded as established? It seems to me that there are two general observations. First, that it is possible and desirable to study people's inner experience directly. Descriptive experience sampling provides information about individuals which is both important and unattainable by any other means.

The second established contribution of the method is that the salient aspects of individuals' (and diagnostic groups') inner experience are likely to be process, not content, characteristics. Of all the characteristics we have described in these two books, only one (Criticalness of Self/Others for our anxious subjects) has been a feature of the "about what" (content) of our subjects' thinking. Much more salient in our sampling research have been aspects of the process, the "how" of thinking and feeling. This is in sharp contrast to most modern cognitive theories of psychiatric disorder, which posit content categories as the cause of disorder. For examples, Beck held that thoughts whose content is about loss lead to depression (e.g., Rush & Beck, 1978, p. 202); and Ellis proposed that thoughts whose content includes "and that would be awful!" lead to emotional upset (Ellis, 1962, p. 50).

There is only one thread of cognitive research that I know of which attempts to give process explanations for cognitive characteristics: that which imports computer terminology such as "inputs," "outputs," "central processors," "serial processing," and "parallel processing" into the theory of human functioning. However, that research is not based on direct observations of inner experience. For example, one of the debates in cognitive psychology has been about whether memory is better regarded as parallel processing or serial processing. In a typical experiment (Sternberg, 1966), subjects were asked to memorize a "positive stimulus set," which might be a short list of digits; later, the subjects were presented a single "test" digit and asked to indicate whether that test digit was or was not present in the positive stimulus set. The variable Sternberg observed was the reaction time between presentation of the test digit and the subject's response; the form of the function between that reaction time and the number of digits to be memorized is the focus of the serial-parallel debate. Sternberg, for example, claimed that the shape of this function demonstrates that the searching of memory is a serial, rather than a parallel, process.

However, from the perspective of our sampling research I would emphasize that these researchers never directly observed in any single person's inner experience anything which resembled either serial or parallel processing; instead, they observed reaction times and *inferred* the presence of serial or parallel processing. This is a distinctly different research procedure from our own. We have demonstrated the occurrence of what might be called parallel processing in some of our subjects—Multiplicity in the inner experience of our bulimic and borderline subjects. However, our own findings are not *inferences about* our subjects, but rather *observations of* them.

Isn't it true that the sampling method deals only with conscious experience and therefore ignores important unconscious material? It is definitely true that the sampling method asks subjects to report only what appears in their awareness. However, these subjects' sampling reports of moment-by-moment awarenesses do in fact contain part (and in some cases the most important part) of what has been called "unconscious" by other writers. It may seem to be a contradiction in terms that reports about awareness can describe the unconscious, so I will present an example to illustrate.

Hurlburt and Sipprelle (1978) studied a patient whose presenting complaint was free-floating, debilitating anxiety. Initial interviews with the patient revealed no cause for the anxiety; he was financially secure and had a happy marriage and family life, and sexuality and aggression did not seem problematic for him. The patient was asked to sample his thoughts using a variant of the technique used in these two books; sampling revealed that the content of a large proportion of his thoughts was anger directed at his children. Thus the facts relevant for the present discussion are that prior to sampling, the patient in all (conscious) honesty denied that he was angry toward his children, but sampling itself revealed the actual presence of frequent angry thoughts.

In the classical sense, this patient's anger would be called "unconscious" since he was not aware of this important characteristic of himself. Some theorists, following Freud, would explain this patient's "unconscious" anger as being the result of angry thoughts being repressed, blocked from his awareness as a means of protection against anxiety.

However, this patient's anger was clearly not "unconscious" when that term means "thoughts blocked from awareness." Angry thoughts *were* frequent visitors to his moment-by-moment consciousness, and, at the moment of each thought's occurrence, he was fully aware of its angry content. Thus, angry thoughts were *not* repressed by this patient but were instead frequently the center of his awareness. It was only when the patient characterized himself *in general terms* that he failed to recognize his anger.

The sampling studies thus require that we distinguish between two distinctly different phenomena that are both sometimes called "unconscious": "truly unconscious" processes, that is, mental processes which actually occur entirely outside of awareness; and "retrospectively-disregarded" processes, categories of thoughts which occur frequently in awareness but which are systematically overlooked or forgotten when an individual characterizes himself in general. Hurlburt and Sipprelle's anxious subject's anger was unconscious in the "retrospectively disregarded" sense, but *not* in the "truly unconscious" sense.

Descriptive experience sampling has no access to true unconscious processes, but it has unhindered access to retrospectively-disregarded categories.

To my knowledge, this distinction between true and retrospectively-disregarded unconscious processes had not been made before the sampling studies began, because making the distinction depends on having access to a random sample of everyday thoughts. It will require further research to ascertain under what conditions which of the two kinds of processes is more important. It is quite conceivable, for example, that truly unconscious processes predominate in depression, with the result that inner experience is stripped of its symbolic representation, while retrospectively-disregarded processes predominate in anxiety. However, at present we have no evidence for or against either possibility; I advance such potentialities simply to illustrate that descriptive experience sampling can be useful in exploring areas of psychology heretofore not investigated.

Do all individuals have inner experience? We speculated in the previous book (Hurlburt, 1990) that schizophrenics when decompensated may have *no* inner experience, that is, had no thoughts, feelings, or sensations in any of the ways (Inner Speech, Unsymbolized Thinking, Images, Feelings, etc.) in which most other people have. We admitted that such a position was largely conjecture, but I wish to state that I still believe such a conjecture should be taken seriously. I have attempted to sample with one individual more psychotically manic than John (the hypomanic subject of Chapter 3). He cooperated with the sampling task, but my impression was again that he simply had no inner experience to report. Thus the tentative speculation is that in psychosis in general (not just in schizophrenic decompensation) inner experience may disappear.

We have sampled with children as young as 11 (Monson, 1989) and found that there seems to be a discontinuity in the ability to report inner experience, ability which occurs at about 12 or 13 years old, although I must emphasize that this is a very tentative observation in need of much further research. At least some children under the age of 12 seem not to be able to report thoughts or feelings with any detail at all, even though they use the words "thought" and "feeling" in ways which are quite externally appropriate. They can correctly use sentences such as "I think the marble is in the black box," or "Yesterday I thought the marble was in the black box," but such usage does not mean that the children had any inner experience of thinking. Thus our tentative speculation is that children under 12, like psychotic adults, may have no inner experience at all. The difference is that psychotic individuals have lost an ability through some kind of disorganization, while children have not yet acquired the ability.

Why haven't the chapters on depression, anxiety, etc., attempted to link the results of descriptive experience sampling with the findings of other research methods? For example, there are studies which show that depressive patients respond to the Rorschach ink blots with less vivid imagery than do normal individuals. That would seem to corroborate our sampling finding that depressives have high frequencies of Unsymbolized ("imageless") Thinking and almost no visual imagery. Shouldn't mention be made of such convergences of results?

There are basically three reasons why I have generally avoided drawing such comparisons in these two books. First, the main focus of these books has been to explore descriptive experience sampling itself, and any hypotheses we have made about schizophrenia, depression, anxiety, etc. have been relatively incidental byproducts of our focus on the method. That is, in the present book we have sampled with depressed individuals not so much to elucidate depression as to demonstrate that the sampling method can be sensitive to a range of inner phenomena; we sampled with normal, schizophrenic, depressed, anxious, bulimic, and borderline individuals primarily to make it likely that we encountered a wide range of phenomena. To seek corroboration of our findings about depression from other modes of research would be to shift our attention towards depression itself and away from the method.

Second, such comparisons strike me as being somewhat premature. The hypothesis that Unsymbolized Thinking is a major factor in depression is a tentative speculation based on a half dozen subjects; clearly, more subjects and different investigators need to be involved before such a hypothesis can be accepted as fact. Only when replication has established the validity of these observations would it be appropriate to explore the relationship of such observations to the other findings about depression.

Third, and most important, I have tried to the extent of my abilities to keep my application of this method as purely sensitive to the phenomena being described as possible; in Chapters 2 and 3 of the first book

(Hurlburt, 1990) I described some of the ways in which I sought to maintain this ideal of objective impartiality in observing inner experience. Perfect objectivity is beyond my reach, but vigilance toward approximating that ideal is not.

In the everyday practice of the descriptive method, I have cultivated in myself a sort of indifference to my own expectations about the characteristics of my subjects' inner experience, because I know that my own preconceptions or biases can diminish my ability to hear accurately what subjects say. I regard as particularly dangerous the feeling, which I sometimes have, of "Ha! I *knew* John's inner experience would be like that!" For me, that feeling of confidence often is both incorrect (the phenomenon is *not*, as it at first seemed, similar to my expectations) and a palpable hindrance to my own concentration and attention: I'm now thinking about myself and my hypotheses rather than listening to the other person.

Just as it seems dangerous when I feel as if I know what to expect from a particular subject, I have come to regard it as equally dangerous when one of my generalizations seems to corroborate the findings of other research. A feeling such as, "Isn't that neat! I've found the same phenomenon as the Rorschach researchers found!" can lead to a numbing of further exploration. Thus, my cultivation of indifference also applies to the findings of other research methods about depression.

To see accurately a phenomenon as it unfolds itself requires genuinely not caring whether the observed phenomenon is a corroboration of past research, a refutation of past research, an authentic discovery of something heretofore unknown, or the observation of a coincidence which replication will disconfirm. I have actively cultivated such a disinterest in myself, and one of the byproducts of that disinterest is that I am not as facile in comparing theoretical positions as I once may have been.

The risks of failing to protect that disinterested point of view can, I think, be great. This was, for example, a prime reason for the demise of the introspections at the turn of the century. The sensationalists were not indifferent—they wanted to *prove* that all thinking involved images. The Würzburgers, in reaction, wanted to *prove* that some thinking was imageless. Both could have been more productive had they eschewed the attempt to prove and satisfied themselves with elucidating phenomena (see Chapter 2).

Does that mean that the facts amassed by other research techniques are not important? No, not at all. It is a question of timing and division of labor. As for timing, it seems a risky business to compare the Rorschach observations with the observations based on sampling until the sampling-based observations are secure in themselves, that is, until they have been replicated by other researchers. Direct description is far too easily influenced by theoretical or other preconceptual influences.

As for division of labor, it is perhaps wise to have one individual (or group of individuals) provide the observations and another individual (or group of individuals) provide the theoretical discussion and discrimination. Alternatively, perhaps other researchers who apply the descriptive method will find that they are less susceptible to the subtle pressures of preconception than I have observed in myself and so would be better able to perform both tasks; that is an empirical question. I can only report that my own ability to describe seems to diminish as any theoretical expectation which I might have increases.

The fact of the matter is that I *do* think it likely that the observation that depressed individuals provide little imagery on the Rorschach ink blots follows from the lack of imagery in the inner experience of depressed individuals. I am not very committed to that position, which is, I think, desirable, since the extent to which I might be so committed would pose a threat to my ability to sample accurately. I will work to suspend it, to put it in "brackets" as the phenomenologists might say, and one aspect of that bracketing is not to explore it prematurely. Later investigators can then attempt to validate the results of both methods against each other.

Given the caveats of the previous two sections, can't we comment on the relationship of our own findings to those that other investigations have provided? Yes, we will provide comments on six relevant research strategies in an attempt to show, at least in a preliminary way, that the descriptive sampling method can be productive in interaction with other methods.

The first related position that we will explore is that of Endel Tulving, who proposed that there are three kinds of consciousness, the "anoetic," the "noetic," and the "autonoetic," which correspond to his three classifications of memory (procedural, semantic, and episodic) (Tulving, 1985). Have we found evidence to support or disconfirm that position?

The anoetic (nonknowing) conscious "refers to an organism's capability to sense and to react to external and internal stimulation, including complex stimulus patterns. Plants and very simple animals possess anoetic consciousness as do computers and learning machines that have knowledge and that can improve it" (Tulving, 1985, p. 388). Tulving apparently included such things as tropisms (a plant turning toward the light, for example) in this class of consciousness. Perhaps Tulving would call anoetic the activities which we called the Just Doing of activities with no particular awareness present—mindlessly buttering toast, for example.

The "noetic" (knowing) consciousness "makes possible introspective awareness of the internal and external world . . . Lower animals . . . [and] very young children . . . may have fully developed noetic consciousness" (Tulving, 1985, p. 388). Noetic consciousness is the source of information about the world which does not depend on the recall of particular events that occurred in the subject's own life. Examples include the knowledge that July follows June, or that the chemical formula for table salt is NaCl (Tulving, 1972, p. 387). Our subjects so far as I am aware do *not* report noetic awareness as occurring at the moment of any beep. Moment-by-moment awarenesses such as our subjects report always have a personal, dated-in-time (and thus "autonoetic") aspect. Noetic consciousness is thus apparently an abstraction rather than a fact of direct experience. Our subjects have reported experiences which we have called Sensory Awareness, where they were absorbed with some particular sensory aspect of their world, noticing a particular shade of green, for example. That may be as close to noetic consciousness as we have found, but that seems to be a long stretch of Tulving's definition.

The "autonoetic" consciousness "allows an individual to become aware of his or her own identity and existence in subjective time. . . , [providing] the familiar phenomenal flavor or recollective experience characterized by 'pastness' and subjective veridicality" (Tulving, 1985, p. 388). Most of our subjects' reports (of Inner Speech, Inner Hearing, Images, etc.) have this knowledge-about-oneself characteristic. Even Unsymbolized Thinking involves a sense of oneself as doing the thinking.

I do not, however, regard such observations as supporting Tulving's ternary classification system, since I believe that similar neither-more-nor-less Procrustean correspondences could be drawn between our own results and memory classification schemes which oppose Tulving's (for example, that memory is unitary or dichotomous rather than ternary as Tulving proposed).

The core of the distinction between my own and Tulving's positions lies in that Tulving incorrectly (in my view) took for granted characteristics of experience on which to base his theoretical position. For example, he wrote that "If 'seeing' things—something that phenomenal experience tells us is clearly unitary—is subserved by separable neural-cognitive systems, it is possible that learning and remembering, too, appear to be unitary only because of the absence of contrary evidence" (Tulving, 1985, p. 386). Our results show that the phenomenal experience of seeing things is clearly *not* unitary. For example, the visual Image-making process appears in experience itself, as we have shown, to be more a coordination of several distinct processes rather than being itself a unitary process. The existence of Imageless Seeing—the act of seeing without the awareness of the thing seen—unambiguously demonstrates that Imaging involves at least two processes, one which generates the experience of seeing, and one which generates the experience of the thing seen.

If learning and remembering appear to be unitary, it is because they have never been subjected to careful description of the kind we have found useful.

The second related position we will consider is that of Mark Williams, who has explored the specificity of personal memories in depression. For example, Williams and his colleagues presented depressed individuals with positive and negative stimulus sentences and asked them to report specific memories which were cued by the sentences (Moore, Watts, & Williams, 1988). They found that depressed individuals report far more general memories (e.g., "My husband always fixes the car for me") than do normal control subjects, and also report far fewer specific memories (about events which occurred on one particular day in the past), even when reprompted to do so. These results replicated an earlier study (Williams & Broadbent, 1986) which used somewhat different stimulus cues (words instead of sentences) and somewhat different subjects (suicide attempters instead of depressed individuals), so this general observation seems rather well established.

Their general conclusion was:

> Depressives' problems in retrieving specific positive memories appear to reside in their gaining access to a general level and being unable to progress beyond it. Recent research has suggested that personal memory is organized as a hierarchy of successively more specific representations of personal information (Kolodner, 1985). Defining a general context may be an essential stage in moving down through such a hierarchy to arrive at a specific memory, and *it is this search for specific instances which depressives find difficult.* The result is that *the cognition of depressed people is likely to be dominated by relatively abstract representations of the past rather than specific instances.* (Moore et al., 1988, p. 275, italics added)

Can our own research shed any light on these observations? First, we have observed that *all* of our subjects (not just the depressed individuals) tend to avoid reporting specific instances, a phenomenon we called the "rush to generalization" in the previous book (Hurlburt, 1990, e.g., p. 12). In fact, one of the cornerstones of our method is the training and constant encouragement of all subjects to avoid generalizing about themselves and to report specific occurrences which were ongoing at the moment of the beep.

Second, while we have not kept explicit records as to this avoidance of specificity (precisely because it is a characteristic we simply try to eliminate as completely as possible from our subjects' reports), it is my impression that this training in specificity is in general more difficult for subjects in all the diagnostic groups we have studied than it is for normal subjects. Thus, the predominance of understanding oneself in general terms may be a characteristic of psychopathology in general rather than a particular characteristic of depression. This impression should be regarded as being very tentative since it is not based on systematic observation.

Third, once our subjects have overcome the hurdle of learning how to report adequately about Unsymbolized Thinking, my impression is that our depressed subjects are just as specific as our other psychiatric groups in reporting their experience.

These results seem rather at odds with Williams' replicated findings. How can we explain that? First, we accept Williams' findings as being in accord with our own experience when engaged in tasks similar to those Williams presented. That is, we agree that depressed subjects frequently report more general memories and have difficulty being specific.

Second, Williams' memory tasks and our own sampling tasks are different in important ways. For example, it is relatively unusual for subjects in any of our sampling studies to report the kind of "pure" memories which Williams' procedure is designed to elicit. That is, subjects only rarely say that at the moment of the beep they were remembering some event which happened in the past. Much more common are reports about thoughts related to current events: what to wear today, etc. Such thoughts are clearly shaped by what is remembered (the decision of what to wear may include an image of something the subject actually owns, and which is thus "stored in memory"), but they are not "memories" per se.

Third, there are two overlapping characteristics of Unsymbolized Thinking which may serve to explain Williams' results: an Unsymbolized Thought in a depressed individual can have a relatively long duration, and Unsymbolized Thinking seems to be under less direct verbal/volitional control than other forms of thought.

The fact that an Unsymbolized Thought may have long duration can affect Williams' memory task because his task was quite time constrained: subjects were allowed only a total of one minute to respond to a given cue. One minute is much longer than the duration of most kinds of thinking in normal subjects; however, Unsymbolized Thinkings can last that long or longer in depressed individuals. In Williams' method, the cue word or sentence was given, followed by a waiting for a response. If the first response was not sufficiently specific, the request was made that a more specific response be given. One minute may not be sufficient for some depressed individuals to progress from one thought (be it general or specific) to another.

The other relevant characteristic of Unsymbolized Thinking is that it does not seem to be under direct verbal/volitional control, that is, it seems simply to occur without being created by the subject himself. While it has been beyond the scope of our research to date to further explore this characteristic, our subjects have reported that Unsymbolized Thinking can be relatively unresponsive to external verbalizations; that is, in depressed subjects, an Unsymbolized Thought can seem simply "to just sit there," continuing to be thought, even though another person may be saying something else (this may be part of the reason why Unsymbolized Thinkings can have long durations). The depressed subject in such instances knows at some level that the other person is talking, and may even know what the person is saying, but the meaning and significance of that conversation does not (at least immediately) impact the ongoing thought process.

Williams' subjects thus may have heard his request that they be more specific but failed to act on it, not because of the characteristics of their memory but instead because of the characteristic slowness of their thinking processes.

I must again underscore the speculative nature of the foregoing discussion. Our research to date has *not* been to explore the function of inner experience. It might be said that we have been exploring the "What" of inner experience (describing the existence of and characteristics of Images, Inner Speech, Unsymbolized Thinking, Partially Worded Thinking, etc.). Speculations such as the one in the preceding paragraphs belong to "What now" research (which attempts to explore the *ramifications* of having Images, Inner Speech, Unsymbolized Thinking, etc.). We ourselves have not undertaken any such "What now" research, and have for the most part assiduously avoided any such speculations. Thus my response to Williams' studies must be recognized as extremely tentative, as opening the door for further research rather than definitively answering a research question.

The third related position that we will consider is that of John Teasdale, who with his colleagues, has demonstrated that the distraction component of cognitive behavior therapy has different efficacies for high or low endogenous (that is, neurotic) depression patients. For example, they showed a series of slides of outdoor scenes to patients who scored high on the Beck Depression Inventory (Fennell, Teasdale, Jones, &

Dample, 1987). Viewing these slides provided a significantly greater decrease in depression for the neurotic depressed group than it did for the high endogenous depressed group.

This result, which generally supported findings by Teasdale and Rezin (1978) and Fennell and Teasdale (1984), suggests that there may well be different kinds of cognitive processing in the two depressed groups. This result points to a serious limitation of our sampling studies as we have carried them out to date. We have not attempted to distinguish between neurotic and endogenous depression, or, for that matter, to make any of the other distinctions between types of depression which Blatt and others have proposed. Our results thus do not clarify the possible differences in inner experience between neurotic and endogenous depression. Our aim was to get a glimpse of some of the phenomena of depressive experience in order to demonstrate that the descriptive sampling method was useful with individuals who are depressed. Some (or all) of our results, such as that the frequency of Unsymbolized Thinking varies directly with level of depression, may be true not for all depressed individuals but only for some subset thereof. For example, it is quite possible that our subjects happened to all be neurotically (rather than endogenously) depressed; were we to sample with other depressed individuals, we may have found other, quite different salient characteristics of depressed inner experience.

Teasdale's research thus suggests a logical next step in our sampling studies: to identify two groups of depressed individuals, one group neurotic and one endogenous, and to use our descriptive sampling technique within each group, comparing and contrasting the differences. Such a study may well provide fascinating new phenomena characteristic of some depressed individuals.

The fourth related position that we will consider is that of Thomas Borkovec, who with his colleagues concluded on the basis of indirect evidence that "worry primarily involves thought" (Borkovec & Inz, 1990, p. 153) where "thought" was defined as "abstract, conceptual, thinking activity" which was held to be distinct from imaginal activity. To explore further whether worry "is primarily a conceptual, rather than imaginal, process" (p. 154), Borkovec and Inz identified generalized anxiety disorder patients and normal controls and asked both groups to relax for a ten-minute period and then worry for a ten-minute period. Subjects were contacted via an intercom three times during each period and asked to report whether their "mental content at the moment of the contact involved thought, image, both, or 'unsure'" (p. 155). During the relaxation period, normal control subjects showed a preponderance of imagery with little thought, while anxiety patients showed approximately equal proportions of thought and image. During the worry period, normal controls' and anxiety patients' responses were quite similar: both showed a preponderance of thought with relatively little imagery.

Borkovec and Inz's conclusion that worry involves primarily thought as opposed to imaginal activity is quite similar to our own reports by anxiety subjects (see Chapters 11 through 13). However, our own experience leads us to speculate that the finding that worry implies non-image may be stronger than Borkovec and Inz reported. We have consistently found with our anxious subjects that they initially over-report the existence of imagery as being ongoing at the moment of the beep. We noted in Chapter 13 that anxious subjects seem to "want" to have visual images and report non-visual thoughts in visual terms. Anxious subjects, in our experience, need rather extensive training to differentiate between an "image" and a non-image, knowing about the visual characteristics of the target of thought. Borkovec and Inz provided no such extensive training, which quite possibly contributed to the fact that anxious patients reported that images occurred at 36% of samples during the relaxation period and 26% of samples during the worry period. My speculation is that these frequencies are spuriously high; many moments reported as being images were likely to have been non-image thoughts. (Another possibility is that our own anxiety sample happened to include subjects with fewer images than Borkovec's anxiety patients.)

Here again, the contribution of our own study is more to the method than to the result. We have demonstrated that at least for some subjects (in fact, for most of our anxious subjects), an exploration of the phenomena of inner experience requires careful training and support, perhaps particularly when they are asked to report images. It is probably not adequate simply to ask subjects to rate inner experience on Likert-type scales without providing rather extensive training in the use of those scales. We have also demonstrated that what Borkovec and Inz called "thought" is actually a quite differentiated spectrum of phenomena ranging from Inner Speech to Unsymbolized Thinking to Unworded Verbalizations, etc.

The fifth related position that we will consider is that of Marcia Johnson. Johnson and her colleagues have called processes by which perceived and imagined events are either discriminated or confused in memory "reality monitoring". The core of Johnson's position is that "memories originating from perception should have more perceptual information (e.g., color and sound), more contextual information (time and place), and more meaningful detail, whereas memories originating from thought should have more information about the cognitive opera-

tions (e.g., sensory, perceptual, or reflective processes . . .) that generated them" (Johnson, Foley, Suengas, & Raye, 1988).

The reality monitoring model is based on Johnson and Raye's (1981)
assumption "that perceptual events produce persistent memory traces
(perhaps in a kind of continuous record of experience . . .) [; they] also
assume that internally generated events produce persistent memory
traces" (1981, p. 69). Our findings *do not* corroborate this position that
memory of inner experience includes information about cognitive operations.

For example, most of our subjects who have frequent Unsymbolized
Thinking are completely surprised by its existence in themselves or others, even though they may engage in it frequently. In fact, many, if not
most, of these subjects resist reporting that kind of thinking because
they naively hold it to be impossible: they believe that one must think in
words or pictures. Clearly these subjects have no access to memory
traces which include the cognitive characteristics of their own experience.

A second example concerns the "memory" for images. We have
sampled with subjects (some of our anxious subjects, for example) who
are convinced prior to sampling that they invariably think in visual
images, only to find that images do not ever occur (or occur extremely
rarely) in their samples. Other subjects are just the opposite: they believe they never have visual images, only to find that such experiences
are frequent in their samples. Such subjects' "memory traces" do not
include information about the operations of their awareness.

Further evidence that internally generated events cannot produce
the kinds of memories of cognitive operations that the reality monitoring
model suggests is provided by the discussion of inferred vs observed
thinking in Chapter 3. There, John reported that at the moment of the
beep he was thinking about looking forward to having a turkey sandwich. Closer questioning of the specifics of this event revealed that he
was seeing a clear visual image of a greasy, green, rather revolting piece
of turkey meat. Our discussion in Chapter 3 noted that the inferred
thought (looking forward to turkey) was quite discrepant with the observed thought (revolting turkey). What, if anything, would be the "persistent memory trace" of this "internally generated event"? It is highly
unlikely that both aspects of this "thought" will be remembered; despite
the fact that the observed characteristic of this thought was an extremely
clear image, it is most likely that there would be no memory trace of this
cognitive event.

The sixth (and last) related position that we will consider is that of
Robert Kunzendorf. One of Kunzendorf's main contributions has been

to refute Hume's sensory continuum theory, the position that most psychologists implicitly adopt (Kunzendorf, 1985–86). Sensory continuum theory holds that individuals differentiate visual perception from visual imaging on the basis of the vividness of the image: perceptions are more vivid than images. Kunzendorf advanced an alternative theory which he called "cognitive-state monitoring" which explains the ability to differentiate image from perception positing that "waking self-consciousness is the phenomenal experience and the neurological process of monitoring *that one is "having" one's sensations:* in particular, *that one is imaging one's sensations* or *that one is perceiving them*" (Kunzendorf, 1987–88, p. 5, italics in original).

Our own observations provide mixed support for Kunzendorf's observations. First, our sampling studies wholeheartedly support Kunzendorf's refutation of sensory continuum theory. Our subjects sometimes report vivid images and sometimes extremely vague or even entirely absent images; they sometimes report clear perceptions and sometimes rather idle, unfocused perceptions. But they never confuse image with perception, regardless of the vividness of either. No subject (including our schizophrenic subjects) has ever wondered whether an experience was an image or a perception; they simply know that this experience is an image, while the other is a perception.

However, Kunzendorf's position that there is a "'cognitive-state monitor' which is part of one's psychological constitution and which sensationlessly registers the central or peripheral innervation of sensory experiences" (Kunzendorf, 1985–86, p. 257) is not supported by our sampling studies. Our subjects frequently report multiple awareness, and their frequent Unsymbolized Thoughts may be called "sensationless"; but it is extremely unusual for a subject to report a sensationless awareness of himself or herself as imaging or as perceiving. Furthermore, subjects have never reported the existence in awareness of anything like a "monitor" which assesses the image/perception distinction. They simply know that this experience is an image while that one is a perception.

Kunzendorf's theory of cognitive-state monitoring, like all other image theories that I know of, also fails to make such distinctions between Images, Imageless Seeing, and Indeterminate Inner Visual Experience that our subjects have described. The terrain of inner visual experience seems to me to be much more differentiated than either Hume or Kunzendorf imagined.

Thus our sampling studies can shed some light on Kunzendorf's experimental results; it is also true that Kunzendorf's experimental work can provide some perspective on our sampling results. For example, we have reported throughout these two books that there are dramatic differences in experience between both individuals and diagnostic groups; in particular we have observed that depressed individuals very infrequently experience words in their thinking. It might be useful to know whether such differences in *experience* reflect differences in underlying *cognition*. There are at least two possibilities. First, it might be that the basic structure of cognition in depressives is in fact essentially different from that in normal individuals; the reason depressed individuals only rarely report words is that their cognition is fundamentally nonverbal, in contrast to other subjects whose cognition is fundamentally verbal. On the other hand, it might be that the essential nature of cognition is identical for both depressives and normals, and that only the *experience* of thinking differs between the two groups. This latter position has been termed the "epiphenomenal" position: awareness is only an epiphenomenon of cognition having no causal or direct connection to the cognition itself. Our own sampling research has uncritically accepted either possibility: we have simply described the contents of awareness without attempting to theorize about the nature of the underlying cognitions.

Does the lack of words in inner experience reflect an essentially nonverbal cognitive process? Kunzendorf and McLaughlin's (1988–89, Experiment 1) results can be interpreted to provide a tentative "Yes" answer.

Kunzendorf and McLaughlin identified a group of mildly depressed individuals and a group of normal controls and measured each subject's ability to discriminate briefly perceived words (.32 msec exposure times) from briefly perceived nonwords. The words were drawn from one of two categories: death-related words (e.g., *cancer*) and neutral words (e.g., *caboose*). Kunzendorf and McLaughlin's hypothesis was that normal individuals would repress the death-related words (that is, their ability to detect death-related words would be diminished in comparison to their ability to detect neutral words), while depressed individuals would not show such repression. The data supported this hypothesis.

Our descriptive sampling research suggests an alternative explanation of these data, consistent with the notion that the nonverbal nature of experience in depressives reflects the nonverbal nature of depressives' essential cognition; that is, the data are consistent with the notion that consciousness is *not* merely an epiphenomenon. Recall that Kunzendorf and McLaughlin presented *words* as the stimuli which either may or may not be 'repressed.' Our own hypothesis might be: if depressives' essential cognition is fundamentally nonverbal, then words themselves might be expected merely to "float on the surface" of cognition, having relatively little direct connection to the more fundamental cognitive or emotional processes (whatever they may be). If that is true, then depressives' responses to words should be indifferent to whether those words are emotionally laden or not. For those normals, on the other hand, whose essential cognition is in fact fundamentally verbal, words themselves should carry more of the "stuff" of emotion, and those individuals should then show a differential response to emotional and nonemotional words. That is precisely what the data in Kunzendorf and McLaughlin's Table 1 (1988–89, p. 7) show. The depressives showed no difference in responding to neutral or death-related words, while normal subjects showed a significant difference.

Let me emphasize that I do not regard this as unambiguous support for the non-epiphenomenality of inner experience. I have tried throughout this work to maintain a posture of indifference as to such theoretical distinctions, and I suspect it will take many demonstrations of causation before I am prepared to abandon that posture.

Prominent psychologists such as B. F. Skinner have urged strongly against so-called "cognitive" studies. Does his criticism apply to the descriptive sampling method? Skinner has recently written, for example, that "cognitive science is the creation science of psychology, as it struggles to maintain the position of a mind or self" (Skinner, 1990, p. 1209). Skinner was arguing against basing cognitive-psychological explanations on "intelligence," "subjective expected utility," "psychological space," etc., and I agree with him entirely. Skinner correctly, in my opinion, pointed out that an explanation such as this "simply moves the bothersome physical-metaphysical distinction a step further out of sight" (p. 1207) without producing fruitful results. I discussed this issue further in the section of Hurlburt (1990) called "Preliminary Comments Designed to Suspend the Introspection Controversy."

I consider Skinner's long and consistent criticism of mental explanations to be an enormous contribution to psychological thought. However, an undesirable side effect of that polemic has been the neglect of careful, accurate observation of inner experience. Such neglect allows Skinner to maintain that "we see the public world about us, but we also feel, hear, taste, and smell it. We do nothing with the inner world but 'see' it" (p. 1208). Such a statement betrays an egregious ignorance about the inner world. Our subjects do "see" in inner experience, but they also hear, smell, feel, talk (Inner Speech), think without talking (Unsymbolized Thinking), see without noticing the thing being seen (Imageless Seeing), talk without words (Wordless Speaking), etc. The variability of inner behavior (as Skinner might call it) is at least as great as that of externally observable behavior. While it is a mistake, as Skinner said, to assign causative implication to any of these characteristics, it is also a mistake to pretend that such characteristics do not exist.

Where should we go from here? The first step is for others not under my direct influence to use descriptive experience sampling and report whether they find phenomena similar to those we have described. Assuming that the answer is in the affirmative, the next step would be to identify other phenomena which differentiate some individuals from others, aspects which my own studies have not uncovered. Then, studies of larger numbers of more carefully selected subjects in various psychiatric groups would be useful, both to test and/or differentiate the hypotheses which the present work has generated and to explore psychiatric diagnoses which have not yet been sampled.

Studies of individuals in two or more conditions will also be useful: before and after the introduction of psychotropic medications to better understand the effects of the drugs; during the titration of antipsychotic medication to ascertain whether the sampling method can be sensitive to the optimum drug dosage necessary to obtain the desired effect; of individuals at risk for schizophrenia (but not yet schizophrenic) and then after its onset, both to better understand the nature of schizophrenia and to ascertain whether sampling can be used as a reliable predictor; repeated sampling with bipolar individuals as they cycle through mania and depression in an attempt to determine whether inner experience changes prior to or after the changes in the expressed mood; etc. Descriptive experience sampling promises a finer-grained understanding of all those phenomena; it remains to be seen whether that promise is realized.

References

Atkinson, R. L., Atkinson, R. C., and Hilgard, E. R. (1983). *Introduction to psychology (8th ed.)*. New York: Harcourt Brace Jovanovich.

Bagley, W. C. (1900). The apperception of the spoken sentence: A study in the psychology of language. *American Journal of Psychology, 12*, 80–130.

Beck, A. T. (1967). *Depression: Clinical, experimental, and theoretical aspects*. New York: Hoeber.

Book, W. F. (1910). On the genesis and development of conscious attitudes (*Bewusstseinslagen*). *Psychological Monograph, 17*, 381–398.

Borkovec, T. D., & Inz, J. (1990). The nature of worry in generalized anxiety disorder: A predominance of thought activity. *Behavior Research and Therapy, 28*, 153–158.

Brennan, J. F. (1982). *History and systems of psychology*. Englewood Cliffs, NJ: Prentice-Hall, Inc.

Brouwers, M. (1988). Depressive thought content among female college students with bulimia. *Journal of Counseling and Development, 66*, 425–428.

Butterfield, P. S., & LeClair, S. (1988). Cognitive characteristics of bulimic and drug-abusing women. *Addictive Behaviors, 13*, 131–138.

Bühler, K. (1907). Tatsachen und Probleme zu einer Psychologie der Denkvorgänge. I. Über Gedanken [Facts and problems of a psychology of thought process. I: About thoughts. *Archiv für die Gesamte Psychologie, 9*, 297–365.

Casper, R. C., Eckert, E. D., Halmi, K. A., Goldberg, S. C., & Davis, J. M. (1980). Bulimia. *Archives of General Psychiatry, 37*, 1030–1035.

Clarke, H. M. (1911). Conscious attitudes. *The American Journal of Psychology, 22*, 214–249.

Crisp, A. H. (1982). *Anorexia nervosa: Let me be* (2nd ed.). London: Academic Press.

Crew, D. F. (1989). *Alltagsgeschichte:* A new social history "from below"? *Central European History, 22*, 394–407.

Danziger, K. (1980). The history of introspection reconsidered. *Journal of the History of the Behavioral Sciences, 16*, 241–262.

Dritschel, B. H., Williams, K., & Cooper, P. J. (1990). Cognitive distortions amongst women experiencing bulimic episodes. *International Journal of Eating Disorders, 10*, 547–555.

Ellis, A. (1962). *Reason and emotion in psychotherapy*. New York: Lyle Stuart.

Elmore, D. K., & de Castro, J. M. (1990). Self-rated moods and hunger in relation to

241

spontaneous eating behavior in bulimics, recovered bulimics, and normals. *International Journal of Eating Disorders, 9,* 179–190.

Farley, D. (1986). Eating disorders: When thinness becomes an obsession. *FDA Consumer, 5,* 20–23.

Fennell, M. J. V., Teasdale, J. D., Jones, S., & Dample, A. (1987). Distraction in neurotic and endogenous depression: an investigation of negative thinking in major depressive disorder. *Psychological Medicine, 17,* 441–452.

Fennell, M. J. V., & Teasdale, J. D. (1984). Effects of distraction on thinking and affect in depressed patients. *British Journal of Clinical Psychology,* 1984, *23,* 65–66.

Fischer, S. C. (1916). The process of generalizing abstraction. *Psychological Monograph, 21,* 1–213.

Garfinkel, P. E., Moldofsky, H., & Garner, D. M. (1980). The heterogeneity of anorexia nervosa. *Archives of General Psychiatry, 37,* 1036–1039.

Garner, D. M., & Garfinkel, P. E. (1984). *Diagnostic issues in anorexia nervosa and bulimia nervosa.* New York: Bruner/Mazel.

Garner, D. M., Rockert, W., Olmsted, M. P., Johnson, C., & Coscina, D. V. (1985). Psychoeducational principles in the treatment of bulimia and anorexia nervosa. In D. M. Garner & P. E. Garfinkel (Eds.), *Handbook of psychotherapy for anorexia nervosa and bulimia* (pp. 513–572). New York: The Guilford Press.

Geissler, L. R. (1912). Analysis of consciousness under negative instruction. *American Journal of Psychology, 23,* 183–213.

Gordon, R. A. (1990). *Anorexia and bulimia: Anatomy of a social epidemic.* Cambridge, Massachusetts: Basil Blackwell.

Hebert, J. (1991). *Sampling the inner experience of anxious and other individuals.* Unpublished master's thesis, University of Nevada, Las Vegas, Las Vegas, NV.

Hsu, L. K. G., & Sobkiewicz (1991). Body image: Time to abandon the concept for eating disorders? *International Journal of Eating Disorders, 10,* 15–30.

Humphrey, G. (1963). *Thinking: An introduction to its experimental psychology.* New York: Wiley.

Hurlburt, R. T. (1990). *Sampling normal and schizophrenic inner experience.* New York: Plenum Press.

Hurlburt, R. T., & Sipprelle, C. N. (1978). Random sampling of cognitions in alleviating anxiety attacks. *Cognitive Therapy and Research, 2,* 165–169.

Jacobson, E. (1911). On meaning and understanding. *American Journal of Psychology, 22,* 553–577.

Johnson, M. K., Foley, M. A., Suengas, A. G., & Raye, C. L. (1988). Phenomenal characteristics of memories for perceived and imagined autobiographical events. *Journal of Experimental Psychology: General, 117,* 371–376.

Johnson, M. K., & Raye, C. L. (1981). Reality monitoring. *Psychological Review, 88,* 67–85.

Kakise, H. (1911). A preliminary experimental study of the conscious concomitants of understanding. *American Journal of Psychology, 22,* 14–64.

Kaufman, L. (1974). *Sight and mind.* New York: Oxford University Press.

Kolodner, J. (1985). The memory for experience. *The Psychology of Learning and Motivation, 19,* 1–57.

Kunzendorf, R. G. (1985–86). Repression as the monitoring and censoring of images: An empirical study. *Imagination, Cognition, and Personality, 5,* 31–39.

Kunzendorf, R. G. (1987–88). Self-consciousness as the monitoring of cognitive states: A theoretical perspective. *Imagination, Cognition, and Personality, 7,* 3–22.

Kunzendorf, R. G., & McLaughlin, S. (1988–89). Depression: A failure to suppress the self-conscious 'monitoring' of dismal cognitions. *Imagination, Cognition, and Personality, 8,* 3–17.

Lacey, J. (1982). The bulimic syndrome at normal body weight: Reflections on the pathogenesis and clinical features. *International Journal of Eating Disorders, 2,* 59–66.

Langfeld, H. S. (1910). Suppression with negative instructions. *Psychological Bulletin, 7,* 200–208.

Martin, M. (1912). Quantitativ Untersuchungen über das Verhältnis anschaulicher und unanschaulicher Bewusstseinsinhalte [Quantitative investigation of the proportion of intuitive and nonintuitive contents of consciousness]. *Zeitschrift für Psychologie, 65,* 417–490.

Mayer, A., & Orth, J. (1901). Zur qualitativ Untersuchung der Associationen [Towards a qualitative investigation of association]. *Zeitschrift für Psychologie und Physiologie des Sinnesorganization, 26,* 1–13.

Misiak, H., & Sexton, V. S. '(1972). *History of psychology, an overview.* New York: Grune & Stratton.

Monson, C. (1989). *Sampling inner experiences of adolescents.* Unpublished master's thesis, University of Nevada, Las Vegas, Las Vegas, NV.

Mook, D. G. (1982). *Psychological research.* New York: Harper & Row.

Moore, R. G., Watts, F. N., & Williams, J. M. G. (1988). The specificity of personal memories in depression. *British Journal of Clinical Psychology, 27,* 275–276.

Moore, T. V. (1919). The evidence against imageless thought. *Psychological Monographs, 27,* 241–282.

Okabe, T. (1910). Experimental study, of belief. *American Journal of Psychology, 21,* 563–596.

Rush, J., & Beck, A. T. (1978). Cognitive therapy of depression and suicide. *American Journal of Psychotherapy, 32,* 201–219.

Russell, G. F. M. (1979). Bulimia nervosa: An ominous variant of anorexia nervosa. *Psychological Medicine, 9,* 429–448.

Shamanek, B. (1991). *Sampling inner experience in learning disabled individuals.* Unpublished master's thesis, University of Nevada, Las Vegas, Las Vegas, NV.

Skinner, B. F. (1990). Can psychology be a science of mind? *American Psychologist, 45,* 1206–1210.

Spearman, C. (1923/1973). *The nature of 'intelligence' and the principles of cognition.* New York: Arno Press.

Sternberg, S. (1966). High speed scanning in human memory. *Science, 153,* 652–654.

Teasdale, J. D., & Rezin, V. (1978). The effects of reducing frequency of negative thoughts on the mood of depressed patients—tests of a cognitive model of depression. *British Journal of Clinical Psychology, 17,* 65–74.

Titchener, E. B. (1910/1980). *A textbook of psychology.* New York: Scholars' Facsimiles & Reprints.

Tulving, E. (1972). Episodic and semantic memory. In Tulving, E. & Donaldson, W. (Eds.), *Organization of memory.* New York: Academic Press, pp. 381–403.

Tulving, E. (1985). How many memory systems are there? *American Psychologist, 40,* 385–398.

Weintraub, D. J., & Walker, E. L. (1966). *Perception.* Belmont, California: Brooks/Cole.

Wertheimer, M. (1987). *A brief history of psychology* (3rd ed.). New York: Holt, Rinehart and Winston.

Williams, J. M. G., & Broadbent, K. (1986). Autobiographical memory in suicide attempters. *The Journal of Abnormal Psychology, 95,* 144–149.

Wood, G. (1981). *Fundamentals of psychological research* (3rd ed.). Boston: Little, Brown and Company.

Woodworth, R. S. (1915). A revision of imageless thought. *The Psychological Review, 22,* 1–27.

Index